Contributions to Jungian Psychology
by
The Psychology Club Zurich

Series Editors
Andreas Schweizer and Regine Schweizer-Vüllers

Volume 4

C.G. Jung
Letters to Hedy Wyss
1936 – 1956

Edited with an Introduction and Commentary
by
Andreas Schweizer

Daimon
Verlag

Translated from the original German book:
C.G. Jung: Briefe an Hedy Wyss 1936 – 1956
Herausgegeben und mit einem Kommentar versehen von Andreas Schweizer

Translator of the Letters:
Alison Kappes-Bates

Translators of the Commentary:
Andreas Schweizer
Judith Dowling
Alison Kappes-Bates

Facing page: C.G. Jung, Photo: Yousuf Karsh, Carl Gustav Jung,
© 1958 Yousuf Karsh, courtesy of the Estate of Yousuf Karsh

Frontispiece: C.G. Jung in his library, 1949. © Photo: Shutterstock Ireland Ltd. /
© Foundation of the Works of C.G. Jung, Zürich

ISBN 978-3-85630-795-0

Contents

Introduction

It has been more than ten years since my colleague Regula Stieger approached me with the opportunity to purchase a collection of some seventy letters of C.G. Jung. The letters, mostly handwritten, were from the legacy of a young artist. The intermediary was the physician Wolfgang Wyss in Zurich, a former schoolmate of Regula and mine. It is to him, and of course to the addressee, Hedy Wyss, that we owe the excellent condition of these letters of C.G. Jung, written to the good 30 years younger artist. Fortunately, the negotiations that then followed with the two heirs, nephews of Hedy Wyss, were successful. Thanks to the encouraging support of colleagues from the *Stiftung zur Förderung der Psychologie von C.G. Jung* [Foundation for the Promotion of Jungian Psychology], of which I was President at the time, we were able to purchase the letters in 2012. They remained, however, in a bank safe deposit box for several years.

One night I dreamed of the keys to this safe deposit box. This aroused my curiosity. I wondered whether the time had come for the letters to be published. Of course, I had read them long ago, but only now, after rereading them again, did I realize what a treasure these documents were. Many of Jung's statements are full of allusions that lead into realms both vast and deep, but only after a careful study of the source material they contain do they reveal their light. In addition to Jung's *Collected Works*, this source material includes personal information of Hedy Wyss, found in her unpublished manuscript bearing the title *Lohengrins Schwarzer Schwan* (*Lohengrin's Black Swan*). In this document Hedy Wyss looks back on her encounters with C.G. Jung – years after his death – in which she intersperses notes from her diaries at the time, her own dreams, and occasionally also some passages from her own letters to C.G. Jung. She notes moments of her family life that must have caused her great suffering, her often difficult relationships with men, but most of all, her analysis with C.G. Jung and her, at times, painful longing for the "old wise man," as she often called him.

The report of Hedy Wyss ends in 1950, the year she met her future husband. The correspondence, however, continued for another six years, albeit with far longer intervals. C.G. Jung's last letter from Bollingen was postmarked October 1, 1956. In this letter Jung reflects on the transience of all things, on old age, and death.

Hedy Wyss, born in 1906, came from a Zurich family of physicians. She became a painter, perhaps in the hope of breaking away from her father and the bourgeois milieu of her family. Since she could sell only very few paintings, she had either to be supported by her family or keep her head above water by teaching at a grammar school, writing art reviews for various newspapers, and other occasional jobs, in order to survive. She was in constant need of money. This, however, did not at all diminish her creativity. In her paintings she often used mythological motifs. It seems that she was forced by the unconscious to express the images of her inner world through her creative work. This might also explain why many of her paintings appealed strongly to Jung, even if their immediacy sometimes also frightened him.

For a deeper understanding of Jung's letters, it is indispensable to consider the work he was engaged in at the time. Some motifs, thoughts and allusions can only be explained when viewed against this background. This holds particularly true for the letters of 1943. In January of that year, Jung had completed the German version of his first major work on alchemy, *Psychology and Alchemy.*[1] From then on, the world of the alchemists never left him. In the years that followed, he was entirely preoccupied with *Mysterium Coniunctionis.* Yet, before its publication in 1955/56, several of his most important works appeared, from which he drew and inserted surprising details in his letters to Hedy Wyss. Sometimes these are only brief allusions that reveal the alchemical background of Jung's thoughts, while clearly showing the sources from which Jung's creative spirit drew inspiration.

This, though, also led to a certain estrangement between Jung and Hedy Wyss, since the world of the alchemists ultimately remained alien to the comparatively young artist. The first signs of this estrangement occurred as early as mid-1942. Nevertheless, in the following year of 1943, triggered by a truly shocking dream[2] of Jung's, their correspondence intensified once again. This also had to do with his preoccupation with *Mysterium Coniunctionis,* especially with the mysterious union of Sol and Luna as part of the alchemical opus. In February, 1944, Jung suffered a heart attack which

1 This version, however, was not published before 1944. This edition was based on two lectures that Jung gave in the years 1935 and 1936. See editorial note to the first edition, CW 12, "Introduction," p. vii. C.G. Jung, *Psychology und Alchemy,* CW 12, Princeton: Princeton University Press, 1993 (1952).

2 See Part II, chapter 8, "Jung's Dream in Geneva," pp. 135.

forced him to reduce all outer contact to a minimum. This is also reflected in the letters to Hedy Wyss, which now became shorter and less frequent.

The publication of this, in part, highly personal material undoubtedly brings with it a certain danger, be it the letters of C.G. Jung to his analysand, or the excerpts from Hedy Wyss' report in *Lohengrin's Black Swan*. In both cases, we are dealing with intimate material that, when torn from its living context, can easily become a source of misunderstanding. It is not my intention to comment on or to analyze the relationship between C.G. Jung and Hedy Wyss in any way. Instead, the letters reproduced here for the first time, as well as the commentary that follows, are intended to convey Jung's struggle to uphold the spiritual veracity of both his analysand and himself. Such veracity can, as Jung once wrote, "create a wider personality whose center of gravity does not necessarily coincide with the ego, but which, on the contrary, as the patient's insights increase, may even thwart his ego-tendencies." "Like a magnet," he continues, using an alchemical image, "the new center attracts to itself that which is proper to it."[3] The individuation process is the basis for any future renewal of life in the individual, as well as in the collective social realm.

Thus, Jung's message – also present in these letters – goes far beyond personal issues, namely to the urgent question of meaning which, after two devastating wars, arose in the 20th century. Jung was deeply convinced that the feminine, and therefore women in particular, has a decisive role to play in this process of renewal. Hence, he wrote, albeit before the catastrophe of the Second World War, "The woman of today is faced with a tremendous cultural task – perhaps it will be the dawn of a new era."[4]

*

At this point I want to express my gratitude to all those people who have supported this publication: first and foremost, the two nephews of Hedy Wyss who made it possible for us to acquire these, in many ways, unique letters of C.G. Jung; Wolfgang Wyss to whom we owe not only the fact that

3 C.G. Jung, *Aion. Researches into the Phenomenology of the Self*, CW 9/2, § 297.

4 C.G. Jung, "Woman in Europe," in: *Civilization in Transition*, CW 10, § 275. For Jung this is the transition from the Age of Pisces to the Age of Aquarius. Just how deeply Hedy Wyss was moved by Jung's work can be seen in her letter of July 11, 1936, to the "Esteemed Professor." See *Appendix*: *Two Letters of Hedy Wyss to C.G. Jung*, p. 233

the letters have survived in such good condition, but also the manuscript *Lohengrin's Black Swan*, in which Hedy Wyss looks back on her years of analysis with Jung. Without this document many passages in the letters would have remained in the dark. Warm thanks also go to my colleagues of the Foundation for the Promotion of Jungian Psychology for their generous support of this project. I am also indebted to the Foundation of the Works of C.G. Jung for granting permission to publish these letters for the first time. I am particularly grateful to Thomas Fischer, former Executive Secretary and now Member of the Board of the Foundation, and to Carl Jung, current Executive Secretary of the Foundation, for their open-spirited collaboration with this project.

With their often singular formulations, these letters were challenging to translate into English. Many a letter went back and forth between Alison Kappes-Bates and me, until even the smallest nuances seemed clearer to both of us. I am very grateful for Alison's meticulous translation. She and Judith Dowling corrected my English translation of the Commentary with great sensitivity and patience. This, too, turned out to be an inspiring adventure and collaboration. To both, I would like to express my deep gratitude. Robert Imhoff is responsible for the layout. With great dedication, he continuously made necessary adjustments to the layout of the text. Special thanks are extended to Robert Hinshaw of Daimon Publishers for publishing also the fourth volume of our series. And above all, I thank my wife Regine Schweizer-Vüllers for her helpful and encouraging presence on this adventurous path.

Zollikon, July 2023

Editorial Notes

We tried to adjust the English translation of the letters as much as possible to the German text.
Occasional remarks of the editor to the letters are placed in square brackets []: for example: [sic], to identify conspicuous spellings or statements of C.G. Jung.
If necessary, personal names were anonymized.
Location and date of the letters, or, if undated, the respective postmark, correspond to the original: i.e., Küsnacht-Zürich 27 VII 1937 or postmark 31.VII.37.
Addresses of sender and addressee are only reproduced in the first letter to avoid unnecessary repetitions.
The letters handwritten by C.G. Jung are marked with {HL} at the end. This applies to all letters from Bollingen.
In the commentary, Latin phrases have been italicized by the editor and, if necessary, translated within square brackets [...].
Underlined and cancelled words or letters correspond to the original.
Freely-formulated quotations, especially all the references to the manuscript *Lohengrin's Black Swan* by Hedy Wyss, are marked by single quotation marks.

Abbreviations

CW *The Collected Works of C.G. Jung.* Edited by Gerhard Adler, Michael Fordham, Sir Herbert Read, William McGuire. Translated by R.F.C. Hull. Princeton: Princeton University Press.
HL Handwritten Letter.

Part I:
C.G. Jung's Letters to Hedy Wyss
(1936 – 1956)

The Letters of December 1936 to November 1943

Prof. Dr. C.G. Jung

Küsnacht-Zürich
Seestrasse 228
December 15, 1936.

Miss H. Wyss,
Wettingerwies, 4,
Zürich

Dear Miss,

Unfortunately, it is quite impossible for me to see you before Christmas, as my vacation is about to begin in a few days, and I will not be back before mid-January.

With the utmost respect,
C.G. Jung

*

Küsnacht-Zürich, March 27, 1937.

Dear Miss,

Unfortunately, it has not been possible for me to see you. I sensed that our last conversation had set all sorts of things in motion, and confusion, within you, and I, too, had hoped to be able to clarify certain things. Unfortunately, this is no longer possible and we will have to leave it till our next appointment after vacation.

In the meantime, I have seen Miss v. Franz, who was able to make quite pleasing progress during the vacation.

With best regards
Your ever-devoted,
C.G. Jung.

PS. Meanwhile, your second letter has arrived. You do not have to take everything I say as an "exhortation to do better." I am merely making a point. And furthermore, it is important to know what your Eros is aiming at. For it is a god and, as Diotima said, "a dangerous poisoner."[5] For God's sake, do not think I am 'moralizing.' For I am simply admiring the beauty of the gentians and trying to understand the song of the birds, and I do this only so that, with the help of art and *Deo adjuvante* [with God's help], nature may become what it is. This is why you need to grasp what you are as a child of nature, beyond good and evil.

Yours truly, once again and as above.[{HL}6]

*

Küsnacht-Zürich 27 VII 1937

Dear Miss!

May I ask you to give the enclosed letter to Miss v. Franz? She has not given me her address and I, heaven knows, do not know it off by heart. So be my good angel = *ángelos* = messenger.

Thank you very much!
Your,
C.G. Jung.[{HL}]

*

5 See: *The Dialogues of Plato*, volume II, "The Symposium." Translated with comment by R.E. Allen, New Haven and London: Yale University Press, 1991, p. 147, 203d.

6 Only the postscript is handwritten.

Küsnacht-Zürich 27 VII 1937

Dear Miss!

I would gladly comply with your wish if I knew an appropriate address. However, I will make inquiries and then get back to you. I was very interested in your pictures. I was only afraid afterwards that my reaction to them might have disturbed you. If that was not the case, so much the better. I have received a weighty letter from M.-L. v. Fr. which I have not yet been able to read because of its bulk. What's more, my secretary[7] is ill. I am drowning in letters. Rather than wishing me '*buon lavoro*,' which, to the devil, of course, means letters, I would rather you wish for Zurich's main post office to have an aerial bomb dropped on it! Nevertheless, I read yours with pleasure.

With my best greetings,

Your devoted,

C.G. Jung.{HL}

*

Küsnacht-Zürich [Postmark 31.VII.37]

Dear Miss!

The address requested is Prof. Eugen Frey, Bahnhofstr. 79, tel. 72525 Zurich.

One must differentiate carefully between those things that must be and those that could be.

With my best greetings,

Yours,

C.G. Jung.{HL}

*

Küsnacht-Zürich January 20, 1939.

Dear Miss,

I have, indeed, heard about your regrettable misfortune. It is decidedly dreadful when fate so callously puts one to bed for two months. But this is often the place where people get to think about all sorts of things, and to think about them deeply, since the long, pleasant period of rest and the plaster cast make it impossible to escape.

7 Marie-Jeanne Schmid. She was Jung's secretary from 1932–1952.

I have due sympathy for you, and I can only hope that you will have the necessary patience to get through this incubation of yourself happily. I also think that it would not be bad if you read some more serious things during this time, because such things are not only educational for the mind, but sometimes also good for the heart. For example, I would recommend you read the sermons of Meister Eckhart.

If you have any other concerns, you know that I can be reached by mail and I will be glad to help you.

With best wishes for a speedy recovery.

I remain,

Your ever-devoted,

C.G. Jung

*

Küsnacht-Zürich February 2, 1939.

Dear Miss,

Unfortunately, I cannot respond to everything in your letter: it would go too far. However, the "thinking" you describe to me "was not meant that way." One can also be thoughtful without thinking anything. That would probably be much more accurate.

I am glad to hear that you have understood Meister Eckhart correctly. If you would like some further serious reading matter, I would recommend the Sermons of the Buddha. There is a German translation by [Karl Eugen] Neumann: "Die Reden Gotamo Buddhos" [The Speeches of Gotamo Buddhos][8] 3 vols. The style is peculiar and somewhat tiring because of the endless repetitions. They are just memorized fragments of speech, which were and are recited with a hieratically-delivered voice. If you read them as if you were listening to them, you will get roughly the right impression. They sound like the half-sung preface of the Mass.

Wishing you further good progress in your recovery and all the necessary patience.

I remain,

Your ever-devoted,

C.G. Jung.

*

8 Siddhārtha Gautama is the historical Buddha who roamed the land as a wandering ascetic before his breakthrough to the awakened one (*buddha*).

Presently, at Bollingen. Ct. St. Gallen. [Postmark 17.VII.39.]

Dear Miss Hedy Wyss!

You will have to wait with your pilgrimage. For the next 12 days, everything is up in the air. After that we can play it by ear. Not only didn't I smile, but I got the creeps from the involuntary God-likeness. Please, no adventure fantasies! I will be able to say "good day" and "hm, hm" to you, as one does, perhaps with a cup of tea and a sandwich.

With kind regards,
Your devoted,
C.G. Jung{HL}

*

Küsnacht-Zürich, 26.8.39.

Dear Miss,

Thank you very much for kindly sending me the Duino Elegies. I should have thanked you on the previous occasion, but the booklet had not yet arrived in Küsnacht when I was there.

I actually do not know the Elegies, for I am very uneducated in modern German literature. Thanks to your efforts, I will now have the opportunity to fill this gap of mine.

With sincere thanks,
Your devoted,
C.G. Jung

*

Küsnacht-Zurich 23 XII 1939

Dear Hedy Wyss!

I was pleased to hear that the "Sermones"[9] were well received by you. I thank you *anticipando* for your good intentions with the little box. I have

9 The "*Septem Sermones ad Mortuos*," the "*Seven Sermons to the Dead*," are a spontaneous product of the unconscious, which, as Jung stated, flowed out of him over three nights in January 1916. Later, he published them privately, and occasionally gave copies to friends. See: *Memories, Dreams, Reflections by C.G. Jung,* recorded and edited by Aniela Jaffé.

indeed received another letter (the missing one) from Miss Gregory. Please give her my regards when you write to her.

I am not actually ill, but very fatigued – the fatigue of a heart muscle that urgently needs rest. The only excursions I am therefore making are to my library, and I am cultivating being silent. However, your letter I had to answer because I liked it, just as I like the expression in your eyes. Yes, that's what it takes to be able to celebrate *dies natalis salvatoris nostri* [birthday of our savior] properly.

With warm Christmas wishes,

Your ever faithful,

C.G. Jung.{HL}

*

Küsnacht-Zürich 26 III 1940.

Dear Hedy Wyss,

Please accept my heartfelt thanks for the charming little box and its contents, as well as for your pleasant letter. My remarks about your behavior towards me were meant illustratively, in that I wanted to show you that you make it too easy for all those who want to escape, while you yourself, however, do not "intrude" (push, pester, etc.) your way enough into the world of reality. The main thing is that you have noticed something.

With best regards and wishes,

Your ever devoted,

C.G. Jung

P.S. I will be happy to pay a visit to your studio after my vacation.{HL}

*

Küsnacht-Zurich August 21, 1940.

Dear Miss Wyss,

I have just received your letter and can only repeat what I have already told you, namely that in this instance, it is difficult to have any good advice.

Translated from the German by Richard and Clara Winston, New York: Vintage Books Edition, 1989, pp. 378 ff. In the following quoted as C.G. Jung, *Memories, Dreams, Reflections.*

If you want to leave home, you must have a place to be [pied-à-terre]. You can't just leave and exist in a void; everyone knows that. On the other hand, you are so attached to your home that it will be difficult for you to find your place outside of it.

For the time being, therefore, I must be the bridge over which you will soon come and go. Meanwhile, I am keeping my fingers crossed for you in the hope that somewhere a shift will occur.

With best regards,
Your ever faithful,
C.G. Jung.

*

Bollingen, 28 VIII 40

My Dear Hedy Wyss!

Yes, my last letter was not exactly emotional. That's because it was typed, meaning, dictated. Of course, I had no idea that you were ill. The sudden change of weather also gave me a cough and rheumatism, as it generally does at an advanced age. (Stupid, how everything has to be repeated!) I had not realized that you are 35. To me, you still seem fabulously young. That's why you were simply in a hurry. A large amount of calculation must have gone into this love, for otherwise it would not have been so "expedient." However, Eros is a great and dangerous god; "a hunter and poisoner," as Diotima (who was obviously no longer quite so young) told Socrates. Intention is always a little bit questionable, even if it is understandable from a human point of view, and congenial for those who are not involved. On the other hand, one must occasionally jump "into the water", i.e., into the ucs. [unconscious], so that God may be served correctly, and in the manner he wishes. Out of this, out of the depths of destiny, come help and strength. Just don't force things!

So now, take good care of yourself and let me know how you get on.

With warm greetings,
Your faithful,
C.G. Jung{HL}

*

Bollingen, 18.XII.1940.

Dear Hedy Wyss!

The year should not end without you receiving the letter you wished for from me. First of all, you know that what I say must not be taken literally. I mostly speak in nuances. Not infrequently, I, too, must speak like the privileged average citizen of the oh-so-laudable city of Zurich, without intending to do so, but often because I intend just the opposite. But it is at times disconcertingly therapeutic to hear how it sounds in everyday language. For despite one's noblest intentions, one also has this within oneself. So, if at times one speaks like this, one is able to intercept in advance possible shocks from unexpected quarters. There are certainly pedigreed and highbred pigs in Epicure's drove. Only suffering, or the suffering of love, drowns out, in a redeeming way, the quieter or more audible grunts from the underworld. Indeed, Tristan and Isolde are as one with the snails, and between them, they form a heaven.

It is therefore natural that love should be both guide and judge – in matters of love. One is not, however, always in love, and, in life, other categories also matter.

Life has more than one meaning. For a woman, however, suffering love is probably of the very greatest meaning, far into the afternoon of her life. But then, one starts to notice something.

It seems to me there's not very much you can do about W. So, for the time being, it looks as if the situation is on hold, and I am helping you pass the time with a long letter. What about your paint brushes and pencils? What does the daemon who takes delight in color and form have to say? In such shadowy times, the ghosts sometimes speak and guide us to other realms where a new future is formed from the remnants of the past.

When you don't know what to do, it's best just to do whatever's next, and then the division ceases.

The sun will soon have passed its lowest point, and we shall secretly celebrate the epiphany of that being who encompasses suffering and joy.

With warm greetings and best wishes,

Your ever devoted,

C. G. Jung.{HL}

*

Küsnacht-Zürich 17 III 41

My Dear Hedy Wyss!

The phenomena you are suffering from are the well-known symptoms of back-flooding which occur when the River Jordan flows backwards (as it did at the time of Christ's baptism), that is, when the flow of libido is suddenly interrupted. You can't "do" anything right now. You can only wait patiently until the beginning of the next number. In life, a lot has to be left up to fate, for one can't "do" anything at all. The most one can do is to do the next and most immediate thing, and even that, we do with a sigh. In any case, I'm with you in this.

I will keep the letter from W. for the time being. You can, by the way, be glad to be rid of a "man" (?!) with this handwriting. It is the handwriting of a 16-year-old anima who is ready for retirement. (Please be discreet.)

Most sincere greetings,

Your ever faithful,

C.G. Jung.{HL}

*

Küsnacht-Zürich 16 IV 41

Dear Hedy Wyss!

I still have to thank you very much for the beautiful camellias that arrived here in pristine condition. I was delighted with this symbol of the southern spring. That you are still in a larger pickle, does not surprise me. It is also not easy to get over such a "death."[10] The dreams of the four points, and of the Chinese man, indicate "wholeness," (that which is "Chinese" wants to unite with you) as an ordering principle, which is superior to the ego. You are still a chaos from which order must emerge.

I shall be back again on the 29 IV.

In the meantime, with best regards,

Your ever devoted,

C.G. Jung.{HL}

*

10 Allusion to the man who left Hedy Wyss. See letter of March 17, 1941.

Küsnacht-Zürich 1.VII.41.

Dear Hedy Wyss!

You were right when you said in your letter that one must live in two worlds. It is, actually, quite natural for a person to live in two worlds. If one tries to live in only one, both can easily bite the dust. The one thrives on the other. You still have to learn the art of not dumping everything into the same hole, but to render unto Caesar the things that are Caesar's, and unto God the things that are God's. It is not a matter of either/or, but of the one and the other. If you cannot be inexpedient, then you also lack the freedom to be expedient. It is not just a matter of falling in love, but of the difficult art of love, which, as we know, does not insist on its own way,[11] but also on the well-being of the other person. You have not yet completely finished with the father, which is why I am still of importance to you. To "go against" [kick against] it is of no use to you at all; one has to see what will help you more in life than 100 disappointments in love. You can have those as well, if you don't believe me, or if it is necessary for other reasons.

Thus, with my best wishes,

Your devoted,

C.G. Jung.{HL}

*

Küsnacht-Zürich 28 VII 1941

Dear Hedy Wyss!

It appears you find yourself in rather rough seas: rejoicing sky high, and then more often its opposite. In any case, I would like to thank you very much for your various greetings, and to say that I hope we will see you in Ascona, so that we at least get to shake hands.

Of course, you have to form the young man to some extent, but the main point is that you redeem what you want.

Always yours truly,

C.G. Jung{HL}

*

11 1 Corinthians 13:5.

Küsnacht-Zürich 18 VIII 1941

My Dear Hedy Wyss!

Unfortunately, I cannot write to you at length as I am not quite well and should rest a lot. But I must tell you that your anxiety dream has to do with Dr. W. She probably won't let Bentinck go and is trying to push you away. According to the dream, you should have spoken to this lady very firmly. The black Madonna is acting as a magic shield. These things are always haunted. The other dreams, too, want to be seen in this light. You have to wrestle for the soul of Bentinck – namely, with the mother witch.

Warmest greetings,
and best wishes,
from your,
C.G. Jung.{HL}

*

Locarno, 15 1 42.

Dear Hedy Wyss!

Not so speedily, indeed with some delay, I am reacting to your non-confessional- confessional letter. Any suitable band-aid in letter form for the known-unknown place – the consolation for the crude ego – is probably only to be achieved by the actuality of a written page, with its pasted-on atmosphere or aura of obliging sympathy. But tomorrow, I return to the domestic gods and will then soon see you face to face and not merely in the rather dark mirror of your letter. Dionysos could have said to the lamenting Ariadne, whom the Minotaur-conquering Theseus had deserted, "I am your band-aid" (instead of "la[by]rinth"), and it would have been true, for I am hellishly ill-suited to be an orphan's father. Since writing letters only creates labyrinthine squiggles of the soul that hopelessly entangle the Minotaur-slayer in an Ariadne-like clew, I will hereby bring my good intentions to an end.

Wishing you a happy and eventful New Year,
I remain,
Your ever-devoted,
C.G. Jung{HL}

*

Küsnacht-Zürich 21 IV 1942.

My Dear Hedy Wyss!

I have already written a letter to you in my mind, but it did not make it into reality, as, firstly, I had to work dreadfully hard on the new edition of an old book, and secondly, because of the battle of food production.[12] I had to dig for days. This is not conducive to letter-writing.

Your situation is, however, unpleasant indeed! If you don't want to return home – which I understand – you must, for God's sake, do something that will bring in the necessary money. But to advise an artist is an impossible task! Your brother should put his wisdom into practice by finding something that would help you. Anyone can make speeches. However, I, too, am also one of those stupid people who can do nothing but talk. But talk I must. I would prefer not to. But if I were to pull out one by one the few remaining hairs I have on my head, I would still be unable to come up with something that would help you. I would have liked to see you in Bollingen at least, but unfortunately, I am so weighed down with obligations to fulfill that I need every minute of the few days that remain of my so-called vacation.

Why not walk up to people and bore as many of them as possible with questions about what is to be done in such a situation? You might hear something that is useful.

Oh dear, I can only assure you of my imbecilic sympathy, as if you had died! And thus, I must remain utterly inadequate.

Your ever-faithful
C.G. Jung.{HL}

*

Küsnacht-Zürich July 1942
[Postmark Bollingen, 10.VII.42]

My Dear Hedy Wyss!

I should have written long ago and thanked you for your "colorful" letter,[13] which touched me in all possible and impossible ways. My vacation, however, has been such that there hasn't been much free time. Your second letter is so perfect that you must nevertheless hear from me immediately. You have infected me with the desire to see you again, and therefore, I hasten

12 Swiss food production during World War II.

13 Hedy Wyss often illustrated her letters with drawings, smaller paintings and other things.

to inform you that next Saturday, I will temporarily be in Küsnacht again. I shall, however, be busy all afternoon, but I could see you around 6.30 p.m. Your new idea is of significance, despite my not understanding it. Somewhere, though, it resonates. You are quite right: we draw from the same substratum, and that is joyful, embarrassing, strange, uncanny, doubtful, indeed, just like life itself.

Warmest regards,
From your ever-faithful,
C.G. Jung{HL}

*

[Postmark Bollingen, 17.VII.42]

Dear Hedy Wyss!

I will be arriving from Rapperswyl tomorrow, Saturday, at 2 o'clock at the main station, and I shall have time until around 3 o'clock, when I must go to a meeting. I shall have lunch at some point. If it suits, we could use this opportunity to meet.

With best regards,
Your devoted,
C.G. Jung{HL}

*

Küsnacht-Zürich 28 VII 1942
[Postmark Bollingen, 28.VII.42]

Dear Hedy Wyss,

Heartfelt thanks for your letters, which again charmed me, despite the horrors they contain. The black eagle or vulture ("lambs" – is good!) has, unimportantly, to do with the parents. More importantly, he is the animus of your own ucs. [unconscious], the ucs. spirit, which swoops down on you so devastatingly. It is the ucs. out of which you paint, and which simultaneously hinders you the most, and will continue to do so until you can understand it. For this, I have to play, or even be, the faithful Eckehart (which is made considerably more difficult by your being such a charming protégé), and to support your apprehension in a long-winded way (this depends on how quick you are to catch on). As long as you are with your parents and under their wing, they will cause you to suffer and you will hold them responsible.

But once you stand on your own two feet, you will gradually realize that you carry the whole parental web within you, and not only that, but also the web in which your parents and your forebears already wriggled themselves to death. *Omnes animae ligatae sunt*: we are all bound. *Attraxit me natura et attractus sum*: nature has attracted me and I am attracted, i.e., bound. Like the sun grows of the night, freedom grows only in captivity. Where bound? Where free? that is the question.

To hell with it – I don't have time and I should be preparing my lecture, but I have to write you a nice letter because you are my daughter, my sister, and who knows what else. Where is the freedom in that? Something always catches us, and it is always precisely as bad as we are ourselves. We have to say yes to it [to what is trapped by the shadow], for otherwise, that which "takes captive your captives"[14] cannot become what it is meant to become. Your letter from the mountain was really good and somehow touched me. Where do you have the bird of prey that you are afraid of?

You probably don't want to go forward with the times, and that's why you crawl back to Papa W.[15] (with the syphilitic first stage chancre on his lip). I, too, am this kind of fool who looks back, who has to look back, because such a nice thing is coming along behind him. Who wouldn't look back? That's what at least half of life is about, isn't it? But you must not look back yet, because you have not yet reached your full potential; behind you are too many hooks still waiting for you. And I can't leave you hanging there, can I? At least, not if you wish for something different. Your will seems to me to be the imperative. (This is a good start.) For the time being, at least, that seems to be the case. But our paths do not always lead only to one side, for otherwise they would all go in circles. One must trust the way, in God's name. (There are things that are smarter than we are).

Are you coming to Ascona this year?

In any case, warmest greetings,

From your,

ever-faithful,

C.G. Jung.{HL}

*

14 Allusion to the Song of Deborah and Barak which is one of the oldest parts of the Hebrew Bible (12th century BC): "Wake up, wake up, Deborah! Wake up, wake up, break out in song! Arise, Barak! Take captive your captives ..." Judges 5:12 (New International Version).

15 Her friend, with whom she had broken up a year earlier.

Küsnacht-Zürich 19 VIII 1942.

Dear Hedy Wyss!

Yes, Dr. Boss[16] was certainly helpfully excited to assist, and he believed it would be possible to tell your father. I am a bit more pessimistic in this respect, i.e., as far as "meddling" in sacred family secrets is concerned. I already had the feeling in Ascona that things were not going all that well for you. But I really could not do anything for you there. Indeed, one cannot properly help you at all, for "something should come to take you away." If I did not already have such a large family in need of money, I would give you the necessary subsidy, so your only lament would be about painting, and about the wickedness of the world in general. We all still have a roof, a bed, clothing and a loaf of bread, and have not yet been deported to Poland, or shot. We must learn to be grateful for even the smallest things, and to marvel at the enormity of our concupiscentia. In times when fools expect more, there is always less.

I will return to Küsnacht for two days at the beginning of September and hope to be able to see you then.

With my best greetings,

Your ever-devoted,

C.G. Jung.

P.S. The pregnant dragon is very promising! A novelty in your menagerie![17]{HL}

*

Küsnacht-Zürich 12 Nov. 1942

Dear Hedy Wyss!

If I recommended for you to take the other path, I did so only in order to have done everything in my power to prove to you that you are not being held fast by me, as appears to be the case in your paintings. For there is a still deeper meaning to the latter, which, however, will only be beneficial for you to know when you are completely sure that the little horse has its stable with

16 Jung wanted to send the analysand to his much younger colleague Dr Medard Boss, the later founder of Daseinsanalysis. He was probably the right man to deal with her sensuality. This triggered a huge crisis in Hedy Wyss, "a solar eclipse," as she said.

17 Hedy Wyss often used the motifs of animals, dragons and other mythical creatures in her paintings.

me. I have an aversion to appearing as a horse thief. I never throw anyone out who is serious and well-intentioned, so I could never bring myself to force you to do anything, as it were, against your will, and of which you are not convinced. I would never have suggested for you to go to Boss if I had not had this dream, and if you had not had signs pointing in a similar direction at the same time. So, calm down. I am always here for you. For now, you need only be patient for a few more days, as I am too busy with work at the moment.

With my kind regards,
Your, as always, ever-present
C.G. Jung{HL}

*

Locarno, until 4 I
Küsnacht-Zürich 1 I 1943

Dear Hedy Wyss!

This bellows (is its name, *'Blasen Sie mir'*?) [18] is large and one of a kind. It will be given a place of honor in Bollingen. Thank you very much! My warmest wishes for the New Year, which is beginning on a hopeful note! Since many things can still come true for you, I shall continue to keep my fingers crossed for you in the New Year, and you have my very best wishes. *À propos* – the food here is very good and I feel accordingly. I hope you also survived a good New Year's dinner.

With my best greetings and
heartfelt, air-pumped thanks,
Your faithful,
C.G. Jung{HL}

*

Küsnacht-Zürich 10 I 1943

Dear Hedy Wyss!

Everything you write to me is quite true and nothing can be done about the fact that it has snowed upon my head, and that the weight of the years has accumulated in my stoop. It is also not necessary for you to agonize over

18 A play of words referring to a German idiom meaning "to ignore the other."

what you might mean to me. I know that I have something to do with your art. As you yourself say, you paint for me. That's how it seems to me, too, and that you paint for me doesn't make it any less meaningful. It simply has "meaning," though I don't know what. For I have discovered that something is only meaningful if you don't know what it means. So, don't fret too much about not knowing the meaning of meaningful things; leave well-meaning and providential secrets up to nature.

Regarding "shock": this need not necessarily be negative. If we could see 100 years into the future, we would all suffer from shell-shock. The future of the world is stranger to us than the hereafter.

I suspect you are a nun *contre coeur*, one who belongs to the order of the *Vita contemplativa* and who has a secret passion for the confessional as a prelude to God's love. These highest forms of culture always shock me, as, hitherto, they have invariably been followed by the dulling of the mind, or mockery, or barbarian invasion.

Meanwhile my warmest
greetings!
Your ever-faithful,
C.G. Jung.{HL}

*

[Poststamp Einsiedeln, 27.II.43]
Mense Februario, on 27th day a.D. [anno Domini] 1843 [sic].

My Most Dear and Amiable Maiden Hedy Wyss!

It gave me great and immense pleasure to have thy highly esteemed letter in my pocket, and then to read it at my leisure with the utmost devotion. Whilst thy letter is very sad, it is so full of beautiful feelings that I felt compelled to sit down and think of something that might bring thee comfort. I will not succeed in putting my good thoughts down on paper, though, for I am so unaccustomed to writing. And because of my advanced age, my thoughts are somewhat embroiled. Nevertheless, may I say that I feel quite like *St. Sebastianus*: pierced many times over by Amor's arrows, I lie wounded at thy feet. How am I to think upon thee, other than with much sighing and the most cordial affection?

Here at the monastery we celebrated a convivial meal, spiced with spiritual conversations. In the peace of this *refugii* I may well recover, and, strengthened with spiritual gifts, I will soon return and, with *fortitudo, continentia, patientia* and *perseverantia*, I shall be able to pass all the tests of a true chevalier.

I kiss thy hand, dearest friend,
Thy most obedient servant,
C.G. Jung[19{HL}]

Mense Februario, am 27ten Tage.
a.D. 1843.

Sehr theuere und liebwerthe Jungfer
Hedy Wyß!

Es war mir ein großes und ungemeines Vergnügen, Euren hochgeschätzten Brief in der Tasche zu wißen und ihn dann in Muße hervor zu holen, um ihn mit Gründlichkeit zu lesen. Euer Brief ist zwar sehr traurig, aber so voll schöner Gefühle, daß ich mich doch hinsetzen muß, um etwas tröstendes für Euch aus=zudenken. Es will mir zwar nicht gelingen, meine guten Gedanken richtig aufs Papier zu bringen, da mir das Schreiben so sehr un=gewohnt ist. Und wegen meines hohen Alters meine Gedanken etwas embrouilliert sind. Ich mag Euch aber doch mittheilen, daß ich mich so recht als ein St Sebastianus fühle, von Amor's Geschoßen vielfach getroffen und verwundet Euch zu Füßen liege. Wie vermag ich der

19 Up to this point, the letter is written in Old German Script with the exception of the words printed in italics. The postscript is once more in normal handwriting.

anders Euer zu gedenken, als mit viel Seuf-
zen und herzlichster Zuneigung?
Wir haben hier im Kloster ein geistliches
Mahl mit geistlichen Gesprächen gewürzt
gefeiert. Im Frieden dieses refugii mag ich mich
wohl erholen und gestärkt mit geistlichen
Gaben werde ich bald zurückkehren, um mit
fortitudo, continentia, patientia, perseverantia alle
Prüfungen eines rechten chevalier bestehen zu
können.
Ich küsse Eure Hand, theuerste Freundin,
Euer gehorsamster Diener

C. G. Jung.

Images 1a and 1b: Jung's letter from Einsiedeln in Old German Script

Forgive the strange theatre in which the grandmother has embroiled me. I have yet to understand it. It's a quirky story, but I know it's nothing bad. It's simply something making a strange detour so that the iron bands can fall off you. The unconscious is not as foolish as conscious man. For now, one gropes in the dark, and one must do so with patience until one once again reaches the light.

With warm greetings,
Always yours,
C.G. Jung.{HL}

*

Bollingen 26 III 1943.
Friday (Dies Veneris)

Dear Hedy Wyss!

Your letter presses deeply into the strings, sounding out chords that reverberate into the unfathomable.

Yes, that's it precisely, and that's what women look like when they love. And I should not beg forgiveness that I exist! This has been the pain and sorrow of an entire life, after realizing early on how women are able to love me, and then, how the Goddess herself descends into them and conjures up an ineffable springtime. That is why I fled from women. It was always "touch and go," because I am only One, one lone small male; but I suspected and feared that, somehow, I was beset by a god, invisible to myself, incomprehensible. In the solitude and silence of nature, or in research work, he was close to me, bearable in tremendous rapture or in abysmal distress and heaviness. But I found him to be unbearably painful when he confronted me in women and, as now, confronts me in you. I felt and feel like a cursed man. I am able to see divine beauty and, being deeply moved, to worship it, but it should not turn toward me, for how should I be capable of a response? I have tried to the point of exhaustion, and I am walled in by my loyalty and devotion. Out of sheer devotedness, I have become an ascetic, a hermit in the pleasure gardens of the earth, surrounded by beckoning butterflies and chirping colorful birds, enveloped by the scent of roses.

The shyest creature of the forest approaches me; the rarest of flowers open beneath my hand. Why? Because I am not a brutal, but a shy and fleeting, animal myself, in the grips of the God who cherishes all living things, of that love which remains ever true to itself and can never deny itself. I have nothing to oppose it with, and that is why I cannot respond. The deity is too big, and I am too small. I can say neither yes nor no. I would prefer to remain silent and to ask God to not appear to me in women. Alone, I can bear his presence, but let him not move me through the woman, for I can give her no answer without presuming some likeness to God. Of me, there is but One, but of women, there are many, and one should give each of them a full answer, for anything else is too little and violates the holy commandment of love. Though I must answer, for it would be inhuman not to, I must tell you that, as I breathe the fragrance of the rose, behold the light of day, and hear the rustle of the wind in the forest, I see the splendor of the eternal Deity in you. I thank nature and women who love for being beautiful. Nature is bearable, for she never expects more of me than my own nature can accomplish. She is satisfied if I breathe deeply, or if I greet the New Moon, or if I sit down quietly in the grass by the wayside, or perhaps just look yearningly out of my window. But what satisfies a woman, and especially one who loves? The only satisfying answer is the one that violates all the laws of love. But if I were to do that, only one woman would have loved me and turned away from me in disappointment. I am loved by so many women precisely because they feel that I am a lover of love and hold its commandments sacred. And yet they all want me to break those very commandments, unaware that I would then no longer be the one they were searching for and loved.

It would be easy for me to heedlessly pass love by, like a Buddha, but this I cannot do for love's own sake. I also cannot follow love, again for love's own sake. I want to tell you "Touch me not."[20] because you are only touching mortal imperfection, "suffering, old age and death"; I am only One. The splendor that surrounds me has been spread by a god. Do not seek this splendor in me, or I will sink into an abyss of shame for my pitiful poverty and limitations. Don't be fooled by my seemingly lengthy response to your feelings: I cannot deny giving you this response. But it is also all that I can do. I cannot pick flowers; I cannot shoot creatures of the forest. I cannot claim any beauty in the world for myself, for I am unable to restore it. For some unknown reason, God has determined for me to be a friendly beast in the forest of this world. It wanders alone, yet it is always surrounded. Wherever it appears, it's springtime. One could also say that it follows the spring. Either way, it can't make spring, and it doesn't do anything with spring, like a white bear that lives according to bear law and can't imagine anything beyond that. Both God and animal come together in humankind, evoking suffering and beauty, and never the one without the other. One is left with only a small garden of flowers and vegetables that demands all that one has to give.

20 John 20:17.

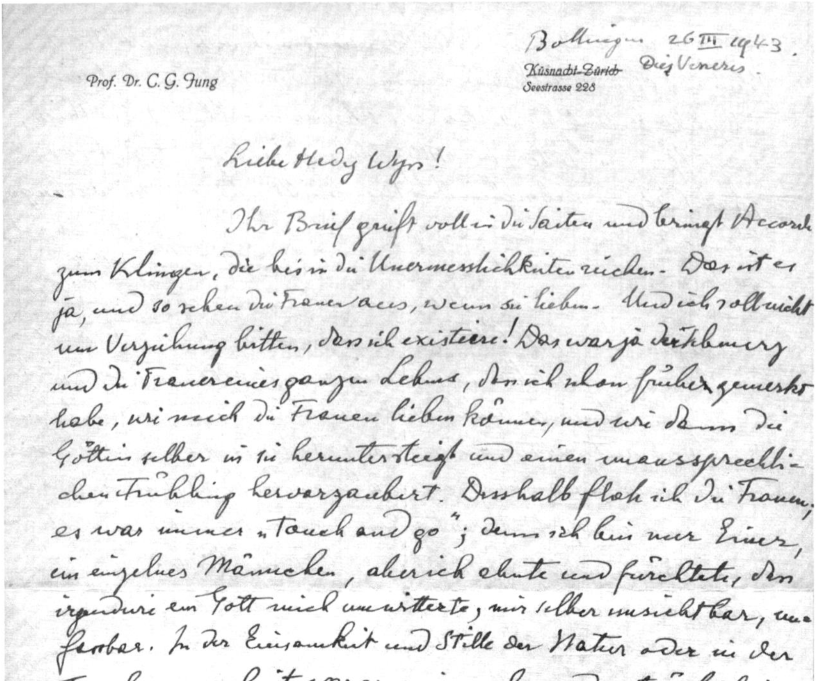

Bollingen 26 III 1943.
Dies Veneris.

Prof. Dr. C. G. Jung

~~Küsnacht-Zürich~~
Seestrasse 228

Liebe Hedy Wyss!

Ihr Brief greift voll in die Saiten und bringt Accorde zum Klingen, die bis in die Unermesslichkeiten reichen. Das ist es ja, und so sehen die Frauen aus, wenn sie lieben. Und ich soll nicht um Verzeihung bitten, dass ich existiere! Das war ja der Schmerz und die Trauer eines ganzen Lebens, dass ich schon früher gemerkt habe, wie rasch die Frauen lieben können, und wie dann die Göttin selber in sie heruntersteigt und einen unaussprechlichen Frühling hervorzaubert. Deshalb floh ich die Frauen; es war immer „touch and go"; denn ich bin nur Einer, ein einzelnes Männchen, aber ich ahnte und fürchtete, dass irgendwie ein Gott mich umwitterte, mir selber unsichtbar, unfassbar. In der Einsamkeit und Stille der Natur oder in der Forschungsarbeit war er mir nahe und erträglich in ungeheurer Entzückung oder in abgründiger Bedrängnis und Schwere. Unerträglich schmerzhaft aber war es mir, wenn er mir in Frauen entgegentrat und, wie jetzt, in Ihnen entgegentritt. Ich kam und komme mir vor wie ein Verfluchter. Ich kann die göttliche Schönheit sehen und in Ergriffenheit verehren, aber sie soll sich mir nicht zuwenden, denn wie sollte ich ihr antworten können? Ich habe es bis zur Erschöpfung versucht und bin in Treue und Ergebenheit eingemauert. Aus lauter Hingebung ein Asket, ein Einsiedler in den Lustgärten der Erde, umspielt von lockenden Schmetterlingen und zwitschernden bunten Vögeln, umschwebt vom Dufte der Rosen.

Image 2: Letter of March 26, 1943 Dies Veneris (extract)

Zimmer's death[21] filled me with sorrow. My best friends died young or relatively early, as if the imminence of their deaths spurred on their understanding. Accordingly, A. K. will go on living for a long time in order to outlive himself.

You have already understood a lot about me; God grant that you may also understand the mere-human about me.

With cordial greetings,
Your faithful,
St. Sebastian.{HL}

*

Küsnacht-Zürich 31 III 1943

Dear Hedy Wyss!

Thank you very much for your kind letter. It was benevolent and I breathed a sigh of relief. I have been going through a strange and devilishly difficult time in which death's bolt of lightning has been striking to my left and to my right. First, Heinrich Zimmer, and then my peer and colleague from my student days Prof. Rud. Staehelin in Bern. When I arrived at the Wettstein Bridge in Basel, an old woman, who had probably had a stroke and died, was being carried away from the square. During the night of 29th-30th, in Geneva, I had a dream that suddenly explained to me where my historical fantasy of 1843 and 1743 came from. In fact, it has to do with my great-grandmother and Mr. von Goethe.[22] My last letter to you was already overshadowed by the dark doom that has been weighing on my soul up to now. I could neither foresee it nor know it – it is too far beyond the human realm. Unfortunately, I can't write more to you at this moment. I will tell you about it in detail later. You were an instrument of fate for me, and without you, I would probably never have been able to fathom this mystery. I feel like it had to do with a birth that I might equally as well have died from. It seems that some insights can be quite life-threatening. Don't be

21 The Indologist Heinrich Zimmer died of pneumonia on March 18, 1943, at the age of only 51. He was a welcome guest and lecturer at Eranos, as well as at the Psychology Club Zurich.

22 According to legend, Jung's grandfather *Karl Gustav Jung*, born in Mannheim in 1794, was an illegitimate son of *Carl Gustav Jung's* great-grandmother Sophie Jung-Ziegler and of Johann Wolfgang von Goethe. See C.G. Jung, *Memories, Dreams, Reflections*, "School Years," p. 35, footnote 1.

concerned, my dear; I won't be walking away from this. Less now than ever before! Much has now been clarified, and a woman's psychology has become much clearer to me. There was something I didn't know. But no one knew it.

Tomorrow, I leave for Bollingen and I shall not forget you. I shall also be able to laugh again, for the curse of the House of Atreus has been lifted. For the moment, I am still just a little bit rattled. "*Reiter und der Bodensee*" feeling.[23]

My warmest greetings and thanks, my dear swan, to speak in the words of Lohengrin.

Your ever-devoted,
C.G. Jung{HL}

*

Küsnacht-Zürich 6 IV 1943

Dear Hedy Wyss!

Thank you very much for your refreshing letter! It is much easier to digest than the sad sort. I could have howled at the moon. And what thoughts the sad devil is able to instil in you! Experiment!!! Do you think I 'experiment' with people for whom I must sweat blood? I just have to be real and, God knows, those around me have to be real, too, because life has to be genuine down to its last fiber; otherwise, it's all substitution and loss. In doing so, my dear black swan, one drowns in ink, for the essence of this world is black – *nigrum, nigrius, nigerrimum* [black, blacker, black as a crow]! But in the darkness, one ultimately encounters the light. This just happened in my dream. You have helped me, unknowingly, onto the right path, and I would not have thought of it if I had not, despite death and the devil, admitted my century fantasy to you. This was not, by heaven, an experiment, but a 149-year-old[24] curse that I still had to solve. A karman [sic] that weighed on me and that I never understood. Like a blind pig, I had to root around in the darkness (1875[25] is the year of the pig according to the Chinese calendar. Šakyamuni [Gautama Buddha] was born in that year. Thank God!) It

23 "The Horseman and Lake Constance," is a German ballad by Gustav Schwab (1826) in which a horseman unknowingly rides across a frozen lake. When he realizes it, he falls from his horse to his death.

24 His grandfather Karl Gustav Jung was born in 1794, 149 years ago.

25 C.G. Jung's year of birth.

started with this fantasy 1743 – 1843 – 1943. In Geneva, after an extremely sad, puritanical rainy-weather twilight of the Calvinist *institutiones* and with the Servetian[26] smell of fire, I had a good dinner on my own that included three dl of Aigle, which did not have the desired effect, but produced instead strange heart symptoms, arrhythmia and similar gallopings. To bed at 9 o'clock, wanting to sleep, but suddenly seized by the fantasy to rewrite the first part of Faust in Basel German, starting at the end, as if it were the beginning. Finishing with the monologue in which Faust finally decides to study medicine. That made me crazy; my pulse got worse. I took quinidine for the arrhythmia and a sleeping pill. At about 1 a.m., I awoke in a wild rage, feeling as if I were having a heart attack, as I once had had in 1941 following a rage dream. But the quinidine (how wise!) helped prevent it and the shot missed. Now comes the dream that ended with anger. Oh God, it is too long. For the time being, I will only mention the basic story: In 1794, my ancestor [Jung's great-grandmother] conceived a son by Goethe. She appeared in the dream and was crazy, thinking I was the Redeemer. I understood only afterwards that I am her redeemer.

Enough for today! Hail to the swan!

Your ever devoted,

Eckehart.{HL}

*

Bollingen. 16 IV 1943

Dear Hedy Wyss!

Please accept my heartfelt thanks for the tea-laden Easter bunny that came hopping in, bringing sweets in its wake. I would have liked to invite you to our hermitage to see the spring, but I am "*au complet*" with my family, and, what is more, I am being brutalized by digging and mucking out and potato planting. But it does me good, and it frees me from suffering on behalf of humanity, 60 to 90 per cent of whom can be written off as hopeless. Real work on Mother Earth is beneficial to the soul, because, like nothing else, it limits one to doing what is next and most immediate. In this way, I am able to regain the strength that is needed to cope to some extent with the onslaught of suffering in this world. Prior to this, I was pretty much at

26 Allusion to the Protestant Michael Servetus, who, at Calvin's instigation, was burned as a heretic in Geneva in 1553, at the age of 44.

the end of my rope, and the dream was just the last straw. My ancestress sat inside of you, from which I must conclude that you bear a special resemblance to her. It is probably an aesthetic sensibility, or lack thereof, which appears so charmingly in you, that caused the 150-year Karman. Reversing this fate is a bitter and difficult task. But I do not want to write a "sad" letter in this beautiful spring season. The "swan" frightened me a little, for it could be pulling an Elsa von Brabant after it, and Lohengrin would not be able to escape, but would have to have the upper hand in order to guzzle up that ink into which life always leads. I have learned to swim; I hope you can too.

In my last letter, I inexcusably, utterly, forgot to congratulate you on your successes and to tell you how pleased I was that you managed to sell a painting to the Social Democratic Party. They seem to be very capable people. I owe my literary prize also to this praiseworthy party.

Springtime is an evil time for love. You should see all the wailing wall notes that I receive these days. The excess makes one cynical – in my own defense, because one also wants to howl, to repent, and to grapple along with them – at least the "it" that claims to be "I" does. But one must remain with one's own karman, so that the life that has been prescribed for one is fulfilled. "All is transition" is written on the bridge in Schmerikon.[27]

With warm regards,
And my best thanks,
Your ever-devoted,
C.G. Jung.{HL}

*

Bollingen. 1 May 1943

Dear Hedy Wyss!

Strange! I did not recognize your handwriting on your letter and, as a result, it has been left unanswered. Even stranger! When you were in Geneva, you were lost to me here. It was as if you were dead, as if your back were turned toward me, and the place where the swan was hatching was empty, and your handwriting was unrecognizable, or it was extremely unlikely that you would write. These phenomena are somewhat alarming. The Anima-haunting is behind it. Caution and consideration seem indicated.

27 A village near Bollingen.

Since you are so insistently interested in my health, I am happy to confirm, "upon receipt of your honored from the xth yz," that I am well. I have dug up and planted 250 square meters of heavy soil and, like a Saturnus, fertilized it with manure, lime and phosphates. I have been able to drink wine again and have done so rigorously.

At the beginning of my vacation, I was overcome with fatigue; the suffering of the world, small, large, near, far, sank like a lead-laden iron ship to the bottom of my sea, leaving the world empty, a stomping ground for ancestral souls and field spirits that hopped around like goats in ruins. It was eerie; and you were drowned, irretrievably it seemed, in the Calvinist, melancholic hole called Geneva. Please, don't let yourself be beguiled by these peripeteia; take only one-half to three-quarters of it seriously, and definitely subtract two-fifths of it. My vacations are namely always a (successful? or failed?) attempt at restoring the so-called reasonable equilibrium in a world that is in itself completely unstable, or has turned upside down, or bottom-side-up, and to do so at that old, most improbable place, namely in one's own *quantité négligeable* called "I".

Thank God that you can swim autodidactically – because that is the safest way. It means I don't have to guard either my pen or my tongue too much, which is a great relief.

I am equally pleased that you want to see clearly. I wish the same for myself. All sorts of things have already been clarified. "But more of that in person," as the saying so beautifully goes. I am a little more optimistic where "clarity" is concerned.

I am grateful if I do not disturb you too much. I hope you have recovered from Geneva.

In the meantime,
With my best regards,
Your faithful,
C.G. Jung.[{HL}]

*

Küsnacht-Zürich 2 July 1943

Dear Hedy Wyss!

You are absolutely right: You have never "said all that there is to say." That's why I reminded you several times that starting a conversation would be desirable. You were surprised that I apologized for that great-grandmother fantasy (even inwardly asked for forgiveness for it); I knew why. *Votre coup a porté.* I have to take the blame. I am now turning 69, and there are still things to be destroyed in me that I cannot master. Arrow wounds heal. The modern cannon shot has a more lasting effect – and it is indescribably painful. *Un coup de grâce* [death blow] – this is how "transferences" are resolved, and never have they been resolved otherwise, except in the sackcloth and ashes of one's own accursedness. The monstrous pain of all living beings is the inexorability of their death. For God's sake, is there no gentle shroud that one could spread over the carrion of beauty biting the dust? I know that you suffer – suffer terribly – the recoil of the cannon! Both the slayer and the slain are one and the same. I ask you and I ask myself not to carry through with the slaying, but for your sake, for my sake, for the sake of the eternal divinity, let us rise again, because one must prove oneself to oneself despite oneself. We are untrustworthy, not credible and not worthy. Why on earth am I even talking? I am only able to devour myself.

Didn't you know that there is something else besides "transference"? Have we never heard of "love" that "bears all things and endures all things," that "does not insist on its own way"[28] but submits? I must believe in this love: without it all our beginnings are meaningless and invariably end in the catastrophe of the transference. And because I believe in you, I must, in spite of my own human weakness, in spite of the most hideous misunderstandings, try again and again to overcome the "transference," the sinister entanglement in the force of destiny [*heimarmene*], through that most difficult art: to love a human being. For me, this means first and foremost to allow someone the dignity of making their own decision.

I cannot believe you are so very different that you would not be able to understand such things. I cannot believe I was so wrong about you. (Nevertheless – the great-grandmother. Forgive this voice from the sidelines; it is aimed at me!) In the same way that "the innermost nature of all grain is wheat, and of all metal, gold," all merely human love bespeaks a higher state, the attainment of which leads into suffering and through the Crucifixio. No one can escape this historical process, and everyone has to make their own bloody contribution.

I am not angry with you, for I do not believe I am a truly evil person, but I find being a human being a heavy burden, and, as a mere human, I must seek an opportunity of finding meaning that is more than senseless desolation.

28 See 1 Corinthians 13:5-7.

I am unable to forget the time that we are living in, the immensity of the suffering! Why do you wage war against me? I know you are under attack by the devil and that you feel abandoned ... but no one can protect us from our own hell. Only the ability to suffer can help, namely to defy all longing to suffer.

Yours,
C.G. Jung.{HL}

*

Bollingen 7.VII.1943.

Dear Hedy Wyss!

I am very grateful for your kind letter. Why should you wage war against me? I do not want to deceive you, take advantage of you, exploit you, enslave you, rape you, bully you, or anything else against which war should be waged. You are surely not so superstitious that if you feel dependent somewhere or in some way, you believe that the other person has put this curse on you. If you feel unfree, it is solely because you desire to be dependent without knowing it. If I take an interest in you, it is only because I do not want you to feel trapped in a sterile dependency, and because I want to give you the opportunity to see why you find yourself in such a situation. Your dream is a part of this:[29] The ghost woman is in you. By virtue of her existence, my unconscious could project the great-grandmother. The ghost woman is the mother-anima of your father. This reveals the key parallel with my "guru" who called himself Philemon. He is equivalent to the father-animus of my mother, who had a pronounced father complex. Philemon is the sage who is in possession of the secret of the self. The key is to open the "*introitum ad occlusum Regis palatium*"[30] [entrance to the locked palace of the king], that "*castrum sapientiae*"[31] [house of wisdom] which is the seat of the self. The figure of your grandmother likewise fetches the keys from the "father" (who is indeed the representative of *sapientia*) in order to open the gate to the self. She is the father-anima form of your self, which wants to free itself from the form of the father-anima. Since I am the unenviable bearer of the father-image, your resistances are thus directed against me, as if I were your

29 Hedy Wyss dreamed of a mysterious, dazzlingly beautiful, black-haired woman who was looking for a key in her paternal grandfather's house.

30 This is the title of a treatise of Philaletha: "*Introitus apertus ad occlusum Regis palatium.*" C.G. Jung, *Mysterium Coniunctionis. An Inquiry into the Separation and Synthesis of Psychic Opposites in Alchemy*, CW 14, § 27.

31 For the "*castrum sapientiae*" see C.G. Jung, ibid., CW 14, § 731.

prison guard. This is a very natural and instinctive reaction. I was once badly bitten by a dog that I had rushed to help because it had caught its paw in a door that had been slammed shut by the wind. Please, do not think that the above is nothing but prosaic science. In reality, it is a desperate attempt to hold on to Ariadne's thread of consciousness in overwhelming darkness. These things are demonic, fateful, and of incalculable danger. Terms like "transference" and the like are hopelessly inadequate to express the mysterious nature of this event, or even to banish it into a formula. I know from my own innermost experience how terrible these forces can be, and therefore, whenever I see these 'super-personal personalities' or whatever one wishes to call them – at work, I try to help. No knowledge, no art helps; only one's own humanity, which one lays on the scales, fully conscious of the danger of doing so. One can only hope and pray that everything will turn out well. It's not a "love affair" that you could whisper about with your girlfriends, but a diabolical test of whether you can ultimately stand and bear yourself. Being alone with oneself, staring oneself in the face with no possibility of escape, that's what it's all about. Being alone has two meanings: it also means being al[l]-one.

If your need seems too heavy, please remember what is happening in the world right now. We are at war on the inside, where it actually belongs, and we must bring it to a good end. We cannot imagine ourselves to be the particular favorites of a "loving" God who spares us the abominations of war. We must learn not to inflict our own torment on others, as the Germans do on principle. I don't like to speak of love. It is too misleading. It seems to me that the only thing that matters is what one does to the other. It is not a matter of forgiving, but of understanding. I like you so much that I have to care about you. Whether one can call that love, I don't know. I am also not sure whether you agree with my doing so, or not. I believe that there is some meaning in my efforts on your behalf. I don't want to acquire or buy you, as it were; I simply want you to blossom like the woodruff, or to become what you are. I cannot stand by and watch plants that could bear beautiful flowers or fruit wither away. Mere weeds are of no interest. I think you will agree with me on that.

I will be back at the end of July, i.e., about 3 days before Ascona, if all hell has not broken loose by then. Should it be before then, I will try to reach you.

In the meantime, best regards from your rest-seeking,

C.G. Jung.{HL}

*

Bollingen 19 July 1943

Dear Hedy Wyss!

Thank you very much for your endearing letter from Basel. I feel very much at home in the Riehen area. I was also pleased to hear that you keep my letters and their contents "in a faithful and attentive heart." The only thing I have to report is that I'm struggling to rest. It's not so easy, but all the more necessary, since I was once again pretty low. I am doing better now. I was able to sail a few times, which is by far the best thing to do when you can't let go. With the wind, you sink into yourself, and then 1000 years pass like a single day. Bearing a likeness to God is an extremely benevolent thing, but less beneficial when it comes to the love of one's neighbor. That's why God himself had to become man, to see how it is if one may not be satisfied with oneself, but always has to integrate a further piece of humanity. Mercifully, human life is of a limited duration and is even interrupted by vacations during which one can imitate a bit of paradise. A fox, a weasel, and a snake have visited me and all knew nothing of the landing in Sicily.[32]

I will let you know when I reappear in Küsnacht.

Meanwhile, with best regards,

Your faithful,

C.G. Jung.{HL}

*

Küsnacht-Zürich 22 VII 1943

Dear Hedy Wyss!

Your dream is certainly very significant. Again, it harkens back to the ancestral story. My grandfather still spoke High German. If I had his extraversion, I would be better able to present myself. Indeed, it was easy for him to come across as a dignified person, whereas I must exist more humbly. I am constantly crushed by the enormity of the things I cannot master. Because I see too much and too many monstrous things, I must constantly struggle with the overwhelming sense of my ineptitude. Your dream says quite correctly that there are thoughts that can kill. There are murderous problems for the sake of which there is, even now, so much murder in the world. I do

32 The landing of the allies in Sicily in July 1943.

not feel up to this demonic situation, and that is why I cannot muster up any decent self-confidence.

By the way, are you also coming to Ascona? I'll be back home on 2nd Aug (Monday) and could see you then at 6 p.m. On 3rd, I am going to Ascona. Don't torture yourself too much, if you can help it.

With warmest regards, Yours, C.G. Jung.{HL}

*

Presently, Bollingen
10 IX 1943

Dear Hedy Wyss!

It is frightening, as it were, to see the ways and methods the dream uses to educate us to be honest. One realizes that one's rough-and-ready existence was only possible because, up to now, one was blissfully unaware of oneself and one's immediate truths and possible truths. Increasing consciousness does not make life easier or simpler. But it is beyond question that one must know, truly know, what one does and what one does not do. Life's outer circumstances and moral values do not change. Also, a brave person with a herd mentality lacks chronic holiness or Luciferian criminality which would allow them to live permanently beyond collective law. The most difficult thing is to be neither god nor pig, and then to have no illusions about one's "decency." For as high-standing as truth is, there is a diabolical twist to it, especially when it is completely true. It is similarly paradoxical with God and sin: he punishes one for those [sins] that one has committed and for those that one has failed to commit. Which of the two he punishes more severely remains an open question.

I hope I don't confuse you with my odious paradoxes; but they form the counterpart to your paradoxical dreams.

Please be patient! This letter should be the plaster for "homesickness" (a "drawing-out" plaster?!). By the way, I am deep in work: I am compiling the material for the timely *mysterium coniunctionis*. This appears to be having a devastating effect, which brings to mind the following verse [of a German folksong]: "And humanity, deeply apprehensive – Of the things yet to come – Sighs deeply." And yet, a proper answer should emerge from this heavenly-hellish question. I feel as one does in the *introitus missae*:[33] God have mercy on me, a sinner – *mea culpa, mea maxima culpa*! And I am in danger of becoming – indeed, of inevitably becoming – a moral pig. "One impulse art thou conscious of, at best; O, never seek to know the other!" That is the inheritance to be digested. I don't grumble, but I sweat. (Animals sweat, gentlemen perspire, ladies are all in a glow! How very apt! I need humor now more than ever!)

Yours, most humbly and obediently[1.)]
C.G. Jung.[{HL}]

Footnote 1.) For God's sake, I hope I haven't addled your brain! It was the "creator" who inspired this letter. I have long been appalled by the demiurge.

*

Küsnacht-Zürich [no date, probably September 15, 1943][34]

Dear Hedy Wyss!

Thank you very much for your kind letter! In the meantime, I have finished reading your diary. It has given me much to think about. I would like to single out only one point: your position on bourgeois morality. This is not "morality," but a psychological medium of a certain average – and therefore exceedingly collective – way of feeling and seeing things. Any violation of this realm is in itself nothing immoral (sometimes to the contrary!); rather it is an uncommon thing that occurs on the outside, which people perceive inwardly as being, at the very least, paradoxical. Seen from a greater distance, its criminal semblance is actually heightened. This collective standpoint is also within us and we cannot escape it. One can silence it for specific purposes and for a certain period of time, but it always returns in order to restore the state of psychic equilibrium. Thus, any violation of the collective standpoint is a serious matter: it causes a dissociation and a disturbance in the psychic equilibrium. As a rule, this disturbance is only clearly perceived by one person, while the other provokes the conflict (as he wishes to be rid

33 Entrance Psalm at Mass.

34 According to a note by Hedy Wyss on an unstamped envelope addressed to her – "after 30 Aug 43 – with diary returned" – Jung must have sent the diary back to her at the end of August.

of it and it is more agreeable to pity the other person). Projection always goes hand in hand with inflation! One's judgment is faulty because one lacks any inner counterpoint. It does not matter who has the conflict. It affects both parties either way – the one directly, the other indirectly – because it is essentially insurmountable. But since standing apart is then a personal imperative (if one is an outsider more or less by nature) then a chronic tension arises between one's personal imperative and the collective norm. This requires moral license which in turn incurs a moral debt to the norm. In the collective vernacular, this psychological debt is called "sin," though the good Lord knows exactly what He understands by this. Only squanderers and fools incur more debt than they can pay. Any violation of the norm constitutes a debt; it is felt as such, and plays out as such. No "spiritual freedom" exempts one from this; only self-deception feigns the moral high ground. Nature itself makes it all so seemingly easy and then, with an almost diabolical reversal of viewpoint, later presents the bill. Faint (?) portents of this earthquake are already vibrating in your diary entries and especially in your points of view. Be glad that I feel and realize this moral conflict on your behalf, and please, do not deceive yourself about the fact that your apparently conflict-free feeling is simply a means of bringing about that very situation in which your inner collective man will demand his payment with even greater force. I will pay my debt by standing by you for as long as you need me. But I will not pay your debt, my dear, for no one else can do that for you. Please understand: If I stand by you and take an active interest in you, I ask nothing of you in return. If you do not believe this, you can put it to the test. I would consider it beneath my dignity as a man to demonstrate it to you. Despite numerous painful disappointments, no woman will ever convince me of the unworthiness of chivalrous feeling.

I am writing to you in such detail about all of this so that you can see clearly how things look from my side, and so that you have no need to interpret, which, as your writings show me, falls very wide of the mark. I am in no doubt that you have to see things the way you do for the time being. But I am as I am. You are as you are. I do not presume to change you; I wish only to give you the chance to correct any errors. But please do not misinterpret my intention. Rather, question me diligently about my perceptions and feelings, and distrust what you think you see, for nature is playing with you, not me.

I know that you are a decent person and I trust you, and I will go on trusting you. But, through self-deception, you are in danger of losing your trust in me and, therefore, in yourself. It is my anxious concern to prevent that catastrophe from happening – Deo concedente. Since you understand neither the nature nor the scope of collective guilt, you perceive my sense of responsibility as being ridiculous. By doing so, you increase my responsibility many times over, for I see that you are blind in this regard. You are by nature a bit too much of an outside observer. Please do not make this burden any bigger, for no one can carry it for you. And if you feel that you are in error somewhere, please stick with it and confess to it, for then you will pay off at least a little of the debt imposed upon you. (This debt is the sins your father did not commit!). One cannot shake off the guilt. Why was it ever made possible for us to forget the terribly true doctrine of the *peccatum originale*?

Please, see me without any wishful fantasies, so that you are able to see where I stand. Just once, try to assume that I am not befuddled by illusions. I know that everything in you resists taking my reality into account. I do not demand that you make my reality your own; nevertheless, you must see it, for otherwise I feel as fictitious and futile as I felt when reading your diary. Where, for example, do you get the idea from that you have beguiled my mind? A woman can beguile my heart, but a whole world cannot beguile my mind. My feeling is amenable, but my mind is a tougher nut to crack. It is not advisable for anyone to underestimate it. It needs to be heard, just as much as the feeling of a woman needs to be heard. Both are nothing less than *quantité négligeable*. Hence, O Diotima, I have bowed most profoundly before your feeling, so that I do not devalue this great divine power. Where it is concerned, I shall be careful not to interfere. But when it comes to your understanding! That is the matter at hand now.

I greet the swans and horses and whatever else hoots and scoots.

I trust you will understand! "Don't fall!"

Your ever-devoted,

C.G. Jung.{HL}

*

Küsnacht-Zürich 19 IX 1943

My Dear Hedy Wyss,

I am grateful to you for writing to me in such a humane and accurate way. Forgive me if I occasionally make things difficult for you, but we must seek the right tones, for otherwise the music will be all wrong. You need a "counterpoint" – one of low and high pitches, of ~~faith~~ harmony, and dissonance.

This is what we have to talk about, and it must resonate with things as they are. Believe me, not for all in the world would I wish to disturb your sense of self. You are quite correct inside – much more correct than I find easy and like. But this inner correctness, though justified in God's eyes, stands in opposition to this diabolical world to which we are bound by our very existence as human beings. One needs to be both correct and not correct, which is why I am both correct and not correct with you. But let's not make things too difficult for each other.

I hasten to get this letter off to you and have someone holding your hand.

Warmest regards,

Your,

C.G. Jung.{HL}

*

Küsnacht-Zürich 24 IX 1943

Dear Hedy Wyss!

I had to neglect everything a little because of my work. It is difficult and emotionally wrenching. In addition, my last close friend, an Englishman with whom I was in Africa, has died.[35] (Please don't offer me your condolences! Ignore such communications!) Death is a part of life: there is a *mortificatio* and *putrificatio* and a *revivificatio*.

It is good if you try to express yourself *par écrit*. Not only does it sharpen one's thinking, but it also objectifies feeling and, moreover, it increases the fluidity of the pen. There is a 'literary' aspect to your art, if I am not mistaken. I may not pay you too many compliments about your letters. My humanity is ruthless. Don't torture yourself more than is necessary. I'll be back next week.

The nature of the relationship men and women have to each other when one or the other says, "I simply love you!" is "the subject of my present investigation,"[36] which, as Jacques de Roquetaillade says, was written for the benefit "*des poures gens evangelisens*," i. e. for the psychotherapists who, as the improvised representatives of the Lord Jesus Christ, have to drag around the super sack of the *peccata mundi* on top of their own pack of sins, and for the edification of the virgins who await their bridegroom with lighted lamps. Or do you know of any other blasphemy? I hope this gives you a sense of

35 Peter Baynes. He died on September 6, 1943.

36 This is related to Jung's work in *Mysterium Coniunctionis*.

how bitter the water of wisdom tastes. I believe it is St. Ambrose who said: *in patientia vestra habetis animas vestras* [Through your patience, your souls prove themselves][37] – This is what I tell myself.

Best regards,
From your ever-devoted,
C.G. Jung.{HL}

*

Küsnacht-Zürich 30 IX 1943

Dear Hedy Wyss!

I must answer your letters so that you have a sign of life from me, i.e., I do not want to wrap myself up in a Zeus-like thundercloud of silence. The story of the great-grandmother is a word-for-word repetition of what is written in Justin's gnosis: after Eloëim together with Edem (earth) created the world as a paradise, he left her and went up to the "good" God. Edem, however, was abandoned and felt resentful. Through Aphrodite, she sowed adultery and divorce among humans and tortured the *pneuma*, planted in humans by Eloëim, so that Eloëim himself would be tortured. In a final step, she brought about the crucifixion of Christ. Edem is a composite being: above, a virgin; below, a serpent. The meaning of the weasel is redemptive, for it is the only animal that can kill the basilisk. (Honorius of Autun). Thus, you are on the right track.

I do not feel very well. Because I am overtired, I am having palpitations. As a result, I must remain very calm. I find analyses or boring lectures particularly exhausting. By the way, my silence has constellated all sorts of things. You will have to be patient until I feel better.

Best regards! Your, C.G. Jung.{HL}

37 Allusion to Luke 21:19.

The Three Entries into the Little Book of Monologues[38]

Monologue in December 1943

Once again, she's writing a beautiful story in the blossom country of the south.[39] There has been no sun here for 14 days and it is dark at 4 p.m., or somewhat darker than at noon; cold misty haze over the lake; 12° C in this room and cold feet. I have to think my life, and life in general, through to the end. I must assemble the mosaic out of a thousand little stones, while she sits on a branch in this land of blossoms where it is so hot and so sad, trilling and lamenting, so hot and so sad, and seems to know nothing of the transalpine Niflheim,[40] of the old people who warm their hands by a fire in the dusky hearth, while thinking of cracks that need plugging against cold rheumatic drafts; of apprehensive rest that one must grant to one's rickety old heart so that it might endure a little longer and not disturb too much while one works on the mosaic, work that is oh!-so indispensable. One can no longer dance; one can no longer catch the fast-receding appearance of things and press it to one's overflowing heart, for it has become frail, like the thinnest of glass that can hold no wine, only the finest scents. Within it sits a homunculus that shall not shatter a second time at Galatea's throne.[41] This time, he must come into being, while on his journey into the beyond? This karma should not become the inheritance of the next century. Gently, I still

38 The *Little Book of Monologues* is a small (4 x 2,76 inches) notebook of Hedy Wyss that went back and forth between Jung and his analysand. Jung made several short entries and three longer ones. An envelope with a postmark of 17.XII.43 seems to belong to the "Monologue in December 1943." After his first longer entry, Jung must have sent the *Little Book of Monologues* back to Hedy Wyss in mid-December 1943.

39 Allusion to Richard Wilhelm's *Dschuang Dsï* [Zhuangzi], *Das wahre Buch vom südlichen Blütenland* [The True Book of the Blossom Country of the South]. For an English translation see *Zhuangzi*, Translation and Introduction by Hyun Höchsmann and Yang Guorong, New York: Longman, 2007.

40 The icy world of Hel, the goddess of death, in Northern mythology.

41 Johann Wolfgang von Goethe, *Faust. A Tragedy*, Translated by Walter Arndt, 2nd ed., New York: W.W. Norton, 2001, Part II, Act II, 8472: "He'll crash at her glittering throne and be shattered ..."

contain this fragile *vitrum sphaericum*,[42] the *noli me tangere*,[43] so that the work of centuries may flourish until it is complete. I am already dead to this age. To the moment, I am no longer bound, nor even a year, but to centuries only.[44] Everything, including what is most recent and immediate, is remembrance from times inconceivably distant, and the inkling of innumerable summers and winters, births and deaths of coming eons. No here, no now, no upswing, no collapse, no hot desiring and no rigid no, no you and no me.

How surprised an old man would be if he were to meet a young man without ever having been one himself! This is how it is for the young: they do not understand the rising waters of timelessness and therefore do not understand the ecstasy of old age, and no one will tell them, for, without noticing, the old have already left the blossoming times and summer lands, their longings and their attachments. All, all, has become remembrance and inklings. And everything he says, does, sings, and laments is that other person whom he remembers. Torn from attachments, he says goodbye at every turn to that other who would like to, who could, who should, who hoped, who feared, and anticipated. His greeting and welcome is inevitably a may-God-protect-you and Godspeed. The morsel remains suspended in the air, and the glass does not reach one's lip. Compassionate joy, compassion for the living? Who can still look back when he knowingly treads the threshold of non-time and non-world? He can – he can truly only retain and carry what he has to lay down at this threshold of splendor, which is precisely what he is still now laboriously and with undivided attention assembling, in order for what has driven him ceaselessly through seven decades to be completed and ready.

Do not perceive me as your defeat. On the contrary: moved by Ariadne's lament, even a god looked back. How should a mortal fare any better? But what can this mortal do? He writes in this diary to remind you. May he be a ray of sunshine that broke through the clouds, a stone of gold for your mosaic. But down here is this curse-laden, fog-afflicted earth upon which God's work is done.

42 The Hermetic vessel of the alchemists representing the celestial sphere.

43 The risen Christ appears to Mary Magdalene at the tomb and says to her: "*Noli me tangere*" – "Touch me not, for I am not yet ascended to my Father." John 20: 17 (King James Version).

44 Reference to Faust's wager with Mephistopheles, "If the swift moment I entreat: / Tarry a while! You are so fair! / Then forge the shackles to my feet, / Then I will gladly perish there!" J.W. von Goethe, *Faust. A Tragedy*, verses 1699-1792.

The verses of Marianne von Willemer[45] and the fitting illustrations that go with them are one peal of the bell-time,[46] sunk for a century and a half – and appropriately so. The silver cord is painfully stretched and the pitcher strikes the edge of the well. The drawings are truly apt. This is how it is in the blossom country of the south. But here, one is approaching the winter solstice. Forgive the *sacro egoismo* – 12°, cold feet, my nose is dripping quietly (not streaming like yours) and I'm glad not to feel unnecessary palpitations right now. I'm looking after myself – what a noble pastime! The joys of old age are strange indeed.

The cruel dissonance between your lovely gift and this, my entry in your diary, weighs upon me, and I see myself as a saturnine, wobbly old man who deadheads flowers in the garden with the sickle moon (instead of worshipping it in the sky). But beyond my unfortunately not-to-be-doubted age, the other within me thanks you.{HL}

*

Locarno 1 Jan 1944

Dear Hedy Wyss!

Here is your little book back again with a wretched little plaster in it, and a few marginal notes. The weather here is wonderful, and one laments the fact that one can no longer romp around on the mountains as one used to, but can only climb small hills at a snail's pace, in a leisurely and affected manner. Even so!

All the best for the New Year
Your ever-devoted,
C.G. Jung.{HL}

*

45 Goethe met Marianne at the home of the banker Johann Jakob Willemer in Mannheim in summer 1814. An intimate and inspiring love relationship developed between the 66-year-old and the young woman Marianne Willemer.

46 An allusion to Friedrich Schiller's famous poem "Song of the Bell" (1799).

Locarno 1. Jan 43. [actually 44][47]

Here comes the little book of monologues running back to you again with many wishes for the new number (1944). Strange that there are still, over and over again, years that one thinks of as "new". They are old, ancient years that were the same as this, when animals were running around with 3 and 5 horns on their heads and didn't know what they had that stuff on their heads for. The past is immeasurably long and the future is very short. It didn't seem that way to me before. There is obviously nothing in it for me, because I am now one of the emigrants to "Batavia". I read some Buddhist stuff the other day. It's sagely right. She, H.W., is somewhat deeply immersed in it, up to where ☉ and ☽ [Sol and Luna] are one and the same thing. That's going a bit too far. She is running after the emigrants. She should aim at being young among the younger, rather than being old with 'Jung.'[48] He was recently studying ☉ and ☽ and saw how one was doing the other's business. It's not quite right for the young to know this, too. But she sees it all from the distance – I have nothing to say about that. I cannot stop anyone breathing the same air as me. God protect me from my own responsibility. At times it swells up so much that it is called Adolf Hitler. Then I feel sick.

The sun shines here as if clouds and fog were mere legend. I stroll along the sunshine and try to shed myself of all responsibility for interminable humanity. I am both well and unwell = indifferent, approaching *nirdvandva*,[49] free of the two = opposites. One has a seat on time's cart and one can't do anything about it. Thus, one heads down No. 1944 on the road of life, the house of moderation where nothing too fast or too much or too intensively or too highly or too deeply can and should be done, under the threat of health-damaging punishments. An interesting place! In addition, one's nose is rubbed into the reheated past, in the form of Basel. Leaving feelings behind, a flight into the world of men, an edition of Once-upon-a-time, so that the circle closes, a bit of introspective adolescence. To this, I shall now drink a cup of tea. The sorrows and joys of a leisurely afternoon in Locarno in one's dotage.{HL}

47 This is a second longer entry in pencil in the *Little Book of Monologues* by C.G. Jung.

48 In German, this is a play on Jung's name: "mit Jüngeren jung zu sein und nicht mit Jung zu alt."

49 A Hindu term for one who is free of opposites. See C.G. Jung, *Aion*, CW 9/2, § 298, "... *nirdvandva*, without opposites, lacking all qualities and therefore unknowable. This describes the state of the unconscious." This passage refers to the Autopator, the highest deity in Valentinian Gnosis.

Epilogue. Bollingen 12 1 1944.[50]

In misty rain and slush. Amen. He sits in the tower, pondering death and life, partaking in Dionysos-Ariadne. "But Hades and Dionysos are the same, to whom they rave in bacchic frenzy," Heraclitus. "You are, O Ariadne, not quite as mad as I thought you were," says Dionysos. "Well, after all, I have always mirrored you so faithfully," says Ariadne. The I who sits in the tower (v/o [vulgo] private nuthouse) once wanted to catch a mouse with two traps (to be certain), and the two traps snapped shut on each other, and the mouse laughed its head off for 24 hours. A 'yes' to life and to death! Who can better that? The powers are so overpowering that we are left with only the mousehole to exist in. The smaller the better – the human scale – this war [World War II] will teach everyone that.

Your most obedient servant,

C.G. J.{HL}

50 Entry in ink on the last pages of the *Little Book of Monologues*. This concludes the booklet.

The Letters of May 1944 to October 1956

Clinic Hirslanden.
12 V 1944

Dear Hedy Wyss!

I would like to thank you warmly for having thought of me so often and so kindly. Hartmann von Aue[51] can allude solely to the leprosy of my soul, for now I am suffering only from an oedematous leg – apart from my general weakness. For the time being, I must meditate daily upon the words of St. Ambrose: *In patientia vestra habetis animas vestras.*

With kind regards,
Your devoted,
C.G. Jung.{HL}

*

Küsnacht-Zürich 19 July 1944

Dear Hedy Wyss!

This morning your letter, so rich in substance, arrived from Mürren. It reminds me of the beautiful alpine flowers you sent me, all of which arrived fresh. Your letter is immensely descriptive and, like most of your letters (not all!!), it contains the charm of naive description that is obviously part of your nature. I can't help but think of you now and again between the lines of my manuscript. Who could fail to be impressed by the problem that you are? As for the meaning of love, there is a lot about that in Paul Claudel's "[*Le*] *Soulier de satin*," though unfortunately in a strangely degenerate form.

I am, indeed, hard at work on my book, which has me crisscrossing the history of the world. But I am glad to have such an enterprising traveling companion, for otherwise my existence – *pedibus ligatus* [with bound feet]! – would be somewhat difficult to bear.

I often have to think of the words of St. Ambrose: *in patientia vestra habetis animas vestras.*

51 Hedy Wyss sent Jung a booklet by the Medieval poet Hartmann von Aue ($12^{th}/13^{th}$ century) to the hospital.

I hope to see you when you are back in Küsnacht.
With heartfelt thanks and best regards,
Your devoted,
C.G. Jung.{HL}

*

Küsnacht-Zürich 30 VIII 1944.

Dear Hedy Wyss!

Since it is raining anyway, I thought I'd add a few drops to the general downpour just for you, so that time doesn't drag on too long for you. Life is long when one is longing. Why shorten life with longing? My letter is thus mercifully short.

With kind regards,
Your ever devoted,
C.G. Jung.

P.S. This is the caution of one who is shocked by the sight of his own face. Enough of that!{HL}

*

Küsnacht-Zürich 1 Sept. 1944.

Dear Miss Hedy Wyss!

There is no need for more fuss than usual. I just wanted to confirm that I have, indeed, been silent, and why. Firstly, all talk is burdensome to me, and secondly, I realized that I have talked too much in the first place. I do not like the image of myself that you mirror back at me (unintentionally!), which I do not impute to you at all, but to myself. I ask you to not get upset about this, for that is precisely what I would most like to avoid as I find it most exhausting. Nothing is pressing and we will have plenty of opportunity to talk about it peacefully.

With best regards, Your faithful, C.G. Jung.{HL}

*

Küsnacht-Zürich 19 IX 1944

Dear Hedy Wyss!

May a mass of visits, letters, my book and my strictly-rationed productivity be my pardon for writing to you only today. Since Marie-Jeanne, my right hand, is on vacation, I must laboriously attend to my own correspondence with my left, and, as the jealous guardian of my solitude's silence, I am quite unable to bear any help. Next Friday, however, at 5 o'clock in the evening, or a little later, a visit from you would be welcome. Do you know one Dr. Montanari? (in Mürren).

With kind regards,
C.G. Jung.{HL}

*

Küsnacht-Zürich
[Postmark Erlenbach, 13.X.44]

Dear Hedy Wyss!

Although I shall be seeing you tomorrow, I must write to you quickly to thank you for the multifaceted picture that evokes all the intricacies of alchemy.[52] Being so busy with my ancient, fascinating texts, I have, without realizing, been silent for too long. To a large extent, I am now permitted to let life pass me by; indeed, I even have to, because I can't keep up with it at all. But it pained me that your pictures, which are at the very least an improvement on the filth that gets exhibited, were not accepted.

I do think of you, but it's a long way from there to a letter, and everything goes slowly for me now. The world seems clouded, and it is only in the world of thought that the sun shines. My heart attack has really knocked the stuffing out of me, and it seems to me that the strength I still have must be used to express everything that comes into consciousness. I was startled by the length of your first letter – a too heavy a task. But I must encourage you to write a proper letter (two kilometers long, if you like) to the art commission, or whatever that animal with the many heads and the brains of a lizard is called. That is where your desire to write ought to run riot.

With kind regards,
Your ever-devoted,
C.G. Jung.{HL}

*

52 This, most likely, refers to figure 32, in C.G. Jung's essay "The Philosophical Tree." Obviously, this painting had fascinated him. C.G. Jung, CW 13, "The Philosophical Tree", figure 32, commentary § 347.

Küsnacht-Zürich 31 X 1944

Dear Hedy Wyss!

Exactly as you describe it is how I imagine an art exhibition of today. Which is why I don't complain about not being able to go to any. Instead of painting from eternity, these devils paint from our time; and instead of painting from the soul, they paint from the world. Basically, I have nothing against your colors but would only wish to see your pictures find an audience. I am doing quite decently, and am winding my way through the jungle of that world of mental images which, in an effort to make themselves visible again, shatter this world. Your pictures – namely those of Hedy Wyss – seem to me to be on the right track, so that I am personally irritated by the bungling of the art commission.

So, for the time being, all the best!

Your devoted,

C.G. Jung.{HL}

*

Küsnacht-Zürich 2 I 1945

Dear Hedy Wyss!

It was very kind of you to paint this beautiful canister for me and to fill it with inner sweetness, a sensitive and meaningful gift! ... yes, that's what one would have said in those days. I reciprocate all your good wishes and add a further one: may this year be less rotten than 1944.

Very slowly, I am feeling a little better. I am caught in the snares of Rex,[53] which I am trying to untangle, going from one entanglement to another ... *o beata confusio – o confusa beatitudo* [o happy confusion – o confusing happiness]! That's pretty much how I feel.

With best thanks and kind regards, Your, C.G. Jung{HL}

*

53 At that time Jung was writing Chapter IV of *Mysterium Coniunctionis*, "Rex and Regina."

Küsnacht-Zürich 1 Febr. 1945

Dear Hedy Wyss!

Your letter comes as a reminder for me to apologize for laying the problem of the fig-leaf on the table yet again. I know that you know, and that your ethos compels you, to give voice to nature. But what if nature is by nature taboo? Must not nature then also be kept secret? You know that it is not out of sheer prudishness that I do not believe in taboos where there are none. Giving full expression to nature is a constant violation of nature. Nature is an ἄρρητον [not to be spoken of]. Speaking about it unleashes its demonic aspect, and this harms the one who is giving voice to it. Nature wants to be, but not to be spoken of, named, designated, pointed to. This has the same effect on her as the evil eye: it annihilates her, and she will take her revenge. Don't look at her so directly; don't talk about her so straightforwardly, for otherwise it will seem as if you were not afraid of nature at all, and could easily conquer her by word or by gesture! In doing this, you are harming yourself by attracting daemons. I want to teach you a wholesome δεισιδαιμονία (fear of daemons), not some fig-leaf hypocrisy. The reckless manner in which you speak about nature is forcing her to distance herself from you.

With best greetings,
From your incorrigible,
C.G. Jung.[HL]

*

Küsnacht-Zürich 10 VIII [sic] 1945
[Postmark Bollingen, 11.VII.45][54]

Dear Hedy Wyss,

That's just it: you are such a very natural little woman. The raunchy color, fable, animal, and daemonic world of the great mother all belong to this being, which is a *tremendum* for the man and terrifies him in the same way a cobra slithering over his foot does.[55] He always wants to appease, dampen, soften, and humanize this side of the eternal feminine, which he really doesn't know at all, for it doesn't even occur to him that the charming

54 Whether this is a clerical error (VIII instead of VII), or the envelope belongs to a lost letter from Jung to Hedy Wyss dated 11.VII.45, can no longer be determined.

55 The letter is Jung's response to a remark made by Hedy Wyss that her new friend had difficulty understanding her paintings.

young lady is surrounded by scorpions and cold-slithering snakes. One doesn't notice it at all, and neither does she. But – horror of horrors – when she paints, the water world of the big green mother comes up with slippery dragons, ghastly, phallic, bull gods, and primeval colors, which put the fearful primeval man in voluptuous panic (pan = fright and goat!). Black Kali is too much for the man. He still wants to be able to believe in his mother. Your images divulge the feminine mysteries, the secrets of the man-bearing uterus and the gruesomely beautiful arcanum of the living protein, the warm blood and magical kitchen of the viscera. There, in that underworld, things still creep, slither, crawl, and swarm as they did in the carboniferous forests, where you could barely see for the swamp and steam.

You certainly paint out of a huge but shattering truth. But for this very reason one whimpers for some soothing veilings, which, of course, does not suit your style of expression. But then you have to rise to a somewhat Luciferian *Quand-même*, which is a risk that no one wants to encourage you to take. Nevertheless, as a counterbalance ...[56]

Your devoted,
C.G. Jung{HL}

*

Küsnacht-Zürich 29 XII 1945

Dear Hedy Wyss!

Thank you very much for the surprising *Gutzi* [cookies]! What can't you do! Next, we'll find out that you are an unappreciated, overlooked snake charmer. I enclose your clippings. This stuff reminds me of reviews of my work. Why the hell shouldn't a woman's paintings be feminine?

Should our age consist of nothing but clippings, worthy of drowning in their own filth? I am pessimistic despite the Ticino sun, which, by the way, is not so brilliant at the moment either. All the best for the New Year! Man will continue to hope for as long as he is capable of making mistakes!

Your devoted C.G. Jung.{HL}

*

56 Namely 'as a counterbalance to your [Hedy Wyss'] infatuation.'

Küsnacht-Zürich 20 III 46

Dear Hedy Wyss!

It really is *peu délicat* of the ucs. to put the great-grandmother – i.e., the history of the earth – on the table once more, particularly if one does not paint. But, as a result, one has written a very beautiful, very interesting letter, the Platonic idea of which was probably put into my hand by Valeri in order for me to tell you about the black mother at the foot of the great mountains, about Gauri and Mahadevi, whose poor cousin dwells with us in the dark forest,[57] and to hear the confession of Casanova. He had to indirectly remind her of her priestly role – Dei locum tenens. Here, it is just cold, so that even one's consciousness freezes.

I don't know if I should greet E.G. Is she crazy, too? I have lost confidence in the Germans, insofar as they were not part of the Resistance. And, to top it off, they lie. I feel no desire to meet again.

With best regards,
Your devoted,
C.G. Jung.{HL}

*

Küsnacht-Zürich 14 IX 1947

Dear Hedy Wyss!

Once again, a breeze flew by with your letter that makes one respond.

Your dream describes the *nigredo* which one always enters into if one does not simply marry and get caught up in procreation. Coal is a raw material out of which all sorts of things are created, including light.

There are women who, despite all their temporality, have more to do with eternity. You are one of them. Anima means love and death and eternity. You touch this in a man. He needs it, because this is how life itself leads him into the vicinity of death and into the great understanding of what you do not understand about yourself.

I'm going to the Rigi for a while for the mountain air. Then – at the end of the month – our paths will cross again.

Meanwhile, I remain,
Your most humble servant,
C.G. Jung.{HL}

*

57 Allusion to the Black Madonna in the abbey of Einsiedeln.

Bollingen, but not after tomorrow!
19 XII 47

Dear Hedy Wyss!

Despite my good intentions, it was no longer possible for me to give you the required sign of life in Küsnacht. Instead, I am doing it from Bollingen, where, for 3 days at least, I may breathe again and clear my head. I would actually need 14 days here to sort myself out. The world is too messy nowadays. At least there has been a good snowfall here. I also slept normally again and dreamed of many Catholic priests who probably have fewer problems to deal with than I do.

I hope that during your vacation you will be able to recover from your pedagogical activity, which is not good for me either.

With my best greetings
and wishes,
Your devoted,
C.G. Jung.{HL}

*

Image 3: Postcard by C.G. Jung to Hedy Wyss, January, 2, 1948.
Woodcut of Jung's House on Lake Zurich

[postcard with postmark Bollingen, 2.I.48]

BEST WISHES FOR THE NEW YEAR
[added by hand:] and many thanks for the original Christmas angel, which has won general approval. I am presently recuperating in the quiet of the tower. Your devoted, C.G. Jung.{HL}

*

Küsnacht-Zurich 16 VIII 1948

Dear Hedy Wyss!

I am better now, but not yet brilliant. Your view of love is quite accurate, but it does not reckon with the anima of the man, or rather, with the animus of the anima, which Freud indeed represents. It's true that the anima "thinks" that she is indispensable, and that a man cannot be anything other than a "man," and a woman is nothing but a woman, i.e., as the insane Schreber thought, her body "is entirely made up of voluptuous nerves." She [the anima] thinks that that is what love is, and the man shares this conviction, but always denies it, because he cannot escape condemning its stupidity. Your friend is no exception to the genus masculinum here. Which is why a woman must keep saying this very clearly and for a long time to a man until he believes it. Freud is therefore as plausible as Hitler is to the Germans: both say what basically everyone thinks, although seldom does anyone blatantly admit to it consciously.[58] So hold on. He loses nothing in the process; on the contrary, it keeps him alive.

Yes, that's how the world works.

Warmly,

Your faithful,

C.G. Jung.{HL}

*

58 See C.G. Jung's lifelong concern about the hubris of modern men: Part II, chapter "Goethe's Faust," pp. 142.

Bollingen, 10 Aug. 1949

Dear Hedy Wyss!

After winding my way through all kinds of vacation obstacles, I have finally been able to get to you. You should not doubt the nature of your love. This is one of the best things about you, which I would dearly like you to accept. I should have told you this some time ago, but I could never find the time. I suffer from thwarted inactivity. What has your Thomas Mann been up to again? What is meant or intended by this Weimar-Goethe magic under the jackass-like and wicked communist régime? Nevertheless, many thanks for the book! I shall obediently read it. I do not doubt that he can write well, but etc.

I regretted that there was not enough time to see you before my departure. I feel atrociously about it, for I realize only too well how important it would be for you. But somehow, I must have time for myself and it must be before I help everyone else become acquainted with themselves, and to maintain that acquaintance to some extent. You are quite right: love has the great disadvantage of not being complete without the other – you said it so much more beautifully! But you have to have the right balance. Most of the time, however, you either have too much "I" or too much "other." Both are regrettable. Μηδὲν ἄγαν don't overdo anything! But what if one is already overdoing it? ...

Devotedly sympathetic,

C.G. Jung.{HL}

*

Küsnacht-Zürich 3 IX 1949.

[Postmark Bollingen, 3 IX 49]

Dear Hedy Wyss!

My main occupation throughout this vacation is stealing time. Although time is always available, for me it only comes in trickles, for all the world gobbles it up. Your moving letter and your dreams, however, have managed to overcome my resistance to letters and have caused me to wave to you, at least from afar, with understanding. I also know all kinds of things about palpitations that come when you go to bed. Hence my sympathy. How much easier it is to know nothing! The all-compassionate Tathagata [Buddha] has wisely worked out how to free oneself from being human. But the art of being thus has not yet been devised. The one seems to be as impossible as the other, and the noble eightfold path turns out to be a path upon which one occasionally has to go on all fours in order to get through.

Affectionately yours,

C.G. Jung.{HL}

*

Küsnacht-Zürich 21 IV 1950.

Dear Hedy Wyss!

There is only one thing to be done in the face of an anima obsession, namely, to not fall into the animus, in other words, to remain constant, conscious, devoted, selfless (among many other disagreeable things). One must be reasonable, even where one's emotion is concerned. This had to happen to you! Occasionally, one must be ready to renounce everything. As it were. One then becomes a mother, which in turn provides the anima with the opportunity to project herself again, that is, to change from saying no to saying yes.

I'm going on a road trip to the Rhineland tomorrow for six days. A peculiar adventure that should be good for God knows what.

Best wishes!

Your faithful,

C.G. Jung.{HL}

*

[Postmark Bollingen, 18.IX.(?)50]

Dear Hedy Wyss!

At last, an evening when I'm not otherwise engaged. Never turn 75. It's devastating. My whole summer was disturbed, when what I needed was peace and quiet. Along with my guilty conscience for having let you down. But what can I do when you're sitting in Venice with your psychology. It is difficult to live between the hammer and the anvil. But that's how you get an iron skin and become so small that you find room inside a small bubble of air within the anvil. Then the blow of the hammer is in vain. Everyone is forged in their own particular way, whether they want it or not, whether they find it useful or not. We simply don't know what came before this damned life, and what will come after. If we knew, we wouldn't be so taken aback. Things are colorful for you right now, but as you are, you are too soft and too colorful

– green and purple, and God knows what else. The green goddess is quite rightly life itself showing you all sorts of things that you obviously need to know in order for you to realize the potential that you are destined to fulfil, after entire generations have tried to buy off the Good Lord with restrictions and appropriate measures.

Unfortunately, I can do no more than to let you know you have my sympathy. There will come a time for you, too, when you will look back on these content-rich summer holidays with satisfaction, because you have "made the most of your talents" and you have not only gone under water with your tail, but also with your head. What more can you do? This entitles you to some later satisfaction and so-called peace of mind. By the end, you may be glad to escape this spa treatment and return to Switzerland.

But right now, I'd like to tell the world to get lost. Too many people, too many letters, too much of everything.

Cordially yours,

C.G. Jung.{HL}

*

Küsnacht-Zürich 19 I 1951

Dear Hedy Wyss,

After a few days of rest and work in Bollingen, I must write you a little letter and thank you for the beautiful Christmas present you surprised me with. It is indeed a good and pleasing picture, whose spring-like atmosphere one readily enjoys. One prefers to look away and forget the gruesome and the abysmal that cruelly thrusts itself upon one in modern art. It catches up with me every day anyway in a different form, so I don't want to see it hanging on walls. I don't feel like going all the way into town to see Chagall's psychic carved-up salad.

Thank you very much for your essays! How mild and measured and well-tempered you stroll along in them! It's hard to believe. Which is why steam is let off in other places in a less well-dosed manner.

Best greetings,

Your,

C.G. Jung.{HL}

*

Küsnacht-Zürich 30 XII 1951

Dear Hedy Wyss,

Unfortunately, it was no longer possible. Because I was indisposed, the work piled up to such an extent that I no longer had any spare time. It seems to me that you need to be reasonable. It is a situation in which you should not drown. As a rule, one fares better with reason, and reasonable people know that a wall is harder than a head. Life, like politics, is the art of the possible. So why be blind when one has eyes in one's head? I will be back on 15th. For the time being, rest is necessary. *Prudenter agas et respice finem*![59]

Your vicarious common sense,

C.G. Jung{HL}

*

Küsnacht-Zürich December 17th 1952.

Dear Fräulein Wyss,

Professor Jung has asked me to write to you for him since, unfortunately, letter writing is still a very laborious matter for him. He wishes me to send you his greetings and tell you that he feels generally better, but is still in a pretty weak and inefficient condition. He has been suffering from Tachycardia and still gets occasional attacks of the same trouble.

With kindest greetings, I am,

Yours sincerely

Una G. Thomas

Secretary

*

[Postmark Bollingen, 4.VII.53]

Dear Hedy Wyss!

There are such phantasies and a bit high up too! The father-sorcerer would produce such miraculous solutions, but – I am afraid – in fairy tales only. In reality this most inconspicuous individual is getting older and older and celebrates birthdays in quick succession.[60]

Best regards and wishes,

Your C.G. J.{HL}

*

59 Act sensibly and be mindful of the end.

60 These two sentences in the original letter are also written in English.

Küsnacht-Zürich 8 July 1953

Dear Hedy Wyss,

Life is a "just-so-story"![61] If it were not for damned Marlus, Frasca's[62] mother-addicted anima would have simply chosen another mask that would have worked just as well, and so on. Oh, you can't change anything that is determined to exist, just as you can't change yourself if it doesn't change. Mostly one must take everything just as it is, and if the Lord Jesus has given us a good Sunday roast and a glass of red to go with it – for once, as an exception – afterwards we must say long and often: "That was good." For the remaining part of life must be taken as medicine. If we have learned our school work well, that our life is existence in and of itself, then the long-term cure begins, that wants to rid us of this error and to teach us that one loses all bets in this game and that this is the prize. This involves living as much nonsense as possible. *Sapit dum desipit*: "Wise becomes he who surrenders to nonsense."

Do not worry too much: everything goes as right and as wrong as it can.

I do not know how much longer I'll last. I am tired and not very efficient.

With best regards,

Your C.G. Jung.[HL]

*

Küsnacht-Zürich 21 XII 1953

Dear Hedy Wyss!

It is excellent and very appropriate that you are in Mallorca. Hopefully you will stay there for quite some time; until time stands still. This only happens on an island in a warm sea. Your description brought back memories of Madeira and the Canary Islands, and of Corfu in the spring. Flowering camellias, red-purple bougainvilleas, the scent of freesias in a London February winter with rain mist, sleet, and cloudbursts. One must stay a long time on an island with red earth and green olea tree gardens. It's so mysterious. The bad moods and illness in Zurich cannot hold a candle to it. It has just

61 Allusion to the book, *Just So Stories*, by Rudyard Kipling published in 1902. This book is still in his Bollingen tower [information from Thomas Fischer].

62 Paul Albert Frasca, the American husband of Hedy Frasca-Wyss, whom she met in 1950. 'Marlus' is the nickname of Marie-Louise von Franz. It seems that the husband of Hedy Wyss has projected his negative mother complex also onto "damned" Marie-Louise von Franz.

rained again here and is now only 2° above zero, and it is also the shortest day, when everyone normally thinks, "Thank God, the light will now begin to increase again." But usually the worst is still to come. One should never use an illness and filial piety as a lever to dislodge some of one's offspring from their self-chosen holes. That is why our Creator has provided us with islands that you must, without fail, once see and experience. Unfortunately, I was never granted the opportunity to be on an island long enough, so I never got to know what happens at the end of an island stay. I was always torn out of the exciting story at the very beginning. Hopefully, this will not happen to you, too. Winter time in particular is the most beautiful, enchanted overture. Your father has obviously never seen the sea through the green veil of olive trees, otherwise he would never get the outlandish idea of wanting to "liberate" you from the colorful glory of the island. After all, this is the very place where you have finally arrived after so many painstaking years, and where you must be left entirely alone. The sea is spread out all around you, wine is growing on red hills, the sun rises and sets, the moon shines in many forms in shifting parts of the night and everything flows into itself. I only hope there is no airport on your island. I have given no thought to this possible dreadful disturbance. As you can see, I am getting old. I am getting along quite well, since I do not have to dislodge any offspring.

With best regards and wishes (not for the New Year, because there is no such thing on islands; there, all years are old – indeed, they're ancient).

Your devoted, C.G. Jung.[HL]

*

Küsnacht-Zürich 11th March 1954

Dear Miss,

Unfortunately, I do not have time at present to write at greater length. Lately, I have been ill and, as a result, I cannot possibly deal with this onslaught of analytical material.

Quite frankly, I do not really understand why Frasca is still preoccupied with these old arguments and has not finally understood that they are his own anima. I shall probably be on vacation at the beginning of April and I most certainly have no intention of concerning myself with Frasca's indigestion.

Spring must be really wonderful on that island of bliss.[63]
Here, too, thank God, it is also beautiful.
With my best regards,
Your devoted,
C.G. Jung

*

[Postmark Bollingen, 2.VIII.54]

Dear H.F-W.!

For the descriptive postcard, many thanks! For your best wishes on my birthday, too! Your good news delighted me. At last, I, too, can enjoy my vacation, except for the letter-writing days, which are marked black in my calendar. Thus, I shall be brief.

My best wishes to you as well!
Your faithful,
C.G. Jung.{HL}

*

Küsnacht-Zurich 12 IX 1954.

Dear Hedy F.-W.!

Apparently, my negative behavior requires some explanation. For more than 50 years, I have had to patiently listen to the whining of the world. But then, one day, it becomes too much, namely when you have to listen to a shriek from a quarter you can do nothing about and, furthermore, for which you have not assumed any responsibility. Then you feel overwhelmed and react accordingly.

It is reasonable for you to raise the question of the subjective aspect of the dream. As is well known, one gains nothing by proving it to another; by doing so, one has simply lost sight of one's own shadow. At the risk of being the bad guy who leaves others in the lurch, I don't wish to make any further comment on this subject. I have to leave a lot of people to their misfortune, for otherwise I would have no time to contemplate my own shadow and its blackness. Therefore, if you think well of me, heap coals of fire upon my head, and if not, then I am as disagreeable to you as I can possibly be, for it

63 At that time, Hedy Wyss and her husband were in Mallorca.

has been irrevocably determined that I was not born to be the Redeemer. That would be detrimental to my health.

Furthermore, you have sunshine in Mallorca, while we have rain clouds and cold winds, pregnant with rheumatism. Why should we be in a good mood? Patient and understanding? We have wet feet and the sniffles, and everyone has enough to do with their own devils and does not want to be annoyed by those of others to boot. Perhaps, you and your spouse could instead see to it that Zurich has better weather.

Shrouded in dripping clouds,
Your devoted,
C.G. Jung.{HL}

*

Küsnacht-Zurich 13 Febr. 1956 [Air Mail]

Dear Hedy née Wyss!

I know that I have long since owed you a letter. But you well know what robbed me of time and inclination. There was also no Christmas for me this year. At my age, it's almost impossible to get out of the deep ditch into which the carriage of life has sunk. My only consolation was not philosophy, but a stone slab that I chiseled. It is alleged, among others also by me, to be good: a self-penned Chinese inscription; a branch of the ginkgo tree in autumn; a withered leaf falls to the ground; a little old man "in modest harmony with nature" observes it. The plate will be placed under a real ginkgo in my garden. On the reverse side, it says:

D[iis] M[anibus]
SACRO ARBORIS
HUIUS NUMINI
FEC. ET. POS. C.G. JUNG
A[NN]O MCMLVI[64]

That's the news. As far as my health is concerned, I live dutifully, observing the rules of the game: no carbohydrates and not too much of anything

64 Dedicated to the spirits of the ancestors [and] to the sacred divine being of this tree. C.G. J[ung] created and placed [this stone] in the year 1956. In memory of Toni Wolff. She died on March 21, 1953 at the age of 64.

at all, including the necessary transgressions, so that I do not constantly lose weight. Thirty pounds have already been written off, and, amid a flurry of sparrows and other songbirds, I look like a hungry, retired lamb-vulture running out of feathers, perched on top of the scrawny tree in the aviary. Also, one has chronic bladder catarrh, and one's heart enjoys *arrhythmia perpetua*. Old age does, indeed, have its own issues. My last book, Mysterium Coniunctionis vol. II, is presently being wrapped in its first diapers. Along with my head, my questions are up against the roof of the above-mentioned aviary. *Nec plus ultra*. No action; I only react now. I just read Priestley's book "Down the Rainbow"[65] and thought of you and of America. I can vividly imagine the situation.

With warm greetings,
Your faithful, C.G. Jung.{HL}

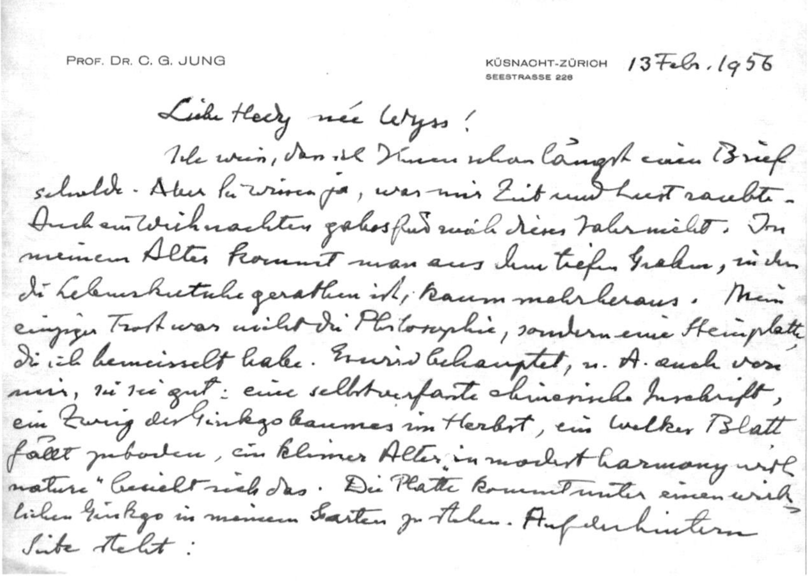

PROF. DR. C. G. JUNG

KÜSNACHT-ZÜRICH
SEESTRASSE 228

13 Feb. 1956

Liebe Hedy née Wyss!

Ich weiss, dass ich Ihnen schon längst einen Brief schulde. Aber Sie wissen ja, was mir Zeit und Lust raubte. Auch an Weihnachten gab es für mich dieses Jahr nicht. In meinem Alter kommt man aus dem tiefen Graben, in den die Lebenskutsche gerathen ist, kaum mehr heraus. Mein einziger Trost war nicht die Philosophie, sondern eine Steinplatte, die ich bemeisselt habe. Es wird behauptet, u. A. auch von mir, sie sei gut: eine selbstverfasste chinesische Inschrift, ein Zweig des Ginkgobaumes im Herbst, ein welkes Blatt fällt zu Boden, ein kleiner Alter, in "modest harmony with nature" besieht sich das. Die Platte kommt unter einen wirklichen Ginkgo in meinem Garten zu stehen. Auf der hintern Seite steht:

Image 4a: Letter of February 13, 1956, front

65 J.B. Priestley and Jacquetta Hawkes, *Journey Down the Rainbow,* New York: Harper and Bros, 1955. The book conveys a dialog between J.B. Priestley, who sets out to explore the so-called higher civilization of city-life in Texas, and his wife, Jacquetta Hawkes, who journeys through the Indigenous People country of New Mexico and Arizona.

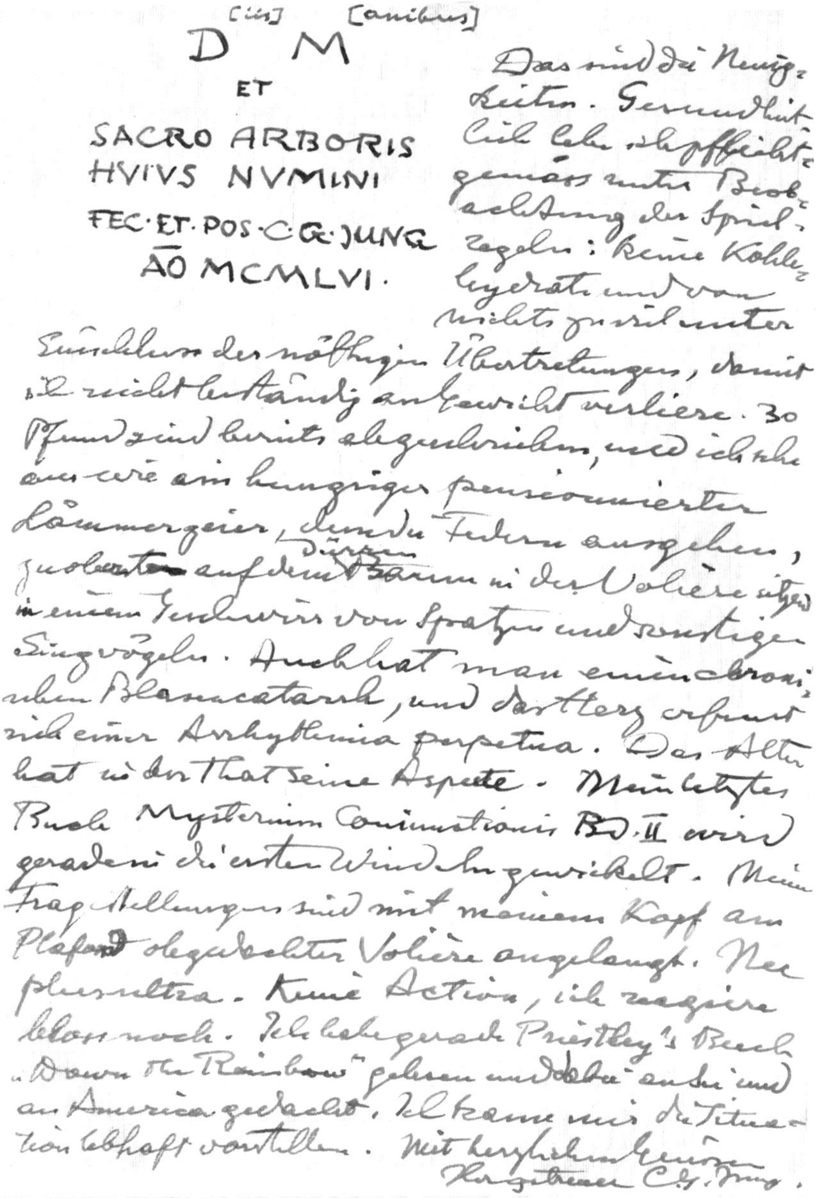

[sic] [omnibus]
D M
ET
SACRO ARBORIS
HVIVS NVMINI
FEC·ET·POS·C·G·JUNG
AO MCMLVI·

Das sind die Neuigkeiten. Gesundheitlich lebe ich pflichtgemäss unter Beobachtung der Spielregeln: Keine Kohlehydrate und von nichts zu viel unter Einschluss der nöthigen Übertretungen, damit ich nicht beständig an Gewicht verliere. 30 Pfund sind bereits abgeschrieben, und ich sehe aus wie ein hungriger pensionierter Lämmergeier, dem die Federn ausgehen, zuoberst auf dem dürren Baum in der Volière sitzend in einem Gewimmel von Spatzen und sonstigen Singvögeln. Auch hat man einen chronischen Blasencatarrh, und das Herz erfreut sich einer Arrhythmia perpetua. Das Alter hat in der That seine Aspekte. Mein letztes Buch Mysterium Coniunctionis Bd. II wird gerade in die ersten Windeln gewickelt. Meine Fragestellungen sind mit meinem Kopf am Plafond obgedachter Volière angelangt. Nec plus ultra. Keine Action, ich reagiere bloss noch. Ich habe gerade Priestley's Buch „Down the Rainbow" gelesen und habe an Sie und an America gedacht. Ich kann mir die Situation lebhaft vorstellen. Mit herzlichen Grüssen

Ihr getreuer C.G. Jung.

Image 4b: Letter of February 13, 1956, reverse

Presently, Bollingen Ct. St. Gall. [Postmark 31.X.56]

Dear Hedy formerly Wyss!

This "formerly" brings to mind the transience of all things. You have lost both of your parents. On the occasion of your father's death, I wrote to you, and I hope that the letter reached you in the proper manner. I did not know that your mother also died shortly thereafter, so I can only offer you my belated, heartfelt condolences. The letter I wrote to you on the occasion of your father's death is the last one I wrote to you. Everything is moving very slowly for me now, and there are days when I don't touch a pen, especially when bad weather is approaching. I have had a tough time recovering from the death of my wife. And from old age ailments of all kinds, altogether! I have pretty much had to pull the plug on any scientific work, because concentrated mental effort tires me beyond measure. My only endeavor is to rest and to find time for resting. In truth, my only exertion is chiseling stones. I have prepared a memorial for my deceased ones in the form of an ancient tombstone[66] and a slab with a ginkgo branch and a Chinese inscription. Right now, I am working on a lengthy Latin inscription concerning my family tree. These are, as I fittingly dreamed, paving stones on the way to the dark gate.

This summer, somewhat overconfidently, I made all kinds of structural changes to the tower so that it may be used by two families as a vacation home.

After your nomadic existence, you will enjoy a settled existence. I still can't quite picture you and the USA together, though. But, oh God, what depths and quirks does the female being not have? That is why people were so late in beginning to think about it, and women themselves were content to say 'yes' or 'no' to what men thought about it. K'an, the Abysmal (Y King)[67] Amen.

I don't know myself just how senile I already am, of course. But I have, as I suspect, a fair touch of it, and therefore I sometimes come precariously close to my feminine side, in any case in a manner in which I begin to understand all sorts of things. It is good that I can no longer write properly about anything, for otherwise I would blurt out my reflections. There is still much insight reserved for posterity. One is a starting point whose beginning

66 Emma Jung-Rauschenbach died on November 27, 1955. The stone stands today in the courtyard of Jung's Bollingen tower.

67 A reference to Hexagram 29, *The Abysmal, Darkness* (Water) in the I Ching.

one doesn't quite know, and an end, and beyond it, one does not know. What happens within the spaceless and the timeless? Before and after? My head has bumped up against a ceiling, but beneath me is unfathomable deep, into which perhaps one sinks.

I wish you all the best and hope that you will cope well with everything *dans ce meilleur des mondes possibles.*

Your devoted,

C.G. Jung

P.S. The arduous thing about old age – which I just now recall – is that if you do anything at all, you do it, or must do it, as if it were for the last time. Hence, this long letter!!!{HL}

[It really was Jung's last letter to Hedy Wyss.]

Jung died on June 6, 1961.

*

Plate I: C.G. Jung, photo: Yousuf Karsh

Plate II: Hedy Wyss – Self-portrait, 1933

Plate III: Hedy Wyss – Parvati, 1941/46

Plate IV: Hedy Wyss – Mignon and the Old, 1942/43

Plate V: The Tower at Bollingen

Plate VI: Hedy Wyss – In the Sign of Pisces, 1943

Plate VII: Bamberger Apocalypse, Staatsbibliothek Bamberg, Msc.Bibl.140, fol. 1r

Plate VIII: Bamberger Apocalypse, Staatsbibliothek Bamberg, Msc.Bibl.140, fol. 9r

Plate IX: Hedy Wyss – Minotaur and the Blonde Citizen Girl, 1943/50

Plate X: Hedy Wyss – Dionysos and Ariadne in the Underworld, 1943

Plate XI: C.G. Jung: *Systema mundi totius*

Plate XII: The Bollingen Stone

Plate XIII: C.G. Jung, Memorial for Toni Wolff, 1956

Plate XIV: C.G. Jung, Memorial for Toni Wolff, reverse, 1956

Plate XV: Memorial for Emma Jung-Rauschenbach, 1956

Part II: Commentary

By Andreas Schweizer

In these hitherto unpublished letters, C.G. Jung searches for answers in ever new and often surprising ways to the problems his analysand Hedwig (Hedy) Wyss, his junior by a good thirty years, experienced in her loves and in her life. Hedy Wyss struggled with her love for various men, but she particularly struggled with her great love for her analyst. These seventy-odd letters of C.G. Jung to Hedy Wyss are a remarkable testimony of Jung's lifelong commitment to human relationship and to love, a commitment he tried to honor, despite all difficulties. They mirror his great awe of Eros, of whom he said in *Memories, Dreams, Reflections,* "[he] was [rightfully] considered a god whose divinity transcended our human limits."[68] An open spirit pervades Jung's letters to the younger woman, and in his openness to love, there is nothing suggestive or hurtful, nor is there any inner retreat by a seemingly detached person about whom it might be assumed that he is above the suffering and lowliness of this world. Thus, we read in a letter from Bollingen:

Küsnacht-Zürich, September 3, 1949
[Postmark Bollingen, 3 IX 49]

Dear Hedy Wyss!
My main occupation throughout this vacation is stealing time. Although time is always available, for me it only comes in trickles, for all the world gobbles it up. Your moving letter and your dreams, however, have managed to overcome my resistance to letters and have caused me to wave to you, at least from afar, with understanding. I also know all kinds of things about palpitations that come when you go to bed. Hence my sympathy.

68 C.G. Jung, *Memories, Dreams, Reflections*, p. 353.

> How much easier it is to know nothing! The all-compassionate Tathagata [Buddha] has wisely worked out how to free oneself from being human. But the art of being thus has not yet been devised. The one seems to be as impossible as the other, and the noble eightfold path turns out to be a path upon which one occasionally has to go on all fours in order to get through.[69]
> Affectionately yours,
> C.G. Jung.

"The art of being thus," namely of being a human being who is aware of the shadow and truly accepts the human – the all too human – in oneself, "has not yet been devised." Jung called this lifelong striving for deeper psychological understanding and its realization in life 'the process of individuation.' Such conscious awareness is indeed a great art which requires most of our vigor and, at times, a perseverance that tests the limits of our forbearance. Therefore, the alchemists said of their art, all that is inauthentic, illusionary, and false has to give way, for only those who can truly accept themselves as they are can become a vessel of the divine. This demands a certain degree of magnanimity toward one's own weaknesses and embarrassments; one must refrain from constantly belittling oneself, from continuously nagging about this or that. How should you be capable of love if you despise yourself? How should you accept your neighbor if you do not accept yourself? (Mark 12:31) In these letters of C.G. Jung, the deeply human aspect of individuation shines through again and again. This is mainly because Jung does not hesitate to share his own fragility and uncertainty – about which he had become repeatedly aware, particularly with a view to the problem of love – with his analysand.

In a letter of March 26, 1943, Jung writes, "It would be easy for me, to heedlessly pass love by, like a Buddha, but this I cannot do for love's own sake. I also cannot follow love, again for love's own sake." And why? Because Eros is a daimon or god, while he, Carl Gustav Jung, is but a human being who cannot free himself of his humanness. He is always aware of his own frailty, of the shadow that creeps into his life again and again. In contrast, Eros is a daimon or god whose divinity transcends human limitations.

69 This, however, does not mean that Jung didn't hold Buddhist teachings in high esteem. Even shortly before his death he was reading the writings of the East. See also his letter to Hedy Wyss of February 2, 1938.

1. Hedy Wyss and Her Manuscript "Lohengrin's Black Swan"

Lohengrin's Black Swan, written some ten years after Jung's death, is Hedy Wyss' report on her encounter and correspondence with C.G. Jung throughout the time of her analysis. Their exchange of letters covers more than twenty years. Only two of Hedy Wyss' letters to the "Esteemed Professor" have survived. She explains she had heard a lot about him recently through friends, which had given her the courage to ask [for analysis]. She then summarizes her painful life situation and, in the most astonishing and honest way, goes on to say:

> Although I have always railed against psychoanalysis in the past, I occasionally came to your lectures and found myself annoyed at the slightly ironic way you spoke about your cases. My friends have taught me otherwise. I am now a little more favorably disposed; I even have confidence in you. [And she ends with the simple question:]
> When may I come?[70]

These two letters reveal the courageous, talented and imaginative writer that Hedy Wyss was. Jung once wrote to her that some of her letters (though not all!) contain "the charm of naive description that is obviously part of your nature. I can't help but think of you now and again between the lines of my manuscript. Who could fail to be impressed by the problem that you are?"[71] Some of her letters touched him so deeply that he had to answer them immediately, because, as he put it, "a breeze wafts by ... that makes one respond."[72] And in another letter Jung exclaims, "To hell with it – I don't have time and I should be preparing my lecture, but I have to write you a nice letter because you are my daughter, my sister, and who knows what else."[73]

The manuscript *Lohengrin's Black Swan* has never been published. It contains much of Hedy Wyss' personal information. Years after Jung's death, as she looks back on her analysis, she reflects on various encounters with

70 First letter is undated, prior to her second letter of July 11, 1936. See *Appendix*: *Two Letters of Hedy Wyss to C.G. Jung*, pp. 233.

71 Letter of July 19, 1944.

72 Letter of September 14, 1947.

73 Letter of July 28, 1942.

him: when she showed him her latest paintings in her atelier; when she visited him in his tower at Bollingen, at the Eranos conferences in Ascona, at the Psychology Club Zurich, and in many other occasions. She often complains about the problems she had with her family, mainly with her father, and with her often difficult relationships with men. She talks about her paintings and the dreams associated with them. Every now and then she intersperses excerpts from the letters she wrote to Jung, as well as diary entries written during the time of her analytic encounters with him. Almost all of Jung's letters to her are carefully reported in the manuscript, mostly verbatim. Only a few have been shortened, and some are missing altogether, particularly ten late letters from the years 1951 to 1956. The account of her analysis with Jung in *Lohengrin's Black Swan* ends abruptly in 1950, the year she met her future husband Paul Albert Frasca. He was an American who came to Zurich to study at the Jung Institute, located at the Psychology Club on Gemeindestrasse, Zurich at that time. The correspondence between Hedy Wyss and C.G. Jung, however, continued for six more years, ending in 1956 with two moving letters of Jung in which he reflects on old age and death.

In addition to much valuable information and many thoughts relating to Jung and his circle, *Lohengrin's Black Swan* also contains some rather naive and occasionally immature passages. This might explain why, at times, and mostly in his late letters, Jung lost patience with Hedy Wyss when she continued to behave in a manner that was too unconscious, or if she wrote overly-long letters to him. It could be said, however, that particularly in his later years, Jung suffered from how unconscious the people around him were. The records of Hedy Wyss in her manuscript are nevertheless of tremendous value.

Less trustworthy, perhaps even misleading, are some passages about her "love-relationship" with C.G. Jung. Fueled by her boundless longing for love, not to mention her illusions, she sometimes loses a sense of reality, and her fantasies and wishful thinking begin to blur her perspective in an alarming way. Even though Jung often emphasizes his old age and how he is surrounded by death – occasionally even referring to his senility – it seems to have had no effect upon the unyielding longing of his much younger analysand. Hedy Wyss is painfully aware of the thirty-year age difference, but she consoles herself with the Song of Songs, where it is written that 'love is stronger than death.'[74]

Image 5: Hedy Wyss: Self-portrait, 1933 (Plate II)

74 *Song of Songs* or *Song of Salomon* 8:6, "Set me a seal upon your heart, as a seal upon your arm, for love is strong as death." (English Standard Version, ESV. Unless otherwise noted, I will use this version).

Who, then, was this woman whose paintings both fascinated and frightened Jung, but nevertheless appealed to him so greatly? Hedy Wyss was born in Zurich on January 20, 1906, and died more than one hundred years later on November 28, 2009, near her home in Gudo, in the southern, Italian-speaking part of Switzerland (Ticino). She came from a traditional bourgeois Zurich family of doctors, from which she was only able to break away to some extent when she was middle-aged, after long and painful disputes. She must have had a rather patriarchal father, which may explain her often complicated relationships with men. Her father, she once said, was so horribly self-righteous that she was almost ashamed to be his daughter. As Hedy Wyss reports, Jung once said to her, 'A father with whom one does not feel a certain animal warmth is disastrous for his daughter, for she will start to have doubts about her womanhood and will be unable to develop a healthy self-confidence.' It would seem that Jung aptly captured her father's character here, as well as his daughter's distress, for Hedy Wyss felt that Jung's comment had hit the mark. She could not expect any help from her mother who was entirely focused on trying to keep the peace in the family. Both parents were obviously very concerned about the family's good reputation. They could neither accept nor understand their daughter's free-spirited, artistic lifestyle, for it was too far removed from their own values.

Since Hedy Wyss could rarely sell her paintings, more often than not she was in severe financial difficulties. The necessity to earn one's bread and butter was always a burden in her life. She earned enough to survive by teaching art at various schools, and by doing other occasional work. The situation became dramatically worse after her father refused to financially support her and her life-style any longer. Unlike Jung, he had not a positive word to say about his daughter's artistic skills. Hedy Wyss often complained about her financial distress. In a letter of August 1942, when her situation was once again particularly precarious – she was already 36 at that time – Jung wrote to her:

Küsnacht-Zürich, 19 VIII 1942

Dear Hedy Wyss!

Yes, Dr. Boss[75] was certainly helpfully excited to assist and believed it would be possible to tell your father. I am a bit more pessimistic in this

75 Jung wanted to send her to his much younger colleague Dr Medard Boss, the later founder of Daseinsanalysis. He was probably the right man, Jung thought, to deal with her sensuality. This triggered a huge crisis in Hedy Wyss, "a solar eclipse," as she put it.

respect, i.e., as far as "meddling" in sacred family secrets is concerned. I already had the feeling in Ascona[76] that things were not going all that well for you. But I really could not do anything for you there. Indeed, one cannot properly help you at all, for "something should come to take you away". If I did not already have such a large family in need of money, I would give you the necessary subsidy, so your only lament would be about painting, and about the wickedness of the world in general. We all still have a roof, a bed, clothing and a loaf of bread, and have not yet been deported to Poland, or shot. We must learn to be grateful for even the smallest things, and to marvel at the enormity of our concupiscentia. In times when fools expect more, there is always less.

I will return to Küsnacht for two days at the beginning of September and hope to be able to see you then.

With my best greetings,
Your ever-devoted,
C.G. Jung.

P.S. The pregnant dragon is very promising! A novelty in your menagerie!

Hedy Wyss was disappointed by this letter. In deep resignation and somewhat reproachfully, she wrote in her diary that even Jung had now reached the end of his wisdom. She, too, was a fool who still expected something to come of her life – despite Auschwitz and Stalingrad, she added, in response to Jung's reference to the deportations to Poland. What she does not seem to realize are Jung's subtle and critically-meant allusions that would have her understand that lamenting is as pointless as flagrant covetousness. His remark 'that something would have to come to take her along' annoyed her the most. This is an allusion to a German poem of Friedrich Rückert,[77] with the recurring wish of a little boy, 'if only someone would come to take me along.' She thinks Jung meant to imply that a man should come to take

76 Reference to the Eranos Conference, Ascona, Switzerland, in 1942, on "The Hermetic Principal in Mythology, Gnosis, and Alchemy." Jung's topic was „Der Geist Mercurius," first published in Eranos-Jahrbuch 1942 (Rhein Verlag, Zurich 1943); revised and expanded in: *Symbolik des Geistes: Studien über psychische Phänomenologie*, in: Psychologische Abhandlungen, VI; Zurich, 1948. See C.G. Jung, "The Spirit Mercurius," in: *Alchemical Studies*, CW 13, §§ 239 ff., Princeton: Princeton University Press, 1967.

77 Poem of Friedrich Rückert (1788–1866), "Vom Büblein, das überall mitgenommen hat sein wollen" (On the little boy who wanted to be taken along everywhere).

her along and marry her. This, indeed, could *also* be true, for Jung loved ambiguities.[78] But in fact, he says that *something* must come and take her along, which refers more to a fateful or archetypal experience that is stronger than one's ego wishes or desires. This, of course, could be the experience of a deep love, but not if love is connected to a secret intention of securing one's livelihood. Psychologically, this would mean a regression to the father, who provides her with everything she needs.

78 See, for instance, Jung's letter to Dr. R. J. Zwi Werblowsky, "The language I speak must be ambiguous, must have two meanings, in order to do justice to the dual aspect of our psychic nature... I strive quite consciously and deliberately for ambiguity of expression because it is superior to unequivocalness and reflects the nature of life. I purposely allow all the overtones and undertones to be heard, partly because they are there anyway, and partly because they give a fuller picture of reality." Letter to Dr. R. J. Zwi Werblowsky, 17 June 1952, in: C.G. Jung, *Letters*, selected and edited by Gerhard Adler, in collaboration with Aniela Jaffé, translations from the German by R. F. C. Hull, in two volumes, Princeton: Princeton University Press, 1973, vol. II, p. 70.

2. The Beginning of Analysis

Out of respect for the feelings that may arise between an analyst and an analysand in deep analytical work, Hedy Wyss' diary entries in *Lohengrin's Black Swan*, will be used with the greatest restraint. They will be referenced only where they are essential, to provide a deeper understanding of Jung's letters.

The analysis began with a bang!

"Live! Make Your Experiments!"

Hedy Wyss saw C.G. Jung for the first time on November 4, 1936, a Wednesday afternoon, in the building that houses the Psychology Club at Gemeindestrasse 27, Zurich, where Jung sometimes received patients. She told him about an unhappy affair with a man with whom she could neither come together nor break away from. According to Hedy Wyss' account of her first meeting with "Prof. Jung," his response to this was, "Live! Make your experiments! Either seduce him or give him the boot!" in slightly coarser language, as she adds![79] This invitation to experiment did not please her at all, since she thought Jung was encouraging her to carry out a psychological experiment, or even misusing her for such an experiment.

What Jung, perhaps, really meant by telling her to 'make [her] experiment' can be gleaned from a report of his farewell speech delivered on the occasion of his visit to New York in 1937, only one year later. Jung gave several lectures at Yale University at that time, the so-called *Terry Lectures*. At the end of what must have been an exhausting week for him, the Psychology Club of New York organized a farewell dinner in his honor. On this occasion he was asked, once again, to say a few words to the participants. It is said that he began with the following words:

79 *Lohengrin's Black Swan*, pp. 2 f.

> "I hardly know what to say to you tonight. I have talked so much, twice already this evening. I do not know what more there is [to say]. I can only hope that something will come to me that I can give you."[80]

But then, as one participant later reported, he burst out with:

> "Jesus, you know, was a boy born of an unmarried mother. Such a boy is called illegitimate, and there is a prejudice which puts him at a great disadvantage. He suffers from a terrible feeling of inferiority for which he is certain to have to compensate. Hence the temptation of Jesus in the wilderness, in which the kingdom was offered to him. Here he met his worst enemy, the power devil; but he was able to see that, and to refuse. He said: 'My kingdom is not of this world.' ... The utter failure came at the Crucifixion in the tragic words, 'My God, my God, why hast thou forsaken me?' ...
> We all must do just what Christ did. We must make our experiment. We must make mistakes ... When we live like this we know Christ as a brother, and God indeed becomes man ... then only does God become man in ourselves ...
> And so, the last thing I would say to each of you, my friends, is: Carry through your life as well as you can, even if it is based on error, because life has to be undone, and one often gets to truth through error. Then, like Christ, you will have accomplished your experiment. So, be human, seek understanding, seek insight, and make your hypothesis, your philosophy of life. Then we may recognize the Spirit alive in the unconscious of every individual. Then we become a brother of Christ."[81]

Jung's speech, only partially reproduced here, must have made a tremendous impression on his audience. For many, his words became a numinous experience, for shortly thereafter, people began to speak of the "Last Supper."

80 William McGuire and R.F.C. Hull (Eds.), "Is analytical psychology a religion?", in: *C.G. Jung Speaking. Interviews and Encounters*, Princeton: Princeton University Press, 1977, p. 95.

81 Ibid., pp. 97-98. I owe the reference to this text to Murray Stein and his contribution "Jungian Psychology and the Spirit of Protestantism," in: Andreas Schweizer and Regine Schweizer-Vüllers (Eds.), *Stone by Stone. Reflections on the Psychology of C.G. Jung*, Einsiedeln: Daimon, 1917, pp. 221-222. For the *Terry Lectures* see C.G. Jung, "Psychology and Religion," in *Psychology and Religion: West and East*, Princeton: Princeton University Press, [2]1998, CW 11, §§ 1-168.

The next day Jung embarked for Europe. With war breaking out, and after suffering a heart attack some years later, Jung never returned to the States. Thus, in a way, it really was a "Last Supper."

"Have the courage to live your own life, even if it is based on errors," is what Jung must have had in mind when he suggested to Hedy Wyss, in their first analytical hour, to risk the experiment of life: "Live your life, take the risk of making your experiment!" His passion for the experiment of life, but also his suffering from it, permeate Jung's letters to the young artist. This is not a therapeutic concept or recipe. Rather, it was his deep conviction. Jung's long experience as analyst and healer had revealed that every single human being must follow his or her own unique path and fulfill their own destiny. The process of individuation, of becoming oneself, demands courage, and it has nothing to do with any kind of egocentricity. On the contrary, it means to "do what Christ has done," to conscientiously follow one's own path, or at least as conscientiously as possible. This is what the ancient Chinese sages meant by following the Tao. Only in this way can God become man in us; only in this way can we come close to living our own unique, individual path.

If we look for the origin of this insight – or better, experience – that everyone must follow their own unique destiny, we must go back to that fateful year of 1913, when Jung, after his separation from Freud, was compelled to surrender to his own "incessant stream of fantasies."[82] Thanks to the publication of *The Red Book* (2009) and *The Black Books* (2020), we are now able to follow Jung's night-sea journey, his descent into the realm of the unconscious. His soul emphatically forced him to live his own life and not to imitate an alien one. Thus, we read in *The Red Book*:

> If you do not acknowledge your yearning, then you do not follow yourself but go on foreign ways that others have indicated to you. So you do not live your life but an alien one. But who should live your life if you do not live it? It is not only stupid to exchange your own life for an alien one, but also a hypocritical game, because you can never really live the life of others, you can only pretend to do it, deceiving the other and yourself since you can only live your own life.[83]

82 See Jung's chapter VI, "Confrontation with the Unconscious" in: C.G. Jung, *Memories, Dreams, Reflections*, p. 176.

83 C.G. Jung, *The Red Book*, ed. and with an introduction by Sonu Shamdasani, New York /London: W.W. Norton & Company, 2009, p. 249b [*The Red Book, A Reader's Edition*,

Accordingly, Jung advises the much younger Hedy Wyss, who had identified with him a bit too much, "She [Hedy Wyss] should aim at being young among the younger, rather than being old with 'Jung'."[84] His admonition not to identify too much with others, regardless of whether one has a positive or a negative projection onto the other person, appears in several of Jung's letters to Hedy Wyss; time and again he encourages her to risk the experiment of living her own life.

Six years after his first encounter with Hedy Wyss, Jung comes back to her initial misunderstanding of his counsel, when he encouraged her to 'make [her] experiment.' Hedy Wyss feels ambivalent about her relationship with Jung; she tends to either overestimate it, or the "it-is-nothing-but" devil plagues her with strong doubts, whispering in her ear that it is nothing but an ordinary experiment. Such doubts – actually, they are self-doubts – destroy the mystery and numinous nature of an analytical relationship, which Jung once called an *opus magnum*.[85]

Jung, however, remained confident that his analysand would be able to overcome her fear of becoming the object of psychological experiments. Accordingly, in a letter six years later, he expressed that, at that time, it must have been a 'sad devil' who strove to convince her that the analysis might be merely a psychological experiment. "Do you think I 'experiment' with people for whom I must sweat blood? I just have to be real and, God knows, those around me have to be real, too, because life has to be genuine down to its last fiber; otherwise, it's all substitution and loss."[86]

The truthfulness Jung brought to his own life he also expected of others, including Hedy Wyss. His intention was not to change his analysand. Such an attempt would certainly fail. This is expressed particularly succinctly in a long and substantial letter dated presumably September 15, 1943:

> ... I am writing to you in such detail about all of this so that you can see clearly how things look from my side, and so that you have no need to interpret, which, as your writings show me, falls very wide of the mark. I am in no doubt that you have to see things the way you do for the time being. But I am as I am. You are as you are. I do not presume to change

p. 188].

84 In German, this is a play on Jung's name: "mit Jüngeren jung zu sein und nicht mit Jung zu alt."

85 C.G. Jung, "The Psychology of the Transference," in: id., *The Practice of Psychotherapy*, CW 16, § 449.

86 Letter of April 6, 1943.

> you; I wish only to give you the chance to correct any errors. But please do not misinterpret my intention. Rather, question me diligently about my perceptions and feelings, and distrust what you think you see, for nature is playing with you, not me.
> I know that you are a decent person and I trust you, and I will go on trusting you. But, through self-deception, you are in danger of losing your trust in me and, therefore, in yourself. It is my anxious concern to prevent that catastrophe from happening – *Deo concedente* ...[87]

Jung wanted to avoid this catastrophe at all costs. In a letter from July of the same year, he called it the catastrophe of the transference. 'What really matters is, for God's sake, to be true, that is, to remain faithful to one's own truth.' One can only fulfill what one is and what one has been from the very beginning. This truth, existing in every human being in a unique way, is the light which the alchemist Gerhard Dorn described as *lumen naturae*. "What madness deludes you? ... The life, the light of men, shineth in us, albeit dimly, and as though in darkness. It is not to be sought as proceeding from us, though it is in us and not of us, but of Him to Whom it belongeth, Who hath deigned to make us his dwelling place ... Thus the truth is to be sought not in ourselves, but in the image of God [*in Imagine Dei*] which is within us."[88] This is the experiment of life, which everyone must dare to live in their own unique way, in search of their own inner light.

87 Undated letter. Hedy Wyss subsequently dated it September 15, 1943. For the discussion of the whole letter see below the chapter "C.G. Jung, Hedy Wyss, and the bourgeois moral."

88 C.G. Jung, *Mysterium Coniunctionis*, CW 14, § 48.

3. Marie-Louise von Franz and Hedy Wyss

The father- or animus devil of "nothing but" not only clouded Hedy Wyss' relationship with C.G. Jung at times, but also darkened her relations with her fellow human beings in general, and not infrequently cast them in a false light. There are times in *Lohengrin's Black Swan* when she speaks of others, mostly women, in a rather dismissive manner, including the circle of women around Jung whom she had met at the Eranos conferences, the Psychology Club, or on other private occasions. Her perspective is often clouded by jealousy, and perhaps by a certain arrogance. Both point to her weak self-esteem as a woman. This is shown, for example, in her ambivalent feelings towards Marie-Louise von Franz, nine years her junior, with whom she had a rather ambiguous relationship. In her manuscript, she sometimes refers to her as 'the girl' or 'the child', or even, because of von Franz's aristocratic background, 'the baroness.' And yet, when recalling the hike she went on with von Franz over the Gotthard Pass – which at the time, was free of cars – for several days while making their way to the Eranos conference in August 1941,[89] she expresses warm feelings for her, referring to her as 'her friend.'

I draw attention to her relationship to Marie-Louise von Franz because in three of his short letters to Hedy Wyss in 1937, Jung, quite surprisingly, refers to von Franz by name. One may wonder why he did so. Hedy Wyss knew Marie-Louise from university and had apparently also met her mother, Baroness von Franz. As she reports, the two young women often sat together in Hedy Wyss' studio, discussing various subjects. They were both enthusiastic about Jung, albeit in different ways.

In the first letter, of March 27, 1937, to "Dear Miss" [*Sehr geehrtes Fräulein*], he wrote quite casually, "In the meantime, I have seen Miss v. Franz, who was able to make quite pleasing progress during the vacation." At that time, Marie-Louise von Franz was only twenty-two years old, but even then, Jung sensed that this young classicist might one day be able to assist him

89 At the Eranos conference 1941 Jung spoke about "Wandlungssymbole in der Messe" (Symbols of transformation in the Mass), later published in a revised version in CW 11, entitled "Transformation Symbolism in the Mass."

significantly in his study of alchemy.[90] In the second letter, he simply asks Hedy Wyss to forward a letter to Marie-Louise von Franz, whose address he did not know: "So be my good angel = *ángelos* = messenger." And finally, in the third letter, he tells her that he has 'received a weighty letter from M.-L. v. Fr. which [he has] not yet been able to read because of its bulk.'[91]

These references to Marie-Louise von Franz are peculiar. They could readily be misunderstood as a breach of professional confidentiality. It seems, however, that in the early stage of the analysis, Jung already had a sense of Hedy Wyss' underlying problem and therefore more or less consciously fostered her contact with Marie-Louise von Franz. He must have intuitively felt that the latter was in a position to help Hedy Wyss understand her dreams on a deeper level. And indeed, few could have interpreted the 'raunchy color, fable, and daemonic world'[92] of the artist more aptly. Be that as it may, Marie Louise von Franz did, in fact, offer a possible interpretation on one or other of the motifs in Hedy Wyss' paintings. Apparently, she often met with resistance, which, given their age difference, was understandable. Despite knowing how broad her younger colleague's knowledge of mythology was, as well as her skill at interpreting dreams, Hedy Wyss nevertheless readily felt 'belittled by what she perceived to be von Franz's schoolmasterly manner,' as she put it in *Lohengrin's Black Swan.*[93] Behind this is perhaps her negative father complex, which, in addition to suffering her father's authority over her, must have caused her to feel belittled many times over.

A short episode that occurred during the aforementioned hike over the Gotthard may illustrate the very different natures of the two young women. In her manuscript, Hedy Wyss describes a moment when the sun came out. Singing and skipping while picking flowers as they made their way down to

90 Marie-Louise von Franz probably became the most important scientific co-worker of C.G. Jung. His alchemical works are inconceivable without her relentless alchemical research and translations of many Latin texts. Jung originally wanted to publish the major work *Mysterium Coniunctionis* in his *and* in Marie-Louise von Franz's name, which was apparently refused. The productive cooperation can be seen, for example, in the first publication of *Aion*, 1951 at Rascher Verlag. This edition includes, at Jung's explicit wish, "*The Passio Perpetuae*" of Marie-Louise von Franz. Today, this work is republished in: *Niklaus von Flüh and Saint Perpetua: A Psychological Interpretation of their Visions,* Volume 6 of *The Collected Works of Marie-Louise von Franz*, Ashville: Chiron Publications, 2022.

91 Both letters of July 27, 1937.

92 "... the raunchy color, fable, animal, and daemonic world of the great mother." Letter presumably July 10, 1945.

93 *Lohengrin's Black Swan*, p. 97.

Airolo, she was warned by her colleague to watch out that her exuberance did not turn into its opposite. But her warning fell on deaf ears. Hedy Wyss wanted to enjoy being happy for as long as she possibly could, no matter what.

This lightheartedness on the part of Hedy Wyss who could be on top of the world one moment, and in the depths of despair the next, proved to be, in the long run, just too foreign for Marie-Louise von Franz's reflective nature. Thus, in the end, they parted ways: their life patterns and individual destinies were simply too divergent. Hedy Wyss looked back on that time with a certain regret; she wondered whether it had been a mistake not to have spoken to Jung about her relationship to Marie-Louise von Franz, for only he could have helped her to properly assess the personality of her "friend." It is the tragedy of the negative father complex that it poisons not only one's relationship to one's own femininity, but often also one's relationships with other women.

Image 6: Hedy Wyss, Parvati 1941/46 (Plate III)

4. The Paintings

Hedy Wyss was an artist. It seems that of all her paintings, the one of particular importance to her was her depiction of the Indian goddess Parvati. Thus, in her conversations with Jung, this painting was often mentioned. Her paintings undoubtedly appealed to Jung, perhaps because of their naturalistic character and mythological background, possibly also because he felt there was a certain psychological truth to them. But at times he was also frightened by the immediacy with which certain motifs burst forth from her unconscious. Why they could evoke a man's fear of the "eternal feminine" as well as his fascination with the "daemonic world" are clearly expressed in one of Jung's late letters. Hedy Wyss had told him that her boyfriend at the time, with whom she had been involved in a short but intimate love affair, had difficulties understanding her paintings. In a letter from Bollingen, Jung writes:

Küsnacht-Zürich 10 VIII [sic] 1945
[Postmark Bollingen, 11.VII.45]

Dear Hedy Wyss,

That's just it: you are such a very natural little woman. The raunchy color, fable, animal and daemonic world of the great mother all belong to this being, which is a *tremendum* for the man and terrifies him in the same way a cobra slithering over his foot does. He always wants to appease, dampen, soften, and humanize this side of the eternal feminine, which he really doesn't know at all, for it doesn't even occur to him that the charming young lady is surrounded by scorpions and cold-slithering snakes. One doesn't notice it at all, and neither does she. But – horror of horrors – when she paints, the water world of the big green mother comes up with slippery dragons, ghastly, phallic bull gods, and primeval colors, which put the fearful primeval man in voluptuous panic (pan = fright and goat!). Black Kali is too much for the man. He still wants to be able to believe in his mother. Your images divulge the feminine mysteries, the secrets of the man-bearing uterus and the gruesomely beautiful arcanum of the living protein, the warm blood and magical kitchen of the viscera. There, in that underworld, things still creep, slither, crawl, and swarm as

they did in the carboniferous forests, where you could barely see for the swamp and steam.
You certainly paint out of a huge but shattering truth. But for this very reason one whimpers for some soothing veilings, which, of course, does not suit your style of expression. But then you have to rise to a somewhat Luciferian *Quand-même*, which is a risk that no one wants to encourage you to take. Nevertheless, as a counterbalance ...
Your devoted,
C.G. Jung.[94]

The scorpions, the cold, slithering snakes, the phallic bull gods, and other motifs of the 'charming young woman' remind Jung of the Hindu goddess Kali, a devastating, bloodthirsty goddess, who is also mentioned in *The Red Book*.[95] The dark goddess threatens not only the life of a man, but also the animus or spirit of a woman who, provided that he is not reduced to conventional opinion, "gives to a woman's consciousness the capacity for reflection, deliberation, and self-knowledge," and thus can become a psychopompos, a mediator between consciousness and the unconscious.[96]

Hedy Wyss, too, seemed to have difficulty in really understanding the daemonic world she depicted in her paintings. Because she spontaneously painted whatever erupted out of the unconscious, the images often overwhelmed her. A true understanding of the unconscious material would have required much self-reflection. She was only able to partially understand, despite having Jung's support over many years. Perhaps her ability to understand was in part blocked by her ambivalent feelings for the 'old wise man.' Clearly fascinated by him, on the one hand, she nevertheless constantly sought to escape the agonizing situation that this engendered on the other, a situation which, as she once noted in her diary, could have best been solved by marriage!

94 Letter presumably July 10, 1945.

95 C.G. Jung, *The Red Book*, p. 248b [*The Red Book, Reader's Edition*, p. 184]. See also Jung's explanation in: Appendix B, ibid., p. 367b [*The Red Book. Reader's Edition*, p. 570]. For some psychological aspects of the goddess Kali see Andreas Schweizer, *The Fierce Dance of the Goddess – Dissolution, Chaos, and Renewal*, in: The Guild of Pastoral Psychology, No. 320, King's Lynn: Minuteman Press, 2015, pp. 19-30.

96 C.G. Jung, *Aion*, CW 9/2, § 33.

Image 7: Hedy Wyss: Mignon and the Old, 1942/43 (Plate IV)

Jung was aware that his analysand's ambivalence had to do with her father. Thus, he endeavored to avoid her propensity to project paternal authority onto him, though without much success. Unfortunately, too much of his analysand's libido flowed in this direction, at the cost of any self-reflection. Projection blurs a clear view of both one's own reality and that of the other person. "Projection always goes hand in hand with inflation," Jung wrote to her in a letter.[97] Whether one feels on top of the world, or in the depths of despair, inflation makes it hard, or even impossible, to become conscious. One lacks the ability to self-reflect and to be objective. In both instances, a certain distance is lacking, be it to one's own inner life (the analysand's unconscious) or to the outer person (the analyst).

97 Letter undated, presumably September 15, 1943.

Jung's many allusions to Hedy Wyss' paintings in his letters reveal his great interest in her art. To give just one example, the end of his letter of September 15, 1943:

> I greet the swans and horses and whatever else hoots and scoots.
> I trust you will understand! "Don't fall!"
> Your ever-devoted,
> C.G. Jung

These swans, horses, and other creatures also have to do with the "water world of the big green mother," that is, to the world of the unconscious which Hedy Wyss expressed in her paintings in ever new forms. Her paintings evoke emotions and feelings. Jung, however, wanted them to evoke her *understanding* of what she painted. He therefore admonishes her emphatically to be more self-critical with respect to her paintings. He begs her to search for their deeper meaning and to choose her motifs more consciously. When she once dreamed of a black eagle, he commented that her suspicion that the dream had to do with her parents was irrelevant. Of far more importance was that this eagle was "the animus of your own unconscious, the unconscious spirit, which swoops down on you so devastatingly. It is the unconscious out of which you paint, and which simultaneously hinders you the most, and will continue to do so until you can understand it. For this, I have to play, or even be, the faithful Eckehart ..."[98]

98 Letter of July 28, 1942. The "faithful Eckehart" is a subtle allusion to a poem by J.W. von Goethe from his "Sturm und Drang" period. Eckart, an old faithful fellow, who likes to play with the children, protects the children from the nightly horror by guiding them to the right way of dealing with the naughty sisters, who then bestow their blessing. Johann Wolfgang von Goethe, "Faithful Eckart," in: *The Works of J.W. von Goethe*, ed. by Nathan Haskell Dole, translated by Sir Walter Scott and others, London and Boston: Oxford Press, Vol. 9, *Poems of Goethe*, p. 147.

5. Facets of Eros

Only a few months after their first encounter, in a handwritten addendum to his first letter to the "Dear Miss" of March 27, 1937, Jung mentions Eros of antiquity as a "a dangerous poisoner":

> PS. Meanwhile, your second letter has arrived. You do not have to take everything I say as an "exhortation to do better." I am merely making a point. And furthermore, it is important to know what your Eros is aiming at. For it is a god and, as Diotima said, "a dangerous poisoner." For God's sake, do not think I am 'moralizing.' For I am simply admiring the beauty of the gentians and trying to understand the song of the birds, and I do this only so that, with the help of art and *Deo adjuvante* [with God's help], nature may become what it is. This is why you need to grasp what you are as a child of nature, beyond good and evil.
> Yours truly, once again and as above.

Diotima's speech on Eros as a "skillful hunter, evil sorcerer, poisoner, and sophist" comes from Plato's *Symposium*.[99] In it, Plato tells of a *symposion* (banquet) in the distant past, to which various learned men were invited to share their notion on the activities of this god. She portrays Eros not as the previous speakers had done, as the great and handsome god of love who ennobles, beautifies, harmonizes, unifies, and delights all things. Rather, she takes a frighteningly sober stance. In doing so, she remains firmly grounded in reality: "He is neither God nor handsome." This does not, however, in any way diminish his inspiring, divine, and cosmic qualities. Like any daemon, he has, as Diotima emphasizes, two very different sides!

Jung's early allusion to the dangerous poisoner in his first letter to his analysand comes as a surprise. Even at this early stage, he addresses Hedy Wyss' fundamental problem, which will remain a central theme in all the

99 Plato, "The Symposium," 203d: θηρευτὴς δεινός ... δεινὸς γόης καὶ φαρμακεὺς καὶ σοφιστής – a skillful hunter ... powerful wizard, poisoner, and sophist (translation mine). For an English translation of the whole dialogue see R.E. Allen, *The Dialogues of Plato*, volume II, "The Symposium." He translates, "clever hunter ... clever at enchantment, a sorcerer and a sophist." Ibid., p. 147.

years to come, namely her difficulty in engaging in relationships with men without harboring excessive expectations, or jeopardizing the relationship through exaggerated self-criticism. This insecurity will also endanger their analytical relationship and the basic trust it requires. Jung evidently felt this from the very beginning and therefore warned her of divine Eros as "a poisoner," which she should not mistakenly take to be a warning based on moral principle. As Jung's letters and especially some of Hedy Wyss' entries in her diary show, this daemon repeatedly shook her trust in men and also in her analyst. At times, her love for Jung inspires her and lifts her to unimagined spiritual heights, while at other times, her daemon leads her into deep, seemingly hopeless, abysses, of self-doubt or a lack of trust in human relationships in general. It is striking to see the sincerity with which Jung repeatedly scrutinizes himself, searching for the fault within himself. Notwithstanding all the difficulties and disappointments that he must have experienced over and over again – and by no means only with Hedy Wyss – Jung seems to hold on to a love that 'does not insist on its own way.' (1 Corinthians 13:5) Jung believes in love and its truth, even though, or perhaps precisely because, he is aware of the 'poisoner.'

In the aforementioned post scriptum of Jung's letter to the "Dear Miss," a surprising reversal takes place.[100] Suddenly, all the gravity of the dangerous poisoner seems to vanish into thin air. This is one of the many enantiodromias,[101] so characteristic of Jung's writing, for he continues by saying that he is simply "admiring the beauty of the gentians and trying to understand the song of the birds." With this reference to nature, Jung brings the overwhelming, even demonic power, of Eros and eroticism down to earth. In contrast to Diotima's sober view which, at bottom, seems to favor Platonic love, Jung emphasizes the beauty of nature and thus the beauty of love. For if, with the help of nature, we are able to take an objective look at love, and to strip away our disturbing attachment to ego, then the 'poisoner', or, as he is called in

100 Letter of March 27, 1937.

101 This term goes back to the presocratic philosopher Heraclitus. It designates the "regulating functions of the opposites," according to which, sooner or later, everything runs to its opposite, day becomes night, summer to winter etc. Jung calls the law of enantiodromia "the most marvelous of all psychological laws," which, however, does not hinder him to speak soon after of the "grim law of enantiodromia," from which only that man escapes "who knows how to separate himself from the unconscious, not by repressing it ... but by putting it clearly before him as *that which he is not*." C.G. Jung, "On the psychology of the unconscious," in: id., *Two Essays on Analytical Psychology*, CW 7, §§ 110 f.

Greek, the *Pharmakeus*, can become a healer. Then the poison turns into a *pharmakon*, that is, into a remedy and elixir.

As in this instance, Jung draws on seemingly unlimited sources from antiquity in many of his letters to Hedy Wyss. He does so not because she had any real knowledge of the philosophical and ancient background of Jung's often amazing allusions – perhaps she did to some limited extent – but rather because as a painter and artist she had an intuitive access to the archaic language of the unconscious and to the ancient world of mythology. Jung cannot and does not want to wrap himself up "in a Zeus-like thundercloud of silence;"[102] rather, he knows about the 'demonic world of the Great Mother,' which is within her and which she attempts to express in ever-new images and motifs.

In an early work of 1917, entitled "*Die Psychologie der unbewussten Prozesse*," Jung mentions the god of love. Here, too, he refers to Plato's Diotima:

> For, at bottom, Eros is a superhuman power which, like nature herself allows itself to be conquered and exploited as though it were impotent. But triumph over nature is dearly paid for. Nature requires no explanation of principles, but asks only for tolerance and wise measure.
>
> "Eros is a mighty daemon," as the wise Diotima said to Socrates. We shall never get the better of him, or only to our own hurt. He is not the whole of our inward nature, though he is at least one of its essential aspects.[103]

It is as if Jung had addressed these sentences to Hedy Wyss. Again and again, these thoughts resonate in his letters to the young woman. Certainly, you can overpower nature – including the nature of Eros – and use it for your own purposes, but you pay a high price, for actually, *Eros overwhelms you*. For this reason, Jung continues, it is better to bear in mind the wise Diotima and thus that daemon whom you can never really manage. Of course, there are those who tell themselves that they are done with love, either because, after too many disappointments, they have said goodbye to it or, conversely, because they have nestled down into a conventional 'love relationship.' But the truth is: "We shall never get the better of him [Eros], or only to our own hurt."

102 Thus in a letter to Hedy Wyss of September 30, 1943.

103 Today published under the title "On the Psychology of the Unconscious," in: *Two Essays on Analytical Psychology*, CW 7, §§ 32-33.

More than forty years later, Jung, in his *Memoirs*, comes back to this great god of antiquity in a similar, yet quite different, way. Although, here too, he makes it clear that we can never conquer Eros, he no longer strives for the scientific language of the early psychoanalytical movement, but rather describes Eros in beautiful, poetic terms. At the risk of repeating often quoted words, I add here a part of his description:

> In classical times ... Eros was considered a god whose divinity transcended our human limits, and who therefore could neither be comprehended nor represented in any way. I might, as many before me have attempted to do, venture an approach to this daimon, whose range of activity extends from the endless spaces of the heavens to the dark abysses of hell; but I falter before the task of finding the language which might adequately express the incalculable paradoxes of love. Eros is a *kosmogonos*, a creator and father-mother of all higher consciousness ...
>
> In my medical experience as well as in my own life I have again and again been fascinated with the mystery of love, and have never been able to explain what it is ... Here is the greatest and smallest, the remotest and nearest, the highest and lowest, and we cannot discuss one side of it without also discussing the other. No language is adequate to this paradox.[104]

In the extensive correspondence that Jung conducted throughout his lifetime with people from all over the world, it is usually when he discusses the problem of love or the meaning of the transference that the name of the god who transcends all human limitations appears. Endless cosmic spaces open up. The sphere of Eros, however, is the inner-psychic cosmos. This is not merely an experience of the 'bliss of being in love,' as Hedy Wyss once expressed it, but of cosmic abysses in the psyche which, as in Dante's *Divine Comedy*, can lead into both infernal depths and paradisiacal spheres in the beyond. More than anything else, Eros is the father-mother of consciousness, a dubious daemon, who, by creating turmoil, paradoxically forces us to become conscious. Precisely because he is a "poisoner" who can abduct one into cosmic dimensions, thereby causing awful mood changes and suffering, it is often so difficult to know what Eros is aiming at, that is, what he really wants from us when he appears.

104 C.G. Jung, *Memories, Dreams, Reflections*, pp. 353–354 (emphasis AS).

"It is Important to Know what Your Eros is Aiming at"

Considering that he had known his analysand for only four months and had seen her only a few times, one may wonder why Jung mentioned Eros as a dangerous poisoner in his first written message to Hedy Wyss. His few handwritten sentences in the letter of March 1937 obviously do not meet the often discussed "analytical distance." The note in the addendum of an otherwise completely official letter to Hedy Wyss, in which he informs her that he can no longer see her before his holidays, must have struck a chord that deeply resonated in the soul of his analysand. At the same time, however, these few impressively clear, even sobering, sentences may have been aimed at helping the artist to keep her feet on the ground when drawing so abundantly from the well of mythical and cosmic motifs in her paintings. Jung concludes his note by pointing out that she 'needs to understand that she is, as a child of nature, beyond good and evil. We find such enantiodromias whenever Jung places emphasis on the wholeness of everything that exists, because "we cannot discuss one side without also discussing the other."[105]

Jung believed that some degree of eros is constellated – that it is given – in every analytical relationship, particularly in one between a man and a woman, providing the analyst permits some level of emotional involvement and does not withdraw to Olympian heights, like a demigod or an all-loving Great Mother. When Jung mentions Eros as poisoner in his initial letter, he is clearly issuing a warning – a warning against the "poison of love" which has destroyed many an analytical relationship and many a love relationship, and will continue to do so. A love based on unconscious calculation always runs the risk of falling victim to the poisoner.

But what is the psychological meaning of the poisoner? He conceals the natural shortcomings of human – all-too human – beings with moral categories. One hopes that through 'love,' one will make progress for the better. As a result, the world of nature and eros, the world of growth and decay, is thrown out of balance, and all of a sudden, once again, one finds oneself back in the murky realm of love's sorrow. This is why, at the very beginning of his addendum to the letter of March 27, 1937, Jung states it is important to know what Eros is aiming at. Is he aiming at some loftier categories, at some beautiful but ultimately useless ideals, or perhaps merely at "just" what one is by nature? Jung writes to the young woman that he simply admires nature's

105 Ibid., p. 354.

beauty, that she [Hedy Wyss] might become what she is, but he goes on to say that fulfillment of one's own nature is only possible through art and with God's help. By 'art' he is referring to her art as a painter, but also to the art of the alchemists, with which he was deeply involved at this time. Presumably, we do indeed need an artistic and, above all, creative streak in order to follow love!

As Jung was working on the visions of Zosimos and on the series of pictures of the *Rosarium* in those years, the world of the alchemists resonates in his letters to Hedy Wyss.[106] In this instance, too. For centuries, the old masters struggled to achieve incorruptible oneness without opposites. "The prerequisite for this, of course, is that the artifex should not identify himself with the figures in the work, but should leave them in their objective, impersonal state."[107] Whenever Jung speaks of eros and love, he is ultimately concerned with the objectivity that is behind any emotional relationship.

Some three years later, Jung again mentions Eros as hunter and poisoner. Prior to the following letter, there had been a small disagreement. Jung had told Hedy Wyss in a letter that her 'clinging' to her family was a problem and that if 'she wanted to leave home, she must find a place to be [a pied-à-terre]. However, as long as she was so attached to her family, it would be difficult for her to find her place outside of it. For the time being, therefore, he must be the bridge over which she could soon come and go.'[108] Jung's comment on her attachment to her family aroused tremendous anger in Hedy Wyss. Defiantly, she argued that any self-respecting Swiss person could have told her as much and she didn't need a man of Jung's standing to tell her that. Nevertheless, it seems that Jung's critical remark was not entirely in vain as it encouraged her to move into her own small flat a short while later. She promptly sent off her letter of protest to which Jung reacted with a surprisingly conciliatory letter:

106 At the Eranos conference of 1935 Jung lectured on "Traumsymbole des Individuationsprozesses" (Dream Symbols of the Process of Individuation), one year later, 1936, on "Die Erlösungsvorstellungen in der Alchemie" (The Idea of Redemption in Alchemy) and again one year later, 1937, on "Einige Bemerkungen zu den Visionen des Zosimos" (Some Remarks on the Zosimos Visions). In the same year he spoke twice about the "Rosarium Philosophorum" at the Psychology Club. The two first contributions have been incorporated in a revised form in Jung's *Psychology and Alchemy*, CW 12.

107 Ibid., CW 12, § 43.

108 Letter of August 21, 1940.

Bollingen, 28 VIII 40

My Dear Hedy Wyss!

Yes, my last letter was not exactly emotional. That's because it was typed, meaning, dictated. Of course, I had no idea that you were ill. The sudden change of weather also gave me a cough and rheumatism, as it generally does at an advanced age. (Stupid, how everything has to be repeated!) I had not realized that you are 35. To me, you still seem fabulously young. That's why you were simply in a hurry. A large amount of calculation must have gone into this love, for otherwise it would not have been so "expedient." However, Eros is a great and dangerous god; "a hunter and poisoner," as Diotima (who was obviously no longer quite so young) told Socrates. Intention is always a little bit questionable, even if it is understandable from a human point of view, and congenial for those who are not involved. On the other hand, one must occasionally jump "into the water," i.e., into the unconscious, so that God may be served correctly, and in the manner he wishes. Out of this, out of the depths of destiny, come help and strength. Just don't force things!

So now, take good care of yourself and let me know how you get on.

With warm greetings,

Your faithful,

C.G. Jung

Just as he complains here about his cough and rheumatism, Jung often bemoans old age and its ailments, perhaps to make the 'still fabulously young' woman – Hedy Wyss was 34 at the time – aware of their age difference, and to help her question through somewhat more critical eyes her transference onto 'the wobbly old man.'[109] Or perhaps he simply wanted to make clear that illness, suffering, and death are part of being human. What followed, however, was a carefully worded, though in fact quite harsh, criticism of how she deals with love. Hedy Wyss was involved in a love relationship at the time, and secretly – or 'expediently,' as Jung put it – hoped to escape the clutches of her father and mother through engagement and marriage, thereby finally being able to leave home. Jung was suspicious of why she was suddenly in such a hurry and he surmised that intention and calculation played a large role in this 'love.' He was aware that those who deal with love in a too unconscious a fashion, or use it to their own advantage, must reckon

109 *Monologue in December 1943.*

with the great and dangerous God, Eros – the hunter and poisoner. To approach this God with any intention is risky, even dangerous.

And then once again, as in his first letter, a surprising enantiodromia takes place, but instead of speaking of flowers that he admires, and birds whose song he tries to understand, this time Jung speaks of the inner nature of love as an immersion into the world of the soul, that is, into the waters of the unconscious. Only thus can God be served correctly, namely in the manner *He* wishes rather than we wish. Strategy and power are always problematic in matters of love; they are an attempt to escape the depths of one's innermost destiny. Those who wish to serve Eros must put their whole being on the line; they must dare to jump into the water and fully accept love without cherishing secret intentions. Only then can those depths of destiny unfold out of which life arises anew evermore.

One may wonder to what extent Hedy Wyss was able to comprehend and accept Jung's messages, particularly his admonitory tone with regard to love. As she recounts in *Lohengrin's Black Swan*, she found this letter to be 'pleasing and a nice little plaster for her poor soul.' But it seems to me that Jung's letter is anything but 'a nice little plaster'! Rather, it spans from heavenly heights down into the depths of destiny. As beautiful and as jubilant as love can be, it is also painful, and sets people on a roller coaster ride of emotions that is sometimes difficult to bear and demands a great deal of steadfastness and stamina. Faced with the greatness of this god or daemon, one becomes all too painfully aware of one's human limitations; at times he blossoms and thrives; at times he withers and dies. It is no coincidence, therefore, that Jung also mentions his physical ailments in this letter.

Given how many unhappy, if not disastrous, relationships there are, it is hardly necessary to mention that Eros is a dangerous poisoner. What is really important to recognize, however, and certainly not only for Hedy Wyss, is Jung's statement that every form of expediency and self-interest poisons true love. The hope of escaping stagnation in one's own life through a new relationship, whether this be liberation from the all too tight bonds of the family, as in the case of Hedy Wyss, or whether it be a professional situation or an inner-psychic stagnation, this hope alone is not a reliable basis for a relationship. In these situations, Eros has, as it were, no target, for by following one's own agenda, all that is other and strange out of which renewal comes is missing.

The Art of Love

In a further letter, Jung is no longer concerned with the aspect of the poisoner, but rather "with the difficult art of love, which, as we know, does not insist on its own way, but also on the well-being of the other person."[110] At that time Hedy Wyss struggled with her erratic relationships with men. Jung had wanted to 'make her believe that her erotic experiences were based on a certain utilitarian intention.'[111] Jung's statement plunged the young woman into an inner uproar. As she noted in her diary, in her distress she wrote Jung 'a silly letter, some sort of a father-complex exposé, beginning with her father, then about C.G. Jung, her relationships with men, and the devil knows what else.' She was ashamed of her letter and immediately regretted having sent it. He, however, answered matter-of-factly and with true honesty, which apparently comforted her.

Küsnacht-Zürich, 1.VII.41

Dear Hedy Wyss!

You were right when you said in your letter that one must live in two worlds. It is, actually, quite natural for a person to live in two worlds. If one tries to live in only one, both can easily bite the dust. The one thrives on the other. You still have to learn the art of not dumping everything into the same hole, but to render unto Caesar the things that are Caesar's, and unto God the things that are God's. It is not a matter of either/or, but of the one and the other. If you cannot be inexpedient, then you also lack the freedom to be expedient. It is not just a matter of falling in love, but of the difficult art of love, which, as we know, does not insist on its own way,[112] but also the well-being of the other person. You have not yet completely finished with the father, which is why I am still of importance to you. To "go against" [kick against] it is of no use to you at all; one has to see what will help you more in life than 100 disappointments in love. You can have those as well, if you don't believe me, or if it is necessary for other reasons.

Thus, with my best wishes,

Your devoted,

C.G. Jung

110 Letter of July 1, 1941.

111 *Lohengrin's Black Swan*, p. 42.

112 1 Corinthians 13:5.

When Jung speaks of 'being inexpedient' here, he is probably expressing the kind of love that has no purpose – one that 'does not insist on its own way.' This requires the willingness to open oneself to the other without desire and wishful thinking which, indeed, is extremely difficult and demands the greatest effort from the one who loves. This is where the problem of transference arises, which will be a recurring theme in the years to come. For now, Jung meant to impress upon his analysand that he was still of importance to her, since she had "not yet completely finished with the father." We will see that the analytical relationship was far more complex than it might at first seem. For Hedy Wyss similarly had touched something in Jung, and he as her analyst did not cover up his feelings with the mist of some therapeutic technique. Only one who is able to open oneself *to the other* without intention and purpose can bring about, or experience in oneself, a real transformation. Only this trust can lead to the renewal of life, a renewal that – in Jung's sense – can certainly be compared to the rebirth that was sought in the ancient mysteries.

At the Eranos conference in 1939, Jung gave two impromptu lectures on various aspects of rebirth. Today they are published in a revised version in volume 9/1 of *The Collected Works*: Here it says, "Therefore, if some great idea takes hold of us from outside, we must understand that it takes hold of us only because something in us responds to it and goes out to meet it." Then there is the possibility "that the man grows with the greatness of his task. But he must have within himself the capacity to grow; otherwise even the most difficult task is of no benefit to him. More likely he will be shattered by it."[113] To this, Jung adds the example of St. Paul, who, on the road to Damascus, was suddenly confronted by Christ. Of course, this conversion experience presupposes the historical Jesus, his life, and his death, but it could never have taken place if *the image of Christ* had not surfaced from the unconscious of the former persecutor of Christians and later apostle of Christ.[114] Now Jung continues with what seems to be the core of his psychological understanding of rebirth: "When a summit of life is reached, when the bud unfolds and from the lesser the greater emerges, then, as Nietzsche says, 'One becomes Two', and the greater figure which one always was but

113 C.G. Jung, "Concerning Rebirth," CW 9/1, § 215. First published in: C.G. Jung, „Die verschiedenen Aspekte der Wiedergeburt," Eranos-Jahrbuch 1939 (Rhein-Verlag, Zürich 1940).

114 To Paul's experience on his way to Damascus see Jung's impressive letter to Pastor Walter Bernet, 13 June, 1955, in: C.G. Jung, *Letters*, vol. 2, pp. 257-264.

which remained invisible, appears to the lesser personality with the force of a revelation."[115]

For Jung, rebirth does not denote becoming someone completely new, as if one could simply get rid of the old existence and be resurrected as a new person. This may be how one feels towards life when one is in love and is blind to the all too human, dark side of love. But in the long run, life does not allow such one-sidedness; on the contrary, it is "quite natural for a person to live in two worlds." The real art of love requires one to live in two worlds, instead of 'dumping everything into the same hole.' This art is expressed aptly in Jesus' response to the Pharisees, "Therefore render unto Caesar the things that are Caesar's, and to God the things that are God's." (Matthew 22:21) But even if the one becomes two, it is still contained within the *whole human being.*

On the left and right edge of the gravestone on the family grave of C.G. Jung in Küsnacht is the sentence of St. Paul's from the First Letter to the Corinthians 15,47: "*Primus homo de terra terrenus / secundus homo de caelo caelestis*" – "The first man [is] from the earth, a man of dust / the second man from heaven heavenly." The first man refers to Adam, the earthly-physical man, the second man to Christ or the second Adam, the heavenly-spiritual man.

In her essay on the inscription "*Percussit petram et fluxerunt aquae*" – "He struck the rock, and the waters flowed" – on the gravestone of Barbara Hannah and Marie-Louise von Franz – Regine Schweizer-Vüllers also included the tombstone of C.G. Jung. Both gravestones, she concluded, "point to and circle around the mystery of the coniunctio, the uniting and becoming one with the divine essence in life and also at life's end, in death. They suggest a continual renewal in this world and in the beyond."[116] This is the bud of rebirth which opens, mentioned by Jung, and out of which the greater emerges from the lesser, where the one becomes two, and the greater man comes face to face with the former man.

115 C.G. Jung, "Concerning Rebirth", CW 9/1, § 217.

116 Regine Schweizer-Vüllers, "'He struck the rock and the water did flow.' The alchemical background of the gravestone of Marie-Louise von Franz and Barbara Hannah," in: A. Schweizer and R. Schweizer-Vüllers (Eds.), *Stone by Stone*, p. 134. To the images of the tombstones see ibid., Plate II and III, pp. 226-227.

6. The Creative Flow of the Unconscious in Jung's Letters

"In the Darkness, One Ultimately Encounters the Light"

In his letters to Hedy Wyss, it is striking how often Jung emphasizes the dark, the abysmal, and the blackness of the world, as well as his own suffering, his frailty, and the tribulations of old age in general. It is as if, in contrast to his analysand's enthusiastic disposition, he wanted to stress the gravity of life. Whoever strives too much towards heaven will soon end up in the deepest hell. Probably not without intention, Jung called the flower-picking Kore a "black swan."[117] Jung's encouragement to take on the experiment of life also includes the conscious perception of its darkness. Thus, he writes in a letter of April 6, 1943, which will be more broadly discussed later:

> ... life has to be genuine down to its last fiber; otherwise, it's all substitution and loss. In doing so, my dear black swan, one drowns in ink, for the essence of this world is black – *nigrum, nigrius, nigerrimum*! [black, blacker, black as a crow] But in the darkness, one ultimately encounters the light.

It is remarkable how many allusions of a profound nature are hidden in Jung's letters to Hedy Wyss, allusions that she probably could only grasp intuitively. We do not know. In any case, these letters are steeped in the most subtle of nuances. Sometimes only a single word resonates within a broad mythological or philosophical background. Now and then, there are

117 In many of his letters Jung alludes to Richard Wagner's romantic opera *Lohengrin*. Therein, Elsa of Brabant (Jung mentions her in his letter of April 16, 1943) is accused of fratricide. A judicial duel between her accuser and a knight chosen by her is to decide her life or death. As she was told in a dream, Lohengrin, the knight sent by God, appears in a boat pulled by a swan in order to fight for her life. He wins the fight, saves her from death and asks her to marry him on the condition that she never asks his name nor where he comes from. When she nonetheless asks his name, he reveals himself as the son of the Grail king Parcival. However, now he can no longer stay with her. The swan returns to take Lohengrin back. Regarding the "flower-picking Kore" see p. 85.

references to literature from all over the world, from antiquity to the Middle Ages through to the present time. Often, one can only intuit their meaning, gradually arriving at a clearer concept over time. What Jung seems to have penned spontaneously opens up almost unfathomable horizons of cosmic dimensions. The only explanation for this seems to be that, in his old age, Jung was perpetually connected to the creative current of the collective unconscious; in other words, his personality No. 2, as he called it, was constantly present and operative in the background.

In her biography of C.G. Jung, Marie-Louise von Franz clearly described Jung's connection with the undercurrent of the unconscious and its effect on the reader:

> [Jung] allowed the unconscious to have its say directly in what he wrote, especially in his later work. ("Everything I have written has a double bottom," he said once.) So that the reader does find a logically understandable argument on the one hand, but on the other finds himself at the same time exposed to the impact of that "other voice," the unconscious, which may either grip him or frighten him off.[118]

The reader of Jung's letters to Hedy Wyss may feel the same way at times. The spontaneity and directness of Jung's language is fascinating, but occasionally also astounding or even frightening. Many of the surprising idioms and formulations we are confronted with can only be explained as the "other voice" from the background of the unconscious. All of a sudden, it is personality No. 2 who speaks, "the 'Other,' who knew God as a hidden, personal, and at the same time, suprapersonal secret."[119] Alone with God, Jung had often lived outside of time, he recounts in *Memories*, and he adds, "I belonged to the centuries; and He who then gave answer was He who had always been, who had been before my birth."[120]

But the "Other" is not the only master in his house. Jung instinctively "knows" this, and since he always keeps an eye on the whole, such passages are followed by surprising, or at any rate unexpected, enantiodromias. Jung suddenly begins to speak of quite everyday things, such as his physical afflictions, the animals that scurry around the tower at Bollingen and the like.

118 Marie-Louise von Franz, *C.G. Jung. His Myth in Our Time*, trans. from the German by William H. Kennedy, Toronto: Inner City Books, 1998, p. 4.

119 C.G. Jung, *Memories, Dreams, Reflections*, p. 45.

120 Ibid., p. 48.

Jung never wished to give the impression of an old sage who sits above the lowlands of every-day life. Hence, probably, his recurring complaints about his old-age ailments.

Looking back on his life and especially personality No. 2, Jung stated that "light reigned, as in the spacious halls of a royal palace whose high casements open upon a landscape flooded with sunlight. Here was meaning and historical continuity, in strong contrast to the incoherent fortuitousness of No. 1's life, which had no real points of contact with its environment."[121] The following example may illustrate how personality No. 2 finds its way into Jung's letters to Hedy Wyss, and the far-reaching implications this may have had. It further shows how creatively Jung used sources from the history of ideas, thus offering an entirely new and surprising view of the old, seemingly well-known traditions of the past.

In his letter of April 6, 1943, he speaks of the light that one meets in the darkness if one perseveres long enough. This, without doubt, refers to the beginning of the Gospel of John where it is said:

> In the beginning was the Word [Logos], and the Word was with God, and the Word was God. In him [Logos] was life; and the life was the light of man. And the light shineth in darkness; and the darkness comprehended it not ... And the Word was made flesh. (John 1:1,4-5 and 14)

Jung, however, significantly modified the Johannine verse, that speaks of the light shining in the darkness, perhaps recalling his descent into the darkness of the unconscious, as he recorded in *The Red Book*. For there, he does not say "the light shines in darkness," but "in the darkness, *one ultimately encounters the light*," namely, when one seeks it out! Not before one "drowns in ink," after one has experienced, endured, and accepted the blackness of this world as far as possible, or, as *The Red Book* puts it, only after one has tasted "the very bottom of hell,"[122] can one – God willing – see the light that shines in the darkness. But it requires human effort. It needs the Logos that became flesh, that is, the vessel of the empirical human being, which can take in the divine spirit; psychologically speaking, it needs the consciousness of a human being. This is Jung's message to the black swan.

Jung perceived the Johannine Logos as divine spirit, that is, an understanding that comes from God, or as we would say, from the depths and

121 Ibid., p. 87.
122 C.G. Jung, *The Red Book*, p. 289a [*The Red Book, Reader's Edition*, p. 316].

heights of the unconscious. This is an understanding that happens within us, that comes to us. It is not an intellectual, scientific endeavor or enquiry, but rather something we can either accept or reject. Basically, the message of 'the Word became flesh' is paradoxical; on the one hand, it refers to an insight that comes to us; on the other hand, it wants to be recognized, 'grasped', realized, and 'become flesh' through us. The divine spirit needs an earthly vessel. Behind this is a deep psychological insight, that "God cannot be experienced at all unless this futile and radicular ego offers a modest vessel in which to catch the effluence of the Most High and name it with his name."[123]

Here, humankind becomes the vessel of the divine, which is probably what Paul meant when he said, "Do you not know that your body (σῶμα) is a temple of the Holy Spirit within you, which you have from God, and that you do not belong to Himself?" (1 Corinthians 6:19)[124]

All of this resonates when Jung writes to Hedy Wyss, "life has to be genuine down to its last fiber," for otherwise "it's all substitution and loss." Only when we succeed in accepting our own darkness do we ultimately encounter the light – God willing.[125] At times, Hedy Wyss seems to have been tremendously conflicted and overwhelmed by her feelings and emotions. This inhibited her from accepting Jung's advice "of not dumping everything into the same hole," but rather to accept the reality of both sides of love and life.[126]

The Creative Daemon in Jung's Letters

In a letter from Bollingen, Jung speaks of the never-ending human dilemma between the necessity of being with oneself, that is, of directing one's energies toward the creative stream of the collective unconscious, versus one's commitment to one's fellow human beings.

123 C.G. Jung, *Mysterium Coniunctionis*, CW 14, § 284.
124 See also 1 Corinthians 3:16 f.: "Do you not know that you are God's temple and the God's Spirit dwells in you? If anyone destroys God's temple, God will destroy him. For God's temple is holy, and you are that temple."
125 Letter of April 6, 1943.
126 Letter of July 1, 1941.

Image 8: The Bollingen Tower (Plate V)

Bollingen, 10 Aug. 1949

Dear Hedy Wyss!

After winding my way through all kinds of vacation obstacles, I have finally been able to get to you. You should not doubt the nature of your love. This is one of the best things about you, which I would dearly like you to accept. I should have told you this some time ago, but I could never find the time. I suffer from thwarted inactivity. What has your Thomas Mann been up to again? What is meant or intended by this Weimar-Goethe magic under the jackass-like and wicked communist régime? Nevertheless, many thanks for the book! I shall obediently read it. I do not doubt that he can write well, but etc.

I regretted that there was not enough time to see you before my departure. I feel atrociously about it, for I realize only too well how important it would be for you. But somehow, I must have time for myself and it must be before I help everyone else become acquainted with themselves, and to maintain that acquaintance to some extent. You are quite right: love has the great disadvantage of not being complete without the other – you said it so much more beautifully! But you have to have the right balance. Most of the time, however, you either have too much "I" or too much "other." Both are regrettable. Μηδὲν ἄγαν don't overdo anything! But if one is already overdoing it? ... [127]

Devotedly sympathetic,

C.G. Jung

Jung's comment that he feels wretched about once again not having time for the other person is no idle talk. It would seem that this conflict of meeting his obligations to the world, on the one hand, and finding time to come to himself on the other, plagued Jung throughout his entire life. The reason he built his tower at Bollingen was not least in order to protect himself from being harassed by people from all over the world, and to finally be able 'to come to himself.' It was in this refuge that Jung lived his essential self, the "age-old son of the mother ... spread out over the landscape and inside things." Here he lives "in every tree, in the splashing of the waves, in the clouds and the animals that come and go, in the procession of the seasons." [128] The time he spent in the tower surrounded by nature helped him to maintain his psychic balance as far as possible. Nevertheless, he is always

127 Written thus in the original letter, no omission.

128 C.G. Jung, *Memories, Dreams, Reflections*, pp. 225 f.

aware of the painful conflict to which he alludes in so many of his letters to Hedy Wyss. There is always a too-much on the one side and a too-little on the other. Thus, he abides by the stoic ideal of not overdoing anything, and, in view of the sometimes overly-emotional, exuberant nature of the addressee, he asks critically, if in veiled form, "But if you're already overdoing it?" The rest is silence.

Jung often contents himself with hinting at things. He has a soft spot for allusions. He avoids teaching, since he knows that there is no recipe for solving the human conflict between one's loyalty to the inner world of the soul and relatedness to the outer world. From Hedy Wyss' records, however, one does not get the impression that she heard Jung's casual question, "But if one is already overdoing it?" She suffers from chronic self-doubt, after having fallen, once again, into the abyss of depression. What she lacks is critical and continuous self-reflection – 'having time for oneself,' as Jung mentions in his letter. Not by chance, the letter ends with the closing words, "Devotedly sympathetic, C.G. Jung." The Greek verb *sym-pathein* means to suffer with (someone), and this sym-pathy is not an empty phrase; it is meant seriously, for Jung really suffered alongside people.

The longing for a loving and devoted partner on the one hand, and the desire or even urge to paint on the other, had always preoccupied the artist. Like Odysseus, she was torn by the waves of the sea, that is, by the chaotic-creative waters of the unconscious. As various letters show – for example the letter from Bollingen in December 1940 – Jung wanted to help her find her balance again. At that time, Hedy Wyss had separated from a man with whom she had been involved in a brief, but passionate love affair. As she wrote in her diary, this particular letter from Jung was one of the most beautiful letters she had ever received from him.

Structures of the Unconscious: The Letter of December 18, 1940

This, however, is not the only reason why this letter is reproduced in full below. Apart from the variety and richness of the issues addressed in its words, we can, if we look at it closely, recognize a meaningful structure in the background, not unlike the characteristic style of a dream or a drama. This structure is not intentional, rather it is a spontaneous product of the unconscious; it illustrates the natural and intimate connection Jung had with the underlying archetypal order of the collective unconscious, that is, with the creative current that flows beneath the surface of the contemporary problems of our age.[129] In the introductory prologue of his biography, Jung offered the image of a plant that lives on its rhizome to illustrate this connection to the underlying current of life. "Its true life is invisible, hidden in the rhizome." What we see "lasts only a single summer. Then it withers away – an ephemeral apparition." And then he adds, "Yet I have never lost a sense of something that lives and endures beneath the eternal flux. What we see is blossom, which passes. The rhizome remains."[130] Fortunate is the one who can say, "I have never lost a sense of an underlying current of life!"

This subterranean stream of deeply meaningful thought can be recognized in the letter that follows, despite its seemingly purely associative accumulation of themes. Rather than gently flowing along, Jung's thoughts resemble more a mountain stream that cheerfully bubbles along until it finally comes to rest in the image of epiphany!

Bollingen, 18.XII.1940

Dear Hedy Wyss!

The year should not end without you receiving the letter you wished for from me. First of all, you know that what I say must not be taken literally. I mostly speak in nuances. Not infrequently, I, too, must speak like the privileged average citizen of the oh-so-laudable city of Zurich, without intending to do so, but often because I intend just the opposite. But it is at times disconcertingly therapeutic to hear how it sounds in everyday language. For despite one's noblest intentions, one also has this within oneself. So, if at times one speaks like this, one is able to intercept in advance possible shocks from unexpected quarters. There are certainly pedigreed and highbred pigs in Epicurus' drove. Only suffering, or the suffering of love, drowns out, in a redeeming way, the quieter or more audible grunts from the underworld. Indeed, Tristan and Isolde are as one with the snails, and between them, they form a heaven.

It is therefore natural that love should be both guide and judge – in matters of love. One is not, however, always in love, and in life, other categories also matter.

129 See Marie-Louise von Franz, "Nike and the Waters of the Styx," in: id., *Archetypal Dimensions of the Psyche*, Boston & London: Shambhala, 1999, p. 263: "The changes in the zeitgeist, however, are based on creative processes in the collective unconscious. This is the hidden current of events that flows beneath the surface of what can be grasped as history."

130 C.G. Jung, *Memories, Dreams, Reflections*, p. 4.

Life has more than one meaning. For a woman, however, suffering love is probably of the very greatest meaning, far into the afternoon of her life. But then, one starts to notice something.

It seems to me there's not very much you can do about W.[131] So, for the time being, it looks as if the situation is on hold, and I am helping you pass the time with a long letter. What about your paint brushes and pencils? What does the daemon who takes delight in color and form have to say? In such shadowy times, the ghosts sometimes speak and guide us to other realms where a new future is formed from the remnants of the past.

When you don't know what to do, it's best just to do whatever's next, and then the division ceases.

The sun will soon have passed its lowest point, and we shall secretly celebrate the epiphany of that being who encompasses suffering and joy.

With warm greetings and best wishes,

Your ever devoted,

C. G. Jung

Jung seems to give free rein to his fantasies, which might initially give the impression that his letter is nothing more than a random collection of thoughts and aphorisms. On closer inspection, however, one recognizes a kind of Ariadne's thread that leads the reader out of the confusion and into a deeper, eternal truth: the epi-phany of the new god, Phanes, the emerging new god of *The Red Book*. Thus, the old year, with which the letter begins, ends with the new, or, as *The Red Book* expresses it, "The Way of What is to Come."[132] To reveal the inner structure of Jung's letter, I have divided it into five sections.

1. "I Express Myself most often through Nuances"

As he himself acknowledges, Jung most often speaks in nuances, which is why he should not be taken literally. He is well able to speak as an average man from the upper class of Zurich, though he freely admits his intention behind doing so is often quite the contrary. This refers to two ways of thinking, as described at the beginning of his *Symbols of Transformation*: on the one hand, non-directed thinking, or the 'merely associative' thinking of

131 The man with whom she had a love relationship.
132 C.G. Jung, *The Red Book*, *Liber Primus*, Prologue.

dreams and fantasies, that is, the symbolic language of the godhead and the daemons; and on the other hand, 'directed' or 'verbal' thinking.[133] To the latter belongs common language, which is also part of who one is, despite one's noblest intentions. Here, Jung seems to be telling Hedy Wyss that, despite one's enthusiasm for mythological themes and one's longing for love, one should never forget one's everyday personality.

2. *Epicurus' Drove*

The "pedigreed and highbred pigs in Epicurus' drove" alludes to one's natural, or everyday self. Epicurus proffered a hedonistic philosophy according to which man could find the meaning of life by accepting the grunts from the underworld, that is, his senses, his pleasure, his lust. However, if we saw his instruction as referring only to carnal lust, in the way that Christian interpreters came to understand it, we would be doing the Greek philosopher an injustice. While it is true that Epicurus does not deny carnal lust, he nevertheless places far greater importance on spiritual desire or strivings than he does on the "flesh" (σάρξ). The goal of the garden of Epicurean philosophy is not carnal pleasure but, on the contrary, the effort not to be ruled by outer influences, to fear neither the gods nor death, and to accomplish one's existence in the garden of life, walking and thinking in serenity and inner peace. Jung, on the other hand, suggests that "the quieter or more audible grunts from the underworld" can only be drowned out by "suffering, or the suffering of love."

3. *Love as a Guide*

One may, of course, be governed by love and make it the sole "guide and judge" of one's life. This may be true as long as one is in love. But one cannot always be in love. In the end, one must see that there are other criteria that rule one's life. For a woman in the first half of life, and, I would like to add, for a man who is more or less unconscious of the anima, the suffering created by love can become the sole focus of life. But eventually one has to realize

133 C.G. Jung, *Symbols of Transformation*, CW 5, §§ 14-20.

that life has more than one purpose, and that, despite the magical allure of a great love, the tedious tasks and duties of daily life cannot be neglected.

4. Where Abides Your Creativity?

When love fades, a turbulent and difficult period of disarray usually begins, when old values no longer satisfy and new ones have not yet been found. In just this situation, Jung addresses Hedy Wyss *the artist*, "What about your paint brushes and pencils? What does the daemon who takes delight in color and form have to say?"[134] In the darkness and blackness of the *nigredo* the colors, or as the alchemists say, the '*multi colores*,' begin to shine. Now the creative daemon awakens, the one who can lead us to "other realms where a new future is formed from the remnants of the past," given that one has the courage to confront one's own darkness and distress. Initially, the daemon's signs might be too vague to know clearly where it all might be heading. At this point it is best to just continue doing one's daily chores. Psychic transformations usually need much time and can sorely try our patience. This is exemplified in the scene from *The Red Book* in which Jung perseveres in the desert for six long days and nights until – on the seventh night – his soul finally speaks to him, although with only a single word: "Wait." To this he responds, "I heard the cruel word. Torment belongs to the desert."[135] This is the torment of the period of disarray, when the creative Spirit of God patiently hovers over the waters of the unconscious until, on the day of creation, She[136] is strong enough to cross the threshold of consciousness into reality.

134 In the penultimate chapter of *Mysterium Coniunctionis*, Jung talks about the great importance of the second stage of the *coniunctio*, of the *unio corporalis*. The *unio corporalis* aims at the *realization* of the insight (*unio mentalis*) gained in the course of the individuation process in concrete life. As in his letter to Hedy Wyss, here, too, he mentions "the usefulness of perceiving and giving shape to the images, whether by pencil and brush or by modelling." Jung is well aware and knows by his own experience that to overcome a merely aesthetic attitude – and here he might have remembered his descent into the unconscious in *The Red Book* – is very difficult, "although it is feasible and leads to satisfactory results." C.G. Jung, *Mysterium Coniunctionis*, CW 14, §§ 754 f.

135 C.G. Jung, *The Red Book*. Chapter 4, "The Desert," p. 236a, [*The Red Book, Reader's Edition*, p. 141].

136 The Hebrew word *ruach* used in Genesis 1:2 is feminine.

5. *The Epiphany*

Then follows the final chord of Jung's letter, written shortly before Christmas. He writes, "The sun will soon have passed its lowest point, and we shall secretly celebrate the epiphany of that being who encompasses suffering and joy." This is an allusion to Christ as referred to by Salome in *The Red Book*, where she declared to Jung, "You are Christ." This is *that* Christ who wants to become manifest in every human being. It is not the Christ of the Christian churches, who, for our sake, took the suffering of the Cross upon himself and redeemed us from our sorrows and hardships, but the Christ within us who embraces the sufferings and joys that we must take upon ourselves. This is the moment when Phanes, the new God, appears, and this is the epiphany Jung mentions at the end of his letter, the epiphany of a being that embraces or encompasses the greatest possible paradoxes within itself.

*

What follows is a five step summary of the enormous arc that Jung's letter spans, from the 'privileged average citizen of the oh-so-laudable city of Zurich' to that paradoxical being that encompasses suffering and joy. In step one, he explains to Hedy Wyss that there are two ways of thinking: rational, directed thinking and non-directed, imaginative thinking. Both are necessary to cope with life; they must offset each other, because, in the end, the one stems from the other, and vice-versa. In this way, he is urging his analysand to transform her sometimes exuberant world of fantasy into a more intelligible form, i.e., that she should try to understand the images that emerge from her unconscious. In step two, he affirms that the Epicurean grunting from the underworld – desire – can only be overcome by suffering love itself, or what love begets. Accepting this suffering requires a great deal of patience. In step three, Jung observes that even accepting this suffering that love begets is not enough, for life makes other demands upon us besides love. The conflict this engenders brings about, in step four, the awakening of the creative daemon which, in the words of *The Red Book*, can show us "the way of what is to come."[137] And lastly, in step five, Jung ends his letter by referring to the epiphany of the divine child who longs to be accepted

137 C.G. Jung, *The Red Book, Liber primus*, "The Way of What is to Come."

by us. Clearly, it was not Jung's conscious intention to impose this outlined structure upon his letter. Rather, he seems to follow quite unconsciously or intuitively an inner pattern that develops spontaneously out of a deep connection with the unconscious, one that makes this and other letters he wrote a true "work of art."

Hedy Wyss recognized Jung's creative spirit at work, both at the Eranos lectures she attended and in his letters. Appreciating his poetic style of writing, she too, for her part, wrote in a poetic and very apt way into a small notebook that was passed back and forth between the two, "[This little book] [138] has now become quite profoundly ennobled by his beautiful handwriting. The writing that does not omit anything, skips no details, and yet sees everything as one unity, heaven and earth, past and future, and also the here and now."

138 This refers to the so-called *Little Book of Monologues*, which will be broadly discussed later.

7. C.G. Jung's Century Fantasy

In the following years of 1942 and 1943, the analytical relationship between C.G. Jung and Hedy Wyss became more intense and thus more complicated, to the point that Jung considered ending her analysis. First evidence of this deepening of their analytical relationship and its consequent disturbing aspect is found in Jung's short note from Bollingen. But for Hedy Wyss, this same short note from Jung was 'a great letter' – indeed, she experienced it as a soothing response to her own 'confused, bold and twisted letter.'[139]

> Küsnacht-Zürich July 1942
> [Postmark Bollingen, 10.VII.42]
>
> My Dear Hedy Wyss!
> I should have written long ago and thanked you for your "colorful" letter, which touched me in all possible and impossible ways ...

The colorful letter Jung is referring to that both touched and confused him had to do with the following: at the time, Hedy Wyss created some truly eerie paintings and drawings, which she often used to illustrate her letters to Jung. Some of her motifs were really strange: They portrayed, for instance, 'a woman's breast pierced by an arrow' (subsequently Jung spoke of her as his 'Sebastiana')[140], or in another image a 'woman [is] tied to a rock with a dagger in her throat, next to a little horse that licks her wound' and so on.[141] When Jung began to dream of these motifs, he wondered whether he was the right analyst for Hedy Wyss. But, as his letter goes on to show, it seems he still trusted their relationship:

> ... My vacation, however, has been such that there hasn't been much free time. Your second letter is so perfect that you must nevertheless hear from me immediately. You have infected me with the desire to see you again, and therefore, I hasten to inform you that next Saturday, I will

139 *Lohengrin's Black Swan*, p. 57.
140 Saint Sebastian died as martyr, pierced by arrows.
141 Thus, Hedy Wyss reports in *Lohengrin's Black Swan*, pp. 69 f.

> temporarily be in Küsnacht again. I shall, however, be busy all afternoon, but I could see you around 6.30 p.m. ...

Bitterly disappointed, Hedy Wyss was unable to see Jung that evening. She tried to reschedule the meeting, but was turned away by his secretary, Marie-Jeanne Schmid. Jung's comment, "You have infected me with the desire to see you again" is quite remarkable. Instead of simply saying he would like to see her again, he says that *she* has infected him with *her* desire!
Jung's letter from Bollingen ends with an amazing remark:

> Your new idea is of significance, despite my not understanding it. Somewhere, though, it resonates. You are quite right: *we draw from the same substratum*, and that is joyful, embarrassing, strange, uncanny, doubtful, indeed, just like life itself.
> Warmest regards,
> From your ever-faithful,
> C.G. Jung[142]

Two weeks prior to this letter, Jung had visited Hedy Wyss in her atelier. The encounter with her paintings seems to have triggered something in him. While some of her motifs impressed him, others shocked and alarmed him. According to her own records in *Lohengrin's Black Swan*,[143] he was primarily 'puzzled by the rigidity of the figures who seemingly had no connection to one another, nor to the viewer.' And yet, fourteen days later, in a further letter to Hedy Wyss, he stated that they both *drew from the same hidden source*. This is the first allusion to an unconscious entanglement between Jung and his analysand that caused the relationship to become more intense in the months that followed. The encounter with Hedy Wyss and her paintings appears to have awakened in Jung a problem he had been wrestling with for many years: his 'century fantasy' – as he put it. It was only with *her* help, he admitted, that he was able to address it, which apparently released him from an old burden.

142 Letter of July 10, 1940 (emphasis AS).
143 *Lohengrin's Black Swan*, p. 56.

The Legend of Jung's Lineage to Johann Wolfgang von Goethe

On several occasions in his letters to Hedy Wyss Jung mentions, with a certain degree of embarrassment, the rumor circulating within his family of their alleged ancestry to Johann Wolfgang von Goethe. Jung calls it the 'great-grandmother fantasy,'[144] the 'curse of the House of Atreus,'[145] or, as mentioned above, the 'century fantasy' which had been hanging over his family history and which he finally wants to be able to dismiss. According to Jung, it was Hedy Wyss who awakened this memory in him. More than this, without her, he thought, he would not have been able to penetrate this secret, or solve the puzzle of the curse. At least, that is how he expresses himself with hindsight: "You have helped me, unknowingly, onto the right path, and I would not have thought of it if I had not, despite death and the devil, admitted my century fantasy to you."[146]

But what exactly was this rumor? In his *Memoirs*, Jung refers to it twice. According to the legend, Jung's grandfather Karl Gustav Jung, born in 1794 in Mannheim, Germany, is said to have been the illegitimate son of Carl Gustav Jung's great-grandmother, Sophie Jung-Ziegler and Johann Wolfgang von Goethe. When writing about his schoolyears, Jung stated, "I should add that there is an annoying tradition that my grandfather was a natural son of Goethe."[147] It seems Jung never fully denied that there could be a certain truth to this rumor; at any rate, he held onto it into old age. In his eightieth year, he told a visitor who had carefully researched the truly adventurous life of C.G. Jung's grandfather, Karl Gustav Jung, that he considered it quite possible that 'there is a certain truth to the tradition of a love affair between Sophie Jung-Ziegler and Goethe.' To this, his visitor simply remarked, that

144 Letter of July 2, 1943.
145 Letter of March 31, 1943.
146 Letter of April 6, 1943.
147 C.G. Jung, *Memories, Dreams, Reflection*, chapter II, "School Years," p. 35. The appendix by Aniela Jaffé about the Jung family, with detailed information about Jung's ancestors that we find in the German edition of Jung's *Memoirs,* does not exist in the English edition. See Aniela Jaffé, "Einiges über C.G. Jungs Familie" (Some remarks on C.G. Jung's family) in: C.G. Jung, *Erinnerungen, Gedanken, Träume*, Rascher Verlag, Zürich 1962, pp. 399 ff. There is, however, a short note about it in footnote 1, p. 35. See also Paul Bishop, *Carl Jung*, London: Reaction Books, 2014, "A Child of Goethe," pp. 22 ff.

'... according to Goethe's biography there isn't the slightest indication for this rumor.'[148]

A further passage in *Memories* better illuminates why Jung sustained his lifelong interest in the legend which, while well-known to his family, was, out of obvious embarrassment, always kept secret. Here he recounts, "This annoying story made an impression upon me in so far as it at once corroborated and seemed to explain my curious reactions to *Faust*. *Faust*," he continues, "struck a chord in me and pierced me through in a way that I could not but regard as personal. Most of all, it awakened in me the problem of opposites, of good and evil, of mind and matter, of light and darkness,"[149] which is what touched him so deeply about Goethe's *opus magnum*. And in reference to alchemy, he adds, "I regard my work on alchemy as a sign of my inner relationship to Goethe. Goethe's secret was that he was in the grip of that process of archetypal transformation which has gone on through the centuries."[150] And just as *Faust* was Goethe's work of old age, so, too, were Jung's works on alchemy, first and foremost *Mysterium Coniunctionis*, his *opus magnum*.

Returning now to Jung's century fantasy: who was this great-grandmother who allegedly had a liaison with Goethe?

Sophie Jung-Ziegler

Not much is known about her, which makes it all the more puzzling why, in a letter to Hedy Wyss on April 6, 1943, Jung refers to his grandfather and his alleged descent from Goethe. He speaks of a 149-year-old curse of the House of Atreus,[151] a curse that Jung felt he needed to solve. The following thoughts represent a speculative approach to the mystery behind this legend. But perhaps a 'tentative' approach, because it is open-ended, might better express

148 See Huldrych M. Koelbing, "Die Berufung Karl Gustav Jungs (1794–1864) nach Basel und ihre Vorgeschichte" [The call of Karl Gustav Jung (1794-1864) to Basel and its antecedents], in: *Gesnerus*: Swiss Journal of the history of medicine and sciences, vol. 34 (1977), p. 318 (translation mine). Koelbing visited Jung in Küsnacht on November 6, 1954.

149 C.G. Jung, *Memories, Dreams, Reflections*, p. 235.

150 Ibid., p. 206

151 This refers to the year 1794 when his grandfather was born, 149 years before. Letter of April 6, 1943: "... a 149-year-old curse that I still had to solve. A karman [sic] that weighed on me and that I never understood."

the secret than a seemingly concise explanation for what is ultimately an ineffable mystery.

The most detailed account of Sophie Jung-Ziegler comes from Jung's own pen, in a letter to his cousin Ernst Jung, dated December 30, 1959.[152] Here, Jung opined that the Ziegler sisters were "lively artistic personalities who did a great deal for the Mannheim theatre at the time of the memorable premiere of Schiller's *Räuber* [The Robbers]" (January 13, 1782).[153] He went on to propose, 'At that time, a transference to Goethe would not have been impossible.' Thus, Jung adhered to the legend, but also considered a possible confusion with Marianne von Willemer-Jung, who, as we shall see, contributed some love poems to Goethe's *West-Eastern Divan,* and with whom Goethe remained in correspondence until the end of his life.[154] Moreover, as his portrait shows, Jung's great-grandfather Franz Ignaz Jung bears a striking resemblance to his son, Karl Gustav Jung, making his own paternity more probable and contradicting the legend of his lineage from Goethe.

However, as Jung wrote in a letter to his cousin, it seems that he was more bothered by and concerned about the alleged *mental illness* of his great-grandmother, Sophie Jung-Ziegler. He does not exclude the possibility that she suffered from a schizophrenic illness, even though her "handwriting shows no schizophrenic traits." C.G. Jung's grandfather, Karl Gustav Jung, had a warm relationship with his mother, Sophie Jung-Ziegler, which would also speak against schizophrenia, and her "emotional ravagement" would rather point to a psychogenic melancholy.[155] Was it the fear of a hereditary illness that frightened Jung? This cannot be completely excluded, for Jung's own mother suffered from severe depression at times. Nevertheless, the actual explanation for Jung's preoccupation with the legend, and why it disturbed him to such an extent, must be sought elsewhere. There are some remarkable hints about this in Jung's letters to Hedy Wyss which, thanks

152 Letter to Dr. med. Ernst Jung, 30 December 1959, in: C.G. Jung, *Letters*, vol. II, pp. 527-529. In the English edition erroneously addressed to *Ewald* Jung.

153 On the friendship between Goethe and Schiller see Rüdiger Safranski, *Goethe & Schiller. Geschichte einer Freundschaft* [Goethe & Schiller. History of a Friendship], München: Carl Hanser Verlag, 2009 (not yet translated into English).

154 Marianne Jung was the illegitimate child of the (not very successful) actress Elisabeth Jung who received the name 'Jung' only through a later marriage. See Dagmar von Gersdorff, *Marianne von Willemer und Goethe. Geschichte einer Liebe*, Frankfurt am Main und Leipzig, 2003 (not yet translated into English].

155 Today we would speak of a psychogenetic depression.

to the publication of *The Red Book* and *The Black Books,* we are in a better position to understand today.

"I, Too, Am Such a Fool Who Looks Back"

On July 28, 1942, only two weeks after those first hints of a mutual psychic entanglement (letter of July 10, 1942), Jung sends another letter from Bollingen to Hedy Wyss. Apparently, she had dreamed of a dark and threatening eagle. While she thought this dream image represented the dark spirit of her parents bearing down on her, Jung saw in it the devastating effect of her animus, which repeatedly swoops down on her, wreaking havoc. The degree to which Hedy Wyss was unconscious about her paintings, her parents, and her various relationships to men deeply concerned Jung.

Küsnacht-Zürich, 28 VII 1942
[Postmark Bollingen, 28.VII.42]

> Dear Hedy Wyss,
> Heartfelt thanks for your letters, which again charmed me, despite the horrors they contain. The black eagle or vulture ("lambs" – is good!) has, unimportantly, to do with the parents. More importantly, he is the animus of your own ucs. [unconscious], the ucs. spirit, which swoops down on you so devastatingly. It is the ucs. out of which you paint, and which simultaneously hinders you the most, and will continue to do so until you can understand it. For this, I have to play, or even be, the faithful Eckehart (which is made considerably more difficult by your being such a charming protégé), and to support your apprehension in a long-winded way (this depends on how quick you are to catch on). As long as you are with your parents and under their wing, they will cause you to suffer and you will hold them responsible. But once you stand on your own two feet, you will gradually realize that you carry the whole parental web within you, and not only that, but also the web in which your parents and your forebears already wriggled themselves to death. *Omnes animae ligatae sunt*: we are all bound. *Attraxit me natura et attractus sum*: nature has attracted me and I am attracted, i.e., bound. Like the sun grows of the night, freedom grows only in captivity. Where bound? Where free? that is the question.

To hell with it – I don't have time and I should be preparing my lecture, but I have to write you a nice letter because you are my daughter, my sister, and who knows what else. Where is the freedom in that? Something always catches us, and it is always precisely as bad as we are ourselves. We have to say yes to it [to what is trapped by the shadow], for otherwise, that which "takes captive your captives"[156] cannot become what it is meant to become. Your letter from the mountain was really good and somehow touched me. Where do you have the bird of prey that you are afraid of?
You probably don't want to go forward with the times, and that's why you crawl back to Papa W. (with the syphilitic first stage chancre on his lip). I, too, am such a fool who looks back, who has to look back, because such a nice thing is coming along behind him. Who wouldn't look back? That's what at least half of life is about, isn't it? But you must not look back yet, because you have not yet reached your full extent; behind you are too many hooks still waiting for you. And I can't leave you hanging there, can I? At least, not if you wish for something different. Your will seems to me to be the imperative. (This is a good start.) For the time being, at least, that seems to be the case. But our paths do not always lead only to one side, for otherwise they would all go in circles. One must trust the way, in God's name. (There are things that are smarter than we are).
Are you coming to Ascona this year?
In any case, warmest greetings,
From your,
ever-faithful,
C.G. Jung

This letter, too, is about fatal entanglements with ancestors, a subject Jung wrestled with in his own family history. The path of individuation permits no avoidance of the confrontation with family ties. That is why he suggests to Hedy Wyss that she needs to "carry the whole parental web within [her], and not only that, but also the web in which [her] parents and [her] forebears already wriggled themselves to death. *Omnes animae ligatae sunt*: We are all bound." Real freedom is only possible when we recognize and accept as best we can our own inner constraints and helplessness, for, as Jung so poetically puts it, "like the sun grows out of the night, freedom grows only in captivity."

156 Allusion to the Song of Deborah and Barak. Judges 5:12 (New International Version).

In any case, it is no solution for Hedy Wyss to go back to "Papa W.,"[157] back to her former lover, in the hope that he might solve her existential woes, i.e., her financial problems. 'One must trust one's own path, in God's name,' and follow it, come what may. Looking back does not help, as Lot's wife experienced bitterly when she looked back at Sodom and Gomorrah and thus became a pillar of salt. (Genesis 19:26) Looking back did not bring good fortune to Orpheus either. He lost his wife Eurydice to the underworld at the very moment when, out of concern, he looked back to see if she was still there. A short while later – according to Ovid's narrative – he was torn to pieces by the Maenads. As so often happens when Jung speaks of a shadow problem, he includes himself. That is why he immediately adds that he, too, is such a fool who looks back, who has to look back, "because such a nice thing is coming along behind him [meaning Hedy Wyss]."[158] It will take almost another year for Jung to speak more plainly about his entanglement with his analysand – as plainly as one may speak within the confines of the difficult problem of the transference.[159]

Solar Eclipse

As mentioned earlier, the degree of unconsciousness that Hedy Wyss brought to her paintings increasingly worried C.G. Jung. Thus, when he began to dream about the images, he wondered if she might need a different analyst. And indeed, he suggested that she see his younger colleague, Dr Medard Boss,[160] with whom she was apparently already acquainted. Jung argued that he was too old for her and that she needed more confrontational work.

157 The boyfriend she broke up with a good year ago (in the letter mentioned by his full name).

158 In a lecture of June 9, 1945 at the Psychology Club Zürich on Gérard de Nerval's *Aurélia* Jung sees the psychological significance of looking back as the denial of life by reaching back to history, "So, like Lot's wife and Eurydice, the author begins to look back and to go back. He does not go forward as life does, because he has indeed rejected life. He goes backward out of life – he goes back into history." C.G. Jung, *On Psychological and Visionary Art*, Notes from C.G. Jung's Lecture on Gérard de Nerval's *Aurélia,* ed. by Craig E. Stephenson, Philemon Series, Princeton: Princeton University Press, 2015, p. 59.

159 See C.G. Jung, "The Psychology of the Transference," especially his commentary on the "*Rosarium philosophorum*," CW 16, §§ 402 ff.

160 Between 1938–1948, Medard Boss, the later founder of Daseinsanalysis was part of the therapeutic group that met monthly in C.G. Jung's house at Seestrasse 228 in Küsnacht.

Moreover, Dr Boss was probably the right man to deal with her sensuality. The whole thing went terribly wrong. For Hedy Wyss, Jung's suggestion came like a bolt out of the blue, so much so that she 'almost lost consciousness.' It was like a veritable 'solar eclipse.'[161] While she did try to work with Dr Boss and actually consulted him, they both immediately realized that she could not, nor did she want to, separate herself from Jung.

Looking back on this episode some three months later, in November 1942, Jung apologized. He explained that he had not wanted to hold her back, which is what her pictures seemed to be saying. He assured her that he would 'never throw anyone out who is serious and well-intentioned.' And he went on to say, "I would never have suggested for you to go to Boss if I had not had this dream, and if you had not had signs pointing in a similar direction at the same time."[162]

Image 9: Hedy Wyss: In the sign of Pisces, 1943 (Plate VI)

161 *Lohengrin's Black Swan*, pp. 70 f.
162 Letter of November 12, 1942. Jung's dream is not known.

Even after this episode, the artist's own lack of conscious awareness about the images she was painting continued to burden their analytical relationship. Jung repeatedly admonished her to grasp the deeper meaning of her work, and to choose her motifs more consciously. Perhaps it was precisely her strong transference onto Jung that made it difficult, if not impossible, for her to understand these motifs. She wanted, as she once put it, to memorialize her love for him on canvas. In other words, she was less concerned with her own inner truth than with painting *for him*. Although Jung knew that he had something to do with her art, he said that she should not worry about what she and her art meant *to him*.[163]

Intermezzo from the Monastery of Einsiedeln

In the midst of this critical phase in their relationship, Jung wrote from the monastery of Einsiedeln an astonishingly open-hearted reply to Hedy Wyss' 'much appreciated letter.' Perhaps inspired by the spirit of the Benedictine monastery hosting him, Jung wrote this letter in Old German Script. In this letter Jung's playful and creative spirit along with his impish and mischievous humor shine through.

> *Mense Februario*, on 27th day *a.D.* 1843
> [Postmark Einsiedeln, 27.II.43]
>
> My Most Dear and Amiable Maiden Hedy Wyss!
> It gave me great and immense pleasure to have thy highly esteemed letter in my pocket,, and then to read it at my leisure with the utmost devotion. Whilst thy letter is very sad, it is so full of beautiful feelings that I felt compelled to sit down and think of something that might bring thee comfort. I will not succeed in putting my good thoughts down on *paper*, though, for I am so unaccustomed to writing. And because of my advanced age, my thoughts are somewhat *embroiled*. Nevertheless, may I say that I feel quite like *St. Sebastianus:* pierced many times over by *Amor's* arrows, I lie wounded at thy feet. How am I to think upon thee, other than with much sighing and the most cordial affection?
> Here at the monastery we celebrated a convivial meal, spiced with spiritual conversations. In the peace of this *refugii* I may well recover, and,

163 Thus in a letter, two months later, on January 10, 1943.

strengthened with spiritual gifts, I will soon return and, with *fortitudo, continentia, patientia* and *perseverantia*, I shall be able to pass all the tests of a true chevalier.
I kiss thy hand, dearest friend,
Thy most obedient servant,
C.G. Jung

In a short addendum in normal script Jung apologizes for "the strange theatre in which the grandmother has embroiled [him]." This is the first time that Jung mentions the entanglement of *his* family legend to Hedy Wyss, an entanglement which, as he believes, is rooted in the unconscious. 'Her old-fashioned face, like anno 1815, time of Napoleon,' he once confessed to her, 'reminds him of a portrait of his grandmother in her youth.'[164]

Ascetic and Hermit in the Pleasure Gardens of the Earth

Only one month later, in the spring of 1943, on a *Dies Veneris* (Friday),[165] Jung once again writes to Hedy Wyss from Bollingen. It is his reaction to one of her letters that had shaken him. Jung's emotional shock reverberates in his letter. He struggles for words to describe the beauty and suffering of love, knowing that he will never find an adequate answer as every true love is beyond human measure. The text of this extraordinary letter will be reproduced again here in full, not only because of its poetic power, but also, as we shall see, because of the dramatic events that followed this confession of love, events that almost cost Jung his life.

Bollingen, 26 III 1943
Dies Veneris

Dear Hedy Wyss!
Your letter presses deeply into the strings, sounding out chords that reverberate into the unfathomable.
Yes, that's it precisely, and that's what women look like when they love. And I should not beg forgiveness that I exist! This has been the pain and sorrow of an entire life, after realizing early on how women are able

164 Thus Hedy Wyss writes in her report *Lohengrin's Black Swan*. See pp. 55 and 80. What is meant is more likely his great-grandmother, Sophie Jung-Ziegler.
165 Letter of March 26, 1943.

to love me, and then, how the Goddess herself descends into them and conjures up an ineffable springtime. That is why I fled from women. It was always "touch and go," because I am only One, one lone small male; but I suspected and feared that, somehow, I was beset by a god, invisible to myself, incomprehensible. In the solitude and silence of nature, or in research work, he was close to me, bearable in tremendous rapture or in abysmal distress and heaviness. But I found him to be unbearably painful when he confronted me in women and, as now, confronts me in you. I felt and feel like a cursed man. I am able to see divine beauty and, being deeply moved, to worship it, but it should not turn toward me, for how should I be capable of a response? I have tried to the point of exhaustion, and I am walled in by my loyalty and devotion. Out of sheer devotedness, I have become an ascetic, a hermit in the pleasure gardens of the earth, surrounded by beckoning butterflies and chirping colorful birds, enveloped by the scent of roses.

The shyest creature of the forest approaches me; the rarest of flowers open beneath my hand. Why? Because I am not a brutal, but a shy and fleeting, animal myself, in the grips of the God who cherishes all living things, of that love which remains ever true to itself and can never deny itself. I have nothing to oppose it with, and that is why I cannot respond. The deity is too big, and I am too small. I can say neither yes nor no. I would prefer to remain silent and to ask God to not appear to me in women. Alone, I can bear his presence, but let him not move me through the woman, for I can give her no answer without presuming some likeness to God. Of me, there is but One, but of women, there are many, and one should give each of them a full answer, for anything else is too little and violates the holy commandment of love. Though I must answer, for it would be inhuman not to, I must tell you that, as I breathe the fragrance of the rose, behold the light of day, and hear the rustle of the wind in the forest, I see the splendor of the eternal Deity in you. I thank nature and women who love for being beautiful. Nature is bearable, for she never expects more of me than my own nature can accomplish. She is satisfied if I breathe deeply, or if I greet the New Moon, or if I sit down quietly in the grass by the wayside, or perhaps just look yearningly out of my window. But what satisfies a woman, and especially one who loves? The only satisfying answer is the one that violates all the laws of love. But if I were to do that, only one woman would have loved me and turned away from me in disappointment. I am loved by so many women precisely because they feel that I am a lover of love and hold its commandments sacred. And yet they all want me to break those very commandments, unaware that I would then no longer be the one they were searching for and loved.

It would be easy for me to heedlessly pass love by, like a Buddha, but this I cannot do for love's own sake. I also cannot follow love, again for love's own sake. I want to tell you "Touch me not."[166] because you are only touching mortal imperfection, "suffering, old age and death"; I am only One. The splendor that surrounds me has been spread by a god. Do not seek this splendor in me, or I will sink into an abyss of shame for my pitiful poverty and limitations. Don't be fooled by my seemingly lengthy response to your feelings: I cannot deny giving you this response. But it is also all that I can do. I cannot pick flowers; I cannot shoot creatures of the forest. I cannot claim any beauty in the world for myself, for I am unable to restore it. For some unknown reason, God has determined for me to be a friendly beast in the forest of this world. It wanders alone, yet it is always surrounded. Wherever it appears, it's springtime. One could also say that it follows the spring. Either way, it can't make spring, and it doesn't do anything with spring, like a white bear that lives according to bear law and can't imagine anything beyond that. Both God and animal come together in humankind, evoking suffering and beauty, and never the one without the other. One is left with only a small garden of flowers and vegetables that demands all that one has to give.

Zimmer's death[167] filled me with sorrow. My best friends died young or relatively early, as if the imminence of their deaths spurred on their understanding. Accordingly, A. K. will go on living for a long time in order to outlive himself.

You have already understood a lot about me; God grant that you may also understand the mere-human about me.

With cordial greetings,
Your faithful, St. Sebastian

How can he turn his attention to the divine beauty of women, he asks, 'when the goddess herself descends into them?' Just as he breathes the fragrance of the rose, beholds the light of day and hears the rustle of the wind in the forest, he sees the splendor of the eternal Deity in women. But how is he to respond to them? He has tried to the point of exhaustion. And thus,

166 John 20:17.
167 The Indologist Heinrich Zimmer died on 18 March, 1943, at the age of only 51.

within the walls of his tower in Bollingen, he ponders upon this *Dies Veneris* with steadfast devotion. Out of this devotedness, he has "become an ascetic, a hermit in the pleasure gardens of the earth, surrounded by beckoning butterflies and chirping colorful birds, enveloped by the scent of roses."

Fifteen years later, Jung confesses in his *Memories* that he falters "before the task of finding the language which might adequately express the incalculable paradoxes of love."[168] But here, in this letter to Hedy Wyss, Jung *does talk* about love, not publicly as in his *Memories*, but to one of his analysands whose love he takes to heart. He chooses to remain silent and to ask God to not appear to him in women. Alone, he believes, he could bear God's presence, but he begs the Deity not to appear to him in the form of a woman. For how could he ever fulfil the onus that a woman who loves puts on him, he who, for some reason, God determined to be "a friendly beast in the forest of this world."

Once Again: Johann Wolfgang von Goethe

The powerful poetic force of Jung's reflection on love is evocative of Goethe's poem "Suleika," in the *West-Eastern Divan,* and thus, of Goethe's relationship with Marianne von Willemer-Jung, mentioned briefly above. It was not only *Faust* to whom Jung felt close, but to Goethe himself.

It was in the summer of 1814 that Goethe met Marianne Jung (1784-1860) for the first time. She was an actress and dancer, 35 years his junior, who, a short while later, became the wife of the Frankfurt banker Johann Jakob von Willemer.[169] A brief but intense love affair soon developed between the poet and the young woman. Their mutual love is reflected in the figures of Hatem and Suleika in the "Book of Suleika," which Goethe was working on at the time. It would seem that Goethe initially tried to resist the burning love of his adoring, young admirer, but once the playful dialogue in the poems they exchanged began to unfold, he was no longer able to resist her poetry and its feminine charm. Marianne developed an astounding and unique talent for responding to him with her own verses, quite equal to the great master.

168 C.G. Jung, *Memories, Dreams, Reflections*, p. 353.

169 In 1800, the 54-year-old banker Johann Jakob von Willemer, twice a widower, took in the 16-year-old actress Maria Theresia Katharina (Marianne) Jung from Vienna as a foster child; he later married her. Goethe met "Dlle. [Demoiselle] Jung," as he noted, for the first time on August 4, 1814.

Goethe included some of these poems, sometimes in partially modified form, in the "Book of Suleika," but without mentioning their authorship! One particularly brilliant example of her poems, from a dialogue between Hatem [Goethe] and Suleika [Marianne], shall be mentioned here. The dialogue begins with the following verses (extract):

Hatem
Thieves are not by chance created
Which itself commits great theft;
Love's remains it appropriated
Which within my heart were left.

All that my full life accomplished,
It has put into your hand
So that now I am impoverished,
Life depends on your command.
...

To this *Suleika* answers:
By your love I am elated,
With occasion find no faults;
Theft on you was perpetrated,
How such theft my joy exalts!
...
Do not jest! No thought of alms!
Does not love have such rich sequel?
When I hold you in my arms
Mine is every fortune's equal.[170]

To Goethe's doubts about their love relationship – "thieves are not by chance created" – Marianne responds, "How such theft my joy exalts!" Rather than feeling "impoverished" by their love, as Goethe [Hatem] feels, Marianne [Suleika] feels enriched: "... When I hold you in my arms / Mine is every fortune's equal."

170 J.W. von Goethe, *Poems of the West and East, West-Eastern Divan*. Bi-Lingual Edition of the Complete Poems. Verse Translation by John Whaley, Bern: Peter Lang, 1998, pp. 249 and 251.

Although brief, theirs was the joyful and inspiring encounter of two creative souls committed to celebrating the Kairos of love. After Goethe left Marianne in the fall of 1815, they never met again. She, however, continued to send him her poems, some of which Goethe included in the *West-Eastern Divan*. Despite the deep pain of separation, their creative exchange continued until Goethe's death in 1832. Marianne was still in his thoughts shortly before his death: he sent her back the letters she had written to him over the years, along with a comment saying, 'some sheets shine in particular; they point to the most beautiful days of my life.'[171]

171 On the relationship between J.W. von Goethe and Marianne von Willemer see Rüdiger Safranski, *Goethe. Life as a Work of Art*, New York/London: W.W. Norton & Company, 2017, chapter 30.

8. Jung's Heart Attack and His Dream of His Great-Grandmother

A Strange and Devilishly Difficult Time

In the spring of 1943, events developed in rapid succession. Only three days after sending Hedy Wyss his letter on love – on March 28/29, 1943 – Jung suffered a life-threatening nighttime heart attack in Geneva. Reporting this attack to Hedy Wyss within a week in two long letters, he describes the dramatic events of that night to her, convinced that in some way she was involved, or, as he put it, that she was "an instrument of fate to him."[172] But what had happened?

He was dining alone somewhere in Geneva when he suffered severe cardiac arrhythmias that continued even after he had returned to his hotel and gone to bed. In his distress, he began to recite the first part of Goethe's *Faust* in Basel German, but this did not calm his heart. His pulse became more irregular; no medicine seemed to help. Finally, he fell asleep, but awoke at 1 a.m. from a shattering dream – the dream of his ancestress (great-grandmother) – that filled him with rage.[173] Jung later understood that this dream solved the mystery of his 'great-grandmother and Herr von Goethe' that had been weighing on him for a long time. "I feel like it had to do with a birth," he writes to Hedy Wyss, that he "might equally as well have died from. *It seems that some insights can be quite life-threatening.*"[174]

"I have been going through a strange and devilishly difficult time in which *death's bolt of lightning* has been striking to my left and to my right,"[175] he

172 Letters of March 31 and April 6, 1943.
173 For Jung's dream see below, "Jung's Dream in Geneva," p. 135
174 Letter of March 31, 1943 (emphasis AS).
175 Ibid. (emphasis AS). Regarding the "*death's bolt of lightning*" see Luke 10:18, where Jesus says, "I saw Satan fall like lightning from heaven." In "Answer to Job" Jung interprets these words of Christ as "a curious metaphysical phenomenon," which explains Satan's "comparative ineffectiveness." It points to "the final separation of Yahweh from his dark son. Satan is banished from heaven ... not cast directly into hell, but upon earth." C.G. Jung, "Answer to Job," CW 11, § 650.

continues. First Heinrich Zimmer had died, then his old friend from his student days Rudolf Staehelin,[176] and finally, in Basel, an old woman had collapsed in front of him on the Wettsteinbrücke[177] and had been carried dead from the square. Jung's choice of words here is significant. What he really meant by "*death's bolt of lightning*" can be observed in his work "A Study in the Process of Individuation," a revised version of a lecture Jung gave at the Eranos conference in 1933.[178] After a lengthy discussion on the symbol of lightning in Jacob Böhme's work, Jung continues, "Lightning signifies a sudden, unexpected, and overpowering change of psychic condition."[179] This is what seems to have happened to him that night in Geneva. A well-known example of such an overwhelming and sudden realignment of life by death's bolt of lightning is precisely what caused Martin Luther's conversion to monastic life. During a thunderstorm, he was dashed to the ground by a bolt of lightning. Terror-stricken, he vowed to St. Anne he would become a monk if he were to survive. A few days later, he abandoned his promising career as a lawyer and, to the bitter disappointment of his father in Erfurt, joined the mendicant order of the Augustinian Hermits.

The day before his short visit to Geneva Jung had apparently been in Basel, where he saw the old woman collapse in front of him on the Wettsteinbrücke. Why Jung was in Basel on Saturday, March 27, 1943, and in Geneva from Sunday to Monday, March 28/29, 1943, can no longer be determined with any certainty. He was almost certainly not in Geneva to give a lecture, for he dined alone there, as he vividly described to Hedy Wyss: "In Geneva, after an extremely sad, puritanical rainy-weather twilight of the Calvinist *institutiones* and with the Servetian smell of fire, I had a good dinner on my own that included three dl of Aigle, [a local white wine], which did not have the desired effect, but produced instead strange heart symptoms, arrhythmia and similar gallopings."[180] The 'Servetian smell of fire' – another one of death's bolts of lightning! – is an allusion to the Protestant Michael Servetus

176 The Indologist Heinrich Zimmer died on March 18, 1943. Rudolph Staehelin was a professor of medicine. He died on March 26, 1943, the same day as Jung wrote his impressive letter about the reality of love in the tower of Bollingen.

177 A bridge crossing the Rhein in Basel.

178 The original title of Jung's Eranos lecture in 1933 was "Zur Empirie des Individuationsprozesses" (On the empirical Evidence of the Individuation Process).

179 C.G. Jung, "A Study in the Process of Individuation," CW 9/1, § 533. In regard to the *Iliaster*, Ruland speaks of "the gliding of the mind or spirit into another world." Ibid., fn. 7. Martin Ruland *Lexicon Alchemiae*, Hildesheim, Zürich, New York: Georg Olms, 1987, p. 264 (Reprint of the original edition, Frankfurt 1612).

180 Letter of April 6, 1943.

who, at Calvin's instigation, was burned as a heretic in Geneva in 1553 at the age of 44! This murder had always deeply outraged Jung, which is why he returns to it repeatedly in his work. His recollection of this scandal – in reality it was a crime – seems to have contributed significantly to his 'wild rage' and his proximity to the dead, described in his letter.

C.G. Jung's Participation in the Resistance Movement

One possible hypothesis for his travels – though it cannot be verified – is that Jung traveled from Bollingen to Basel and Geneva to ask two friends, Albert Oeri in Basel and Carl Jacob Burckhardt in Geneva, their advice on an important and highly secret matter.[181] Albert Oeri was a friend from his student days. He later became editor-in-chief of the *Basler Nachrichten* and a member of federal parliament. He was one of the most important exponents of the Intellectual National Defense and co-founder of the group "*Aktion nationaler Widerstand*" (National Resistance Campaign), which opposed the National Socialists. It seems Jung met Prof. Dr. Carl Jacob Burckhardt in Geneva. At the time, Burckhardt was a university lecturer at the Geneva *Institut universitaire de hautes études internationales.* In 1935 and 1936, he visited concentration camps in Germany as a member of the Red Cross. In 1944, he was elected president of the Red Cross. What, then, were Jung's visits about?

During the war, Jung was involved in two completely independent projects in the fight against the Nazi regime in Germany. One group had set itself the goal of ending the war, in defiance of the dictator, by orchestrating a peace treaty with the Allies.[182] Since some of these people knew about

181 Deirdre Bair suspects that behind these visits was the so-called "Schellenberg plan." Deirdre Bair, *Jung. A Biography*, Boston, New York, London: Little, Brown and Company, 2003, p. 484: "Jung said he was 'interested' in Schellenberg's plan but first wanted to consult 'two outstanding political friends.' The first was Prof. Karl Burckhardt in Geneva ...; the second was Dr. Albert Oeri, editor of the *Basler Nachrichten* and a representative of Basel in the *Nationalrat*, the federal parliament, and his lifelong friend." Earlier, in March 1934, Albert Oeri gave a talk at the Psychology Club Zurich on "Psychische Wirkung nationaler Bedrängnis" (Psychic Effect of National Hardship).

182 According to Deirdre Bair, the group that addressed C.G. Jung united under the leadership of General Walter Schellenberg, number one of the German Intelligence Service. Before the rout of Stalingrad, he confessed that National Socialism was "completely wrong." Also the German psychiatrist and later analytical psychologist, Wilhelm Bitter – he was the intermediary for C.G. Jung – joined that group. For him it was clear that

Jung's good relations with England, they asked him for his help. Apparently, neither his wife Emma nor Toni Wolff were informed of these plans. Only Barbara Hannah was privy to them, for, as an Englishwoman, it was decided that it would make most sense for her to covertly hand-deliver a message to England.

However, a dream Barbara Hannah had a year before the nighttime events in Geneva made it clear that there was little chance the plan could succeed. She dreamed that Jung's son – in the dream still a very young man – was running the project. A voice in the dream told her that nothing could come of it. It went on to say that Jung should not be reproached for this, for "he was motivated by the very purest love of humanity." Jung was alarmed when he heard Barbara Hannah's dream and, because it was his own son who was "still a very young man" in the dream, he wondered if he had been too naïve. Finally, however – and this seems to be typical of Jung's prudent, assessing attitude – he decided to 'wait and see what happens, before making a decision of any sort.'[183]

In spring 1943, through the agency of Mary Bancroft, a member of the Psychology Club Zurich from 1946–1952, C.G. Jung was contacted by Allen W. Dulles, who later became the influential head of the Central Intelligence Agency (CIA).[184] Dulles arrived in Switzerland in November 1942. His secret mission was to support members of the German resistance with important information. He was soon in active communications with Jung. Jung's task was to create psychological profiles of political and military leaders, including Hitler, in order to improve resistance plans. Jung, for his part, received his information mainly from the aforementioned German psychiatrist and analytical psychologist Wilhelm Bitter, as well as from

"only immediate unconditional surrender could save Germany from future occupation by Bolshevik Russia." (D. Bair, *C.G. Jung*, p. 483) For details of Schellenberg's plan see Geoffrey Cocks, *Psychotherapy in the Third Reich. The Göring Institute*, New Brunswick (USA) and London: Transaction Publishers, ²1997, pp. 243 f. As to the dating of these events see ibid., p. 250, fn. 101. Also D. Bair, *C.G. Jung*, pp. 482–485. It was not possible for me to check the accuracy of all the facts discussed by Deirdre Bair.

183 Barbara Hannah, *Jung. His Life and Work. A Biographical Memoir*, Wilmette, Illinois: Chiron Publications, 1997, p. 273 (emphasis AS). Barbara Hannah had this dream on March 9, 1942 (I owe this information to Emmanuel Kennedy who administers the estate of Barbara Hannah), i.e., one year before the events around Schellenberg's plan. Geoffrey Cocks suspects that Barbara Hannah was mistaken in the dating of the events. This, however, can hardly be true, given the date of Barbara Hannah's dream. G. Cocks, *Psychotherapy in the Third Reich*, p. 250, fn. 101.

184 For Allen W. Dulles see D. Bair, *C.G. Jung*, pp. 486–495.

other Swiss conspirators. It seems that Jung's assessments were very helpful. Dulles highly valued Jung's observations and repeatedly expressed his gratitude for Jung's cooperation. When the war was over, Dulles remarked in a conversation with William Kennedy, "nobody will probably ever know how much Professor Jung did for the Allied cause during the war ..."[185]

The year of 1943 was a "devilishly difficult time" for Jung. The war and its related tasks must have been a heavy burden for him to bear. But in light of the dream he had about his ancestress (C.G. Jung's great-grandmother) on that eventful night in Geneva, the question now arises if the suffering engendered by the war raging in Europe and Jung's commitment to peace are connected in some way to his great-grandmother fantasy. Jung's comment that the knowledge he gained that night 'had to do with a birth that he might equally as well have died from' indicates the deep suffering this well-kept family secret caused him.[186] But why was this particular dream, which will be explored shortly, able to solve the mystery that had so long weighed upon him down?

We may wonder why Jung says that his previous letter from Bollingen, with those poetic statements on love, "was already overshadowed by the dark doom that [had] been weighing on [his] soul up to now." It is as if his reflections on the paradoxes of love were the trigger of this dark doom – as if these very thoughts had finally awakened in him the desire to get to the bottom of it. This doom that has to do with *Faustian hubris*, i.e., with the complicity of the Faustian man in crimes of war, will be discussed at length below.

What, then, was the message from Jung's great-grandmother that disturbed him so much?

Jung's Dream in Geneva

In his first letter to Hedy Wyss from Küsnacht,[187] only two days after his heart attack in Geneva, Jung only hints at his dream of his great-grandmother, saying he will share the whole dream with her when they next meet. This meeting took place in May 1943. Soon afterwards, on April 6, 1943, he

185 D. Bair, *C.G. Jung*, pp. 493 f.
186 Letter of March 31, 1943.
187 Jung paid just a short visit to his house in Küsnacht, probably to celebrate the sixty-first birthday of his wife Emma Jung (March 30, 1943). The next day he went back to

writes her another long letter in which he once again mentions the strange heart symptoms and arrhythmia that he experienced in Geneva, and the 149-year-old curse that he had yet to solve. It was a karma[188] which weighed on him and that he had never understood. Quite the contrary: 'Like a blind pig, he had to root around in the darkness,' he wrote to Hedy Wyss in the same letter. He then refers to the dream of his great-grandmother that shook him so deeply:

> Now comes the dream that ended with anger. Oh God, it is too long. For the time being, I will only mention the basic story: In 1794, my ancestor [Jung's great-grandmother] conceived a son by Goethe. She appeared in the dream and was crazy, thinking I was the redeemer. I understood only afterwards that I am her redeemer.
> Enough for today! Hail to the swan! Your ever devoted, Eckehart[189]

Jung did not see Hedy Wyss again until May 7, 1943, a month after his eventful night in Geneva. Once again, he referred to this dream. Hedy Wyss carefully recorded this encounter in *Lohengrin's Black Swan*. It is from this source that we can glean some important details of Jung's dream. With few exceptions, the facts and details she recounts that I was able to verify proved to be accurate. We may assume, therefore, that her account of the dream corresponds to what Jung disclosed to her. His dream was as follows:

> Together with some other women, his great-grandmother [Sophie Jung-Ziegler] came out of the water of Lake Zurich into his garden in Küsnacht. Jung was very annoyed. There were also intruders in the house itself, people laughing stupidly and impudently. Jung grew angry. The old woman [Jung's great-grandmother] held a book in front of her which she was reading. It was the Apocalypse, and she pointed her finger at him,

Bollingen (This hint I owe to Thomas Fischer).

188 Jung does not use the word *karma* in the sense of Indian religions and their belief in the cycle of rebirths, according to which man's life is shaped in both a positive and negative sense by previous incarnations. For Jung karma refers to *psychic prefigurations* inherited from previous generations and their cultural environments. These include mainly unsolved problems and the unfulfilled tasks of the ancestors.

189 Letter of April 6, 1943. Jung alludes to the dream of March, 28/29, 1943, that he had in Geneva.

fuming, and said, "You are the redeemer." Jung got so angry, yelled at her, and woke up with a heart attack.[190]

This report reveals several elements that were quite central to Jung's life, which Hedy Wyss could not have known about. This confirms not only the authenticity of her rendition of the dream, but also the great importance that this dream must have had for Jung. First, there is the motif of his great-grandmother who came out of the lake. In the "*Protocols*,"[191] published in part only recently in German, Jung recounts his struggle to maintain a relationship with Toni Wolff, after their brief analytical work together had been concluded. All passages concerning Toni Wolff are missing in Aniela Jaffé's official biography. In the *Protocols*, however, Jung mentioned that he had had several dreams about her at that time. Yet, he hesitated to get involved with her until the following happened: One day he was swimming far out in the lake when he got a terrible leg cramp. He vowed that if he survived, he would surrender to his feelings for Toni Wolff. He did survive and that was the evening Jung assented to the relationship.[192] Toni Wolff became Jung's most important companion during the difficult years of his descent into the unconscious. He shared his active imaginations with her – which we can now read in both *The Red Book* and *The Black Books*. Her support proved essential to Jung's survival in those strenuous years of his immersion into the world of the unconscious. In the dream, however, it is not he who emerges from the lake, but an "old woman" whom Jung recognizes as his great-grandmother. Be that as it may, it is out of the lake, or rather the unconscious, that his fate emerges.

The people laughing stupidly or impudently is the second motif. This brings to mind the dead who filled his house at Seestrasse 228 in Küsnacht,

190 *Lohengrin's Black Swan*, p. 101.

191 The *Protocols*, originally only privately circulated, contain the text Aniela Jaffé noted from Jung's narratives about his inner and outer life. From these texts she assembled the biography, *Memories, Dreams, Reflections of C.G. Jung*, published soon after Jung's death. However, the first and last chapters of this book were written by Jung himself. In 2023, a collection of Jung's reflections in the *Protocols*, which are not integrated in the official biography, have been published in English under the title *Reflections on the Life and Dreams of C.G. Jung by Aniela Jaffé from Conversations with Jung*, Einsiedeln: Daimon, 2023. An English publication of the *Original Protocols* will follow soon: C.G. Jung and Aniela Jaffé, *The Original Protocols for Memories, Dreams, Reflections*. Edited by Sonu Shamdasani, with Thomas Fischer and Robert Hinshaw as Consulting Editors [status July 2023; see www.cgjung-werke.org].

192 C.G. Jung, *Protocols*, p. 98.

in January, 1916, forcing him to answer their unresolved questions. As mentioned earlier, it was from this experience that the *Septem Sermones of the Dead* emerged. Both his experience in 1916 and his dream about his great-grandmother deal with the redemption of the dead.

The old woman in Jung's dream who is reading the Apocalypse and pointing her finger at him is the third motif. Quite a few years were to pass before Jung gave his full attention to the *Book of Revelation*, in his paper "Answer to Job," published in 1952. All three motifs, therefore, point to events in Jung's life that were of the utmost importance: his relationship to Toni Wolff, the *Septem Sermones ad Mortuos*, and Jung's confrontation with the ambivalent image of God as described in his "Answer to Job."

The Ancestress: "You Are the Redeemer"

In his initial and brief description of the dream, Jung addressed none of these three motifs. And yet, it is precisely these details that offer significant hints of its tremendous importance. Perhaps they explain why the family legend of being descendants of Goethe irritated Jung so very much, and why up until this dream he had refused to deal with it. Jung was now 69 years old.

"You are the redeemer" the old woman [Jung's great-grandmother] says to him. This enrages Jung. He calms down by thinking that he is *her* redeemer, in other words, that he has redeemed *his ancestress* from the family curse of infidelity, or as he called it, from the curse of the House of Atreus. This seems to be what he relayed to Hedy Wyss, as she recorded in her manuscript: 'At last, the curse of the House of Atreus that lay heavily upon him was resolved. Now he understood that he was not the Redeemer, as his ancestress clearly had wanted to persuade him he was, but rather that he had redeemed her, whereby her restless soul could now be at peace.'[193] In my view, however, this does not get to the heart of the matter, which a glance at Jung's encounter with the anima in *The Red Book* would appear to confirm.

193 *Lohengrin's Black Swan*, p. 102.

Salome: "You Are Christ"

The comment of his ancestress "You are the redeemer" brings to mind the remark of blind Salome, who, in Jung's imagination, said to him in *The Red Book*: "You are Christ."[194] Salome's words deeply shocked Jung at the time, probably no less than his great-grandmother's claim in his dream that he was the redeemer. His encounter with Salome, with his anima, had taken place thirty years earlier, but Jung was still indignant about the audacity of her remark! In *The Red Book*, in which Jung recorded his active imaginations, Salome is not just any figure from the unconscious. Along with her father, the prophet Elijah, who later transforms into the figure of Philemon, she is one of the most important inner figures Jung encounters during his immersion into the depths of the unconscious.

According to his own statements, the dream of his ancestress freed Jung from a dark doom that had never ceased to weigh upon his soul. It did nothing short of "reversing this fate, [and that] is a bitter and difficult task."[195] Salome's redemption from her blindness, as described in *The Red Book*, was no less agonizing. The scene is preceded by long dialogues with Elijah, the old wise man, and Salome, his daughter. That Salome is said to be the prophet's daughter deeply shocked Jung. His dismay was even greater when she asked him if he loved her. How could he ever love the woman who has the blood of the saint (John the Baptist) on her hands, he asks himself. After long and painful arguments, there is a breakthrough. Here is a summary of the scene that begins with the touching image of the divine child:

> Jung sees a child; it is the divine child with a white serpent in his right hand, and a black serpent in his left hand. Then he sees the cross of Christ on the green mountain. A stream of blood flows from the summit of the mountain. Again he sees the cross and Christ in his final hour and agony. Now Salome comes to him and says, "You are Christ." He stands with outstretched arms like someone crucified, his body horribly entwined by the serpent. "You, Salome, say that I am Christ?" he asks her. Blood streams from his body, spilling down the mountainside. Salome bends down to his feet wrapping her black hair around them. Then she cries, "I see light!" At that moment the serpent falls from his body. He kneels at

194 C.G. Jung, *The Red Book*, p. 252b [*The Red Book, Reader's Edition*, p. 197]. Imagination of December 25, 1913. See also C.G. Jung, *The Black Books*, vol. 2, p. 195.

195 Letter of April 16, 1943.

> the feet of the prophet Elijah, the Old, who says, "Your work is fulfilled here. Other things will come. Seek untiringly, and above all write exactly what you see."[196]

Jung's encounters with Elijah and Salome, which he calls the "Mystery Play," are some of the most impressive scenes in the entire *Red Book.* His imaginations, as recorded in the "Mystery Play," contain the essence of Jung's later remarks on God's incarnation in every human being and its stages of transformation in our time. Unlike in Christian dogma, the focus here is not on the work of redemption done by Christ, but rather on the redemptive work of *the human being.* This is the work of redemption both Salome and his great-grandmother were referring to.

In his 1940 lecture on the dogma of the Trinity, given at both Eranos and the Psychology Club, Jung speaks of the drama of redemption "...whereby God descends into the human realm and man mounts up to the realm of divinity."[197] Thus, Jung continues, the Christian definition of God as the *summum bonum*, which excludes evil and the devil from being a part of God, can no longer be understood.[198] In his work *Aion*, published ten years later in 1951, Jung expounds upon the one-sidedness of the Christian image of God. The tendency to deny any reality of evil within the image of God is the origin of the often-quoted axiom of the Syrian Christian apologist Tatian (2nd century AD): "*Omne bonum a Deo, omne malum ab homine*" – All good comes from God, all evil from man.[199] This view, shared by many of the Church Fathers, excludes from the outset the participation of man (who tends toward evil) in the redemptive work of God (who is only good).

Marie-Louise von Franz was particularly succinct in formulating how the image of God is changing today. Almost at the end of her extensive commentary on the *Aurora consurgens* of Thomas Aquinas in a passage that could be seen as the quintessence of her entire commentary, she says with regard to the mystery of the continuing incarnation of God:

> In [the Aurora] the mediator who unties the pair in place of the Holy Spirit is the spirit Mercurius, who [...] manifests himself in many

196 C.G. Jung, *The Red Book*, p. 252b [*The Red Book, Reader's Edition*, pp. 197 f.].

197 C.G. Jung, "A Psychological Approach to the Dogma of the Trinity," CW 11, § 241. The original title was "On the Psychology of the Idea of the Trinity."

198 The Christian definition of God as *summum bonum* excludes the Evil One right from the start. See ibid., CW 11, § 252.

199 See mainly C.G. Jung, *Aion*, CW 9/2, §§ 95-98.

> individuals. This means that God becomes manifest in the individual man. [...] Man becomes God's redeemer, uniting in him his two aspects as man and woman.[200]

"Man becomes God's redeemer," says Marie-Louise von Franz; "You are the redeemer," Jung's ancestress tells him. Both indicate that the empirical human being is definitively involved in the divine drama, sharing co-responsibility with God. This could explain Jung's suffering in the "Mystery Play" when Salome calls him Christ. But it might also explain Jung's violent rage and the heart attacks he suffered in connection with the dream of his ancestress. Every effort to unite the opposites – every step of carrying the cross – is fraught with deep suffering. Without this suffering, Salome's blindness could not have been healed. The tremendous terror and rage that overtook Jung that night in Geneva show just how aware Jung was from the beginning of the difficulty of the task before him. While writing down his thoughts on the dogma of the Trinity – and probably also with a mind to his encounter with Salome in *The Red Book* – Jung describes what he means by 'carrying the cross':

> If, however, God is born as a man and wants to unite mankind in the fellowship of the Holy Ghost, he must suffer the terrible torture of having to endure the world in all its reality. This is the cross he has to bear, and he himself is a cross. The whole world is God's suffering, and *every individual man* who wants to get anywhere near his own wholeness knows that this is the way of the cross.[201]

Salome's "You are Christ" and his ancestress' "You are the redeemer" could be readily misunderstood, as if Jung were about to replace Christ, as if he alone were the long-awaited Messiah and Redeemer. That would be an egregious misunderstanding. Just how much Jung feared this is revealed in his active imaginations recorded in *The Black Books*. Here Jung vehemently opposes the anima, who conjures up the danger of adulation or, to put it psychologically, of inflation and hubris. This becomes particularly apparent

200 Marie-Louise von Franz, *Aurora Consurgens. A Document Attributed to Thomas Aquinas on the Problem of Opposites in Alchemy*, ed. with a commentary by M.-L. von Franz, transl. by R.F.C. Hull and A.S.B. Glover, Toronto: Inner City Books, 2000, p. 398. In the German text this passage corresponds to § 576).

201 C.G. Jung, "A Psychological Approach to the Dogma of the Trinity," CW 11, § 265 (emphasis AS).

in one of his active imaginations in October 1916. His soul asks him seductively, "Weren't you covered just now by a shimmering light? What was that golden glow? ... I saw it around you, the golden shimmering flowing just now around you. Never have I have seen the like ..." And later she even says, "The gold shone from you!" To which Jung answers, "Sick with pain, petrified from suffering – and you speak of shining gold?" The anima, however, insists that she has seen him in a divinely shimmering light. Now Jung is seized by an almost panicky fear of, as he put it, the 'worst and most diabolical of all temptresses.' He harshly rejects her and warns her, "Don't seduce me into the madness of holiness, into stupid and unjust arrogance ..."[202]

This fear of the hubristic Promethean misunderstanding of holiness and of the gold shining through was probably what led Jung to conceal from Hedy Wyss, and perhaps from himself as well, the true meaning of the message of the ancestress, namely, the incarnation of God in *each* human being. The time was not yet ripe for him to acknowledge this. It was only in later years that Jung addressed the theme of God's incarnation more frequently. In the same way he pointed out in *The Black Books* when conversing with the soul, Jung repeatedly emphasized how important it was for each and every individual who strives for wholeness to take upon themselves the cross of uniting the opposites. Only through bearing the cross can one become the redeemer, can one become "Christ." In a similar way, Marie-Louise von Franz speaks of the alchemical spirit of Mercurius which manifests in *many individual people*. This means that each person can become "Christ," the redeemer; each person can make his or her contribution, however small, to healing the painful and dangerous divisions of this world.

Goethe's *Faust*

As mentioned above, the dark doom that descended on Jung around the issue of possibly being a descendant of Goethe's *also* has to do with a Faustian hubris and complicity in the crimes of never-ending wars. Only a few months before his fateful dream in Geneva, Jung completed his work *Psychology and*

202 C.G. Jung, *The Black Books, 1913-1932. Notebooks of Transformation*. Edited by Sonu Shamdasani. Translated by Martin Liebscher, John Peck, and Sonu Shamdasani, Philemon Series. In collaboration with the Foundation of the Works of C.G. Jung, 7 volumes, New York/London: W.W. Norton & Company, 2020, vol. 6, pp. 269 f.

Alchemy.[203] In its "Epilogue" and in reference to Nietzsche's Superman, he examines Faustian hubris at length, that is, the hubris of modern humankind in relation to nature. This hubris stands in complete contradiction to the alchemists' spirit of humility.

Against this background, it is remarkable that on that fateful night when he was stricken with menacing cardiac arrhythmia, Jung attempted to rewrite in Basel German Faust's monologue in Part One, beginning at the end, "as if it were the beginning," and ending with the "monologue in which Faust finally decides to study medicine" after all.[204] What a strange idea, to reverse Goethe's *Faust*! And yet, there seems to be a kernel of truth in it as well.

Jung had always been fascinated by Goethe's *Faust*. It really was as if he had to "reverse" *Faust* in order to find the very medicine that the alchemists had been seeking for centuries. In Mercurius, they found the *medicina catholica* and the *alexipharmakon* – the "preserver [*servator*] of the world."[205] It was this medieval-alchemical spirit, or at least its echoes, that so fascinated Jung in Goethe's *opus magnum*. With *Faust*, he stated, alchemy had reached its "historical turning-point." This is expressed, for example, in the tragedy of the Paris-Helena-scene in *Faust*, Part Two, at the end of Act I. On this passage Jung writes:

> To the medieval alchemist this episode would have represented the mysterious *coniunctio* of Sol and Luna in the retort; but modern man, disguised in the figure of Faust, recognizes the projection and, putting himself in place of Paris or Sol, takes possession of Helen or Luna, his own inner, feminine counterpart.[206]

203 Jung wrote the Foreword to the Swiss edition in January 1943.

204 Letter of April 6, 1943. See the beginning of Faust's monologue, "I have pursued, alas, philosophy, / Jurisprudence, and medicine, / And, help me God, theology, / With fervent zeal through thick and thin. / And here, poor fool, I stand once more, / No wiser than I was before." J.W. von Goethe, *Faust. A Tragedy*, Part I, verses 354 ff.

205 C.G. Jung, "The Spirit Mercurius," CW 13, § 283.

206 C.G. Jung, *Psychology and Alchemy*, Epilogue, CW 12, § 558. "Faust begrudges Paris the beautiful Helena, takes his place, wants to seize Helena, but instead falls down fainting." Id., "Faust und die Alchemie," in: Irene Gerber-Münch, *Goethes Faust, Eine tiefenpsychologische Studie über den Mythos des modernen Menschen* (Goethe's Faust. A Depth Psychological Study on the Myth of Modern Man), Egg ZH: Verlag Stiftung für Jung'sche Psychologie, 1997, p. 27 f. (translation mine).

Faust, however, is no match for the goddess, the beautiful Helena. He is overwhelmed by her and loses himself in her, which is why the astrologer soberly and aptly cautions when she appears :

He who beholds her must distracted sigh,
He who possesses her won a bliss too high.[207]

Whoever she, the goddess of love, appears to is in grave danger of being so enraptured, they will take flight from the earthly-human realm. As the sight of any two people in love proves, this is a fairly normal phenomenon. In the background, however, lurks the danger of losing one's sense of self. Psychologically speaking, whenever Eros, the poisoner, plays his hand too forcefully, one is in danger of succumbing to inflation.

Jung was clearly aware of this danger. In his aforementioned letter on love, he speaks of the magical power of women have and he writes, "[I realized] early on how women are able to love me, and then, how the Goddess herself descends into them and conjures up an ineffable springtime. That is why I fled from women."[208] Jung *knew* that he should not fall blindly for the archetype of female beauty and its divinity. Faust, however, was completely overwhelmed by the vision of Helena:

To you alone I vow my striving art,
My strength, affection, life with passion twined,
My worship, frenzy, love, my inmost heart."[209]

Her lady-in-waiting probably is not entirely wrong when she remarks:

I see she's [Helena] planning to become his teacher;
In such a matter all you males are dense,
He fancies too he is the first to reach her."[210]

Such concerns do not bother Faust. He forcefully seizes Helena, or his image of her, whereupon everything dissolves into mist. On this, Jung says in the Epilogue of *Psychology and Alchemy*, "Consequently Faust cannot resist

207 J.W. von Goethe, *Faust. A Tragedy*, Part Two, Act I, pp. 86f., verses 6485 f.
208 Letter of March 26, 1943 (emphasis AS).
209 J.W. von Goethe, *Faust. A Tragedy*, Part Two, Act I, p. 87, verses 6498 ff.
210 Ibid., p. 88, verses 6522 f.

supplanting Paris in Helen's affections, and the other 'births' and rejuvenations, such as the Boy Charioteer and the Homunculus, are destroyed by the same greed. This is probably the deeper reason why Faust's final rejuvenation takes place only in the post-mortal state, i.e., is projected into the future."[211] But Faust's blind striving has yet a further and fatal consequence.

Because of his demonic desire, Faust – and all of us today – gave rise to the murder of Philemon and Baucis.[212] This murder never ceased to infuriate Jung. As we learn in *Memories*, in light of Faust's hubris and inflation, Jung felt personally impacted by, and even complicit in, the murder of Philemon and Baucis, "quite as if [I myself] in the past had helped commit the murder of the two old people."[213] The legend of his grandfather being the natural son of Goethe exacerbated his sense of guilt. Only gradually did he become aware that the unresolved problem of Faust was not his alone, but rather the problem of modern humanity in general.

Jung addresses this collective and contemporary aspect of Goethe's *Faust* in his contribution "After the Catastrophe," published in 1945, a year after the publication of *Psychology and Alchemy*. In this work, he reflects upon the manifestation and significance of the Faustian problem during World War II. In this paper, Jung no longer merely speaks only of the hubris of Faust, but of the hubris of Faustian man, that is, of the threat encompassing the entire modern world – as the war, or rather both World Wars, have clearly shown. Despite the horrific catastrophes of the twentieth century, this threat remains. The clarity that Jung brings to this paper – and even more so in "Answer to Job" – concerning the threat of the opposites remaining split is, in my view, not solely based upon his war-time experience. Rather, behind both works is the deadly "bolt of lightning" that Jung suffered with his first and second heart attack in the spring of 1943 and in February 1944, respectively.[214]

With a view to the collective exaggerated expectations, especially at the beginning of World War II, when a real enthusiasm for war was present, Jung writes in his paper "After the Catastrophe":

211 C.G. Jung, *Psychology and Alchemy*, CW 12, § 558.
212 Ibid., CW 12, § 561.
213 C.G. Jung, *Memories, Dreams, Reflections*, p. 234.
214 After his heart attack in February 1944, Jung, in a state of unconsciousness and in imminent danger of death, experienced images and visions that influenced his entire future work. See chapter X "Visions," in: C.G. Jung, *Memories, Dreams, Reflections*.

> In him [Faust] we experience the loftiest flight of the mind and the descent into the depths of guilt and darkness, and still worse, a fall so low that Faust sinks to the level of a mountebank and wholesale murderer as the outcome of his pact with the devil. Faust, too, is split and sets up "evil" outside himself in the shape of Mephistopheles, to serve as an alibi in case of need. He likewise "knows nothing of what has happened," i.e., what the devil did to Philemon and Baucis. We never get the impression that he has real insight or suffers genuine remorse [...] He never attains the character of reality: he is not a real human being and cannot become one (at least not in this world). He remains the German idea of a human being, and therefore an image – somewhat overdone and distorted – of the average German.[215]

But the problem is not limited to the German people alone, as Jung makes unmistakably clear a little later. Here he speaks of a 'God-likeness' which, rather than elevating one to be on a par with the Divine, only elevates one to an arrogance that arouses all the evil within. And he adds, "This is not the fate of Germany alone, but of all Europe. We must all open our eyes to the shadow who looms behind contemporary man. We have no need to hold up the devil's mask before the Germans."[216] Today, almost eighty years later, it must be said, however, this arrogance seems to have a grip on almost the entire human race.

What a contrast Jung's life-long devotion to Philemon and Baucis is to Faust! Above the entrance of what he called the chapel – Jung's small tower in Bollingen where he used to retreat when he needed to draw renewed energy from the silence and depth of the unconscious – are the words *Philemonis sacrum – Fausti poenitentia:* Philemon's Sanctuary – in Repentance of Faust. Jung never ceased to be shaken by the nefarious murder of the god-fearing old couple who had once welcomed and entertained the gods Jupiter and Mercury, disguised as wretched wanderers, into their hut.[217] He once told Hedy Wyss that he had built the tower in order to atone for Faust's crime, that is, for the arrogance of Faust's godlike and superhuman nature.

215 C.G. Jung, "After the Catastrophe," in: CW 10, § 423.

216 Ibid., CW 10, § 440.

217 About the story of Philemon and Baucis see Ovid, *Metamorphoses*, Book VIII, verses 618-720.

Image 10: Bamberger Apocalypse,
Handing over the Book of Revelation to John.
"The revelation of Jesus Christ, which God gave him to show to his servants the things that must soon take place." Revelation 1:1, fol. 1r (Plate VII)

Image 11: Bamberger Apocalypse,
Christ demands John: "And to the angel of the church in Laodicea write ..."
Revelation 3:14 ff., fol. 9r (Plate VIII)

The Ancestress, the Book of Job, and the Apocalypse of John (Book of Revelation)

In Jung's dream, his ancestress is reading from the Book of Revelation, while pointing her finger at him. It would seem that her presence in the dream and her alleged liaison with Goethe have something to do with the core message of the Apocalypse. But what could that be? John's visions of the Son of Man are bleak: from out of his mouth comes a sharp, double-edged sword; the cosmic woman, clothed with the sun, with the moon under her feet and a crown of twelve stars on her head, is pursued by a great red dragon that intends to devour her newborn child; war reigns in heaven; the woman's child is caught up to God and to his throne, from where he does not return; seven angels carry golden bowls full of God's wrath, and more besides. None of this bodes well. In the face of such violence threatening humankind, who could presume to be the Redeemer, as the ancestress seems to demand? Who would not be scared to death by having her finger pointing at them, as if they, a mere human being, would be able, like Jesus, to cast out demons by [pointing] God's finger?[218]

Jung addressed these dark, apocalyptic images almost ten years later in his "Answer to Job." This work is *Jung's* answer to the idea, suggested by his ancestress, that the human being, and especially "the guilty man is eminently suitable and is therefore chosen to become the vessel for the continuing incarnation, not the guiltless one who holds aloof from the world and refused to pay his tribute to life, for in him the dark God would find no room."[219] Thus, the human being becomes the redeemer of the inner-divine conflict.

I think it is fair to say that this paper is C.G. Jung's most radical, arguably his most controversial, and most emotionally-charged work. Jung was acutely aware that his interpretation of the dark prophecies of the Revelation, which he discusses in detail in the second part of "Answer to Job," would shake the very foundations of the Christian God-image. For this reason, he prefaced "Answer to Job" with a "*Lectori benevolo*" – a plea to the reader to receive what follows with good will – followed by a quotation from David's lament for Saul and Jonathan: "*Doleo super te frater mi* ... – I grieve for you, my

218 Luke 11:20, "But if it is by the finger of God that I cast out demons, then the kingdom of God has come upon you."

219 C.G. Jung, "Answer to Job," CW 11, § 746. See also ibid., § 659: "He [man] becomes a vessel filled with divine conflict."

brother Jonathan ..."[220] And as he predicted, the book has not been well received by all of its readers. Especially among theologians, including his friend Victor White, Jung's thoughts were met with a more or less complete lack of understanding, sometimes even with indignant rejection. Jung reacted extremely sharply to some of these criticisms, particularly to the letter he received from the "joyous Christian" in America, who proclaimed that all would become quite clear if one merely acknowledged that *God is Love*. Why should one fuss with the mythology of old fables, "like monkeys with a picture-puzzle of parts that don't fit anyway."[221]

In "Answer to Job" Jung firstly states that, from a psychological point of view, the author of John's Letters could be the author of the Book of Revelation. These books tell us "that God is light, and in him is no darkness at all ... But if we walk in the light, as he is in the light, we have fellowship with one another and the blood of Jesus his Son cleanses us from all sin." (1 John 1:5.7) We are the children of God to whom our Father has given His eternal love. Jung raises the heretical question of why, then, does this love have to be paid for by human sacrifice – by the crucifixion of Christ. Such a one-sided view, he continues, creates a counter-position in the unconscious against this loving Father. And it is this counter-position, wherein evil originates in heaven, i.e., in the inner divine world, that is the content of the Apocalypse of John (Book of Revelation) with its brutally depicted dark prophecies.[222]

"Answer to Job" offers a fascinating, coherent response to the question of what Jung calls the continuing "incarnation of God in an empirical human being."[223] This has its origin in the antinomy of Yahweh himself, the antagonism of the opposites within, for all that is separated longs for unification. While Job's friends hold fast to the righteousness of God – "God will not reject the blameless man" (Job 8:20) – Job recognizes Yahweh's dual nature: "It is all one; therefore I say, He destroys both the blameless and the wicked." (Job 9:22) Job understood that humankind is engulfed in *divine conflict*. This prompts him to voice freely his grievance with God; he wants to know

220 2 Samuel 1:26.

221 C.G. Jung, *Letters*, vol. 2, Anonymous, Letter of 7 May 1960. The footnote with the mentioned quote is from the German edition of Jung's letters; it is missing in the English version. To the mythic aspect of Christ's birth, see C.G. Jung, "Answer to Job," CW 11, chapter VII, §§ 643-648, where Jung, among other topics, raises the question, "What is the use of a religion without a mythos since religion means, if anything at all, precisely that function which links us back to the eternal myth?"

222 Ibid., CW 11, § 698.

223 Ibid., CW 11, § 657.

why God is at odds with him. (Job 10:1-2) But he receives no answer and concludes that it is obviously not "God's purpose to exempt a man from conflict and hence from evil."[224]

The *Apocalypse of John* does not speak of the God of Love, but of His wrath. When the once-so-spotless Lamb opens the Book with seven seals (Revelation, chapters 5, 6 and 8), "a veritable orgy of hatred, wrath, vindictiveness, and blind destructive fury that revels in fantastic images of terror breaks out and with blood and fire overwhelms a world which Christ had just endeavored to restore to the original state of innocence and loving communion with God."[225] The sky darkens, the earth trembles, Jerusalem is destroyed and with it, the heart of the Israelites, with whom Yahweh had once made a covenant.

Against this background, Jung's rage at the old woman's proclamation that he, Jung, was the redeemer becomes understandable. How was he, a mere human being, to take a stand against a catastrophe of such cosmic proportions? His anger was so great that his heart barely survived the emotional violence that erupted in his dream.

Returning to the Apocalypse, a sun-woman appears in the midst of the most terrible destruction (Revelation 12). With her cosmic attributes, Jung calls her the *anima mundi*, the world-soul: "She is the feminine anthropos, the counterpart of the masculine principle ... She adds the dark to the light, symbolizes the hierogamy of opposites, and reconciles nature with spirit."[226] In great agony, she gives birth to a son, who, when threatened by the great dragon – that ancient serpent known as the devil and Satan (Revelation 12:9) –, is raised up to heaven. In this now-divine Son, the opposites that violently collide with one another in Yahweh are reconciled.[227] But having been raised up to heaven, the divine Son has not yet reached the sphere of man. Only two millennia later, in our present era, will this come to pass, as indicated in Jung's dream of the ancestress; astrologically speaking, in the transition from the Aion of Pisces to the Aion of Aquarius, as prophesied by John in the twentieth chapter of the Book of Revelation.

C.G. Jung has described this event in impressive, but frightening, words:

224 Ibid., CW 11, § 659.
225 Ibid., CW 11, § 708.
226 Ibid., CW 11, § 711.
227 This brings to mind the divine child in *The Red Book* that holds the black serpent in his left hand and the white serpent in his right hand. C.G. Jung, *The Red Book*, p. 252a [*The Red Book, Reader's Edition*, pp. 196 f.].

> [In his vision, John] divines that the reign of Antichrist will begin after a thousand years, a clear indication that Christ was not an unqualified victor. John anticipated the alchemists and Jakob Boehme; maybe he even sensed his own personal implication in the divine drama, since *he anticipated the possibility of God's birth in man* which the alchemists, Meister Eckhart, and Angelus Silesius also intuited. He thus outlined the program for the whole Aion of Pisces, with its dramatic enantiodromia, and its dark end which we have still to experience, and before whose – without exaggeration – truly apocalyptic possibilities mankind shudders.[228]

How could Jung not shudder at his great-grandmother's words? Jung intuitively grasped that her pronouncement, "You are the redeemer" meant that he and all of humankind today are confronted with an immensely difficult and grave task. And in the passage quoted above, he went on to say that the gloomy end to this time of transition had not yet been reached, despite the two World Wars that had brought profound apocalyptic darkness down upon humanity!

However, there was also a glimmer of hope, namely the dogma of the *Assumptio Mariae*, proclaimed by Pope Pius XII, in 1950. According to it, "Mary as the bride is united with the son in the heavenly bridal-chamber, and, as Sophia, with the Godhead."[229] It was Jung's faint hope that this ultimately *inner-divine* event to which the dogma alludes would have a healing effect on the terrible brokenness of the world. Perhaps it could heal, at least partially, the world's unstable, chaotic state by referring to, on the one hand, the *coniunctio*, that is, to the necessary union of the opposites, and on the other hand, to the *quaternio* – to wholeness. This event was presaged almost two thousand years earlier by John's vision of the sun-woman and her son who was raised up to heaven. "*God wanted to become man, and still wants to.*"[230]

People today are still actively involved in this process that Jung's ancestress revealed to him with her ruthless statement, "You are the redeemer." But as soon as a person gets involved in the drama of redemption in a personal way, they are in danger of being overwhelmed by the archetype of the *Redeemer* and of identifying themselves with it. This has led to the dangerous hubris

228 C.G. Jung, "Answer to Job," CW 11, § 733 (emphasis AS).
229 Ibid., CW 11, § 743.
230 Ibid., CW 11, § 739. To the "Woman closed with the sun" see Revelation 12.

of our age, prophesied in Goethe's *Faust* and in Nietzsche's *Thus Spoke Zarathustra.* Rather than seeing ourselves as participants in the drama of redemption, we think, instead, with Promethean levels of inflation, that we are the redeemer. "The rationalistic hubris is tearing our consciousness from its transcendent roots," out of which, like a tree with roots reaching down into the earth, we were always able to arise anew.[231]

An immense power of destruction has been placed into the hands of Faustian man. Never before have we had the capacity to destroy the entire planet. Whether or not Faustian man can resist the temptation of using this power, we do not know. And thus, Jung continues in "Answer to Job,"

> [Faustian man] will hardly be capable of doing so on his own unaided resources. He needs the help of an "advocate" in heaven, that is, of the child who was caught up to God and who brings the "healing" and making whole of the hitherto fragmentary man.[232]

For centuries, alchemists searched for a symbol of wholeness that could unite the opposites of good and evil and thus, the paradoxical image of God that threatens to tear man apart. They searched and found it in the *filius sapientiae*, the *homo altus*, the *lapis philosophorum* – some of the terms used to describe the sought-after treasure. But these symbols remained projected into the retort. Now, in the wake of the alchemists, we suspect that the divine Son wants to dwell within us. As Jung's ancestress prophesied, we suspect we are, indeed, caught up in the divine drama of redemption. This, however, provokes the superhuman power of Faust within us.[233] Thus, at the very end of "Answer to Job," Jung mentions St. Paul and his split consciousness. Unlike us, St. Paul was aware of being split: "For when I am weak, then I am strong." (2 Corinthians 12:10)[234] Jung concludes Job with the following, truly remarkable statement, "... even the enlightened person remains what

231 See C.G. Jung's elaboration on "Gnostic Symbols of the Self," in *Aion*, CW 9/2, § 346, where he says, "These specific attainments [the growth of the human personality and the development of consciousness] are now gravely threatened in our antichristian age, not only in sociopolitical delusional systems, but above all by the rationalistic hubris which is tearing our consciousness from its transcendent roots and holding before it immanent goals."

232 C.G. Jung, "Answer to Job," CW 11, § 745.

233 C.G. Jung, *Psychology and Alchemy*, CW 12, §§ 558 f.

234 Not unlike John, the author of the New Testament Apocalypse, Paul was a visionary, moved by experiences of God that affected him in his innermost being.

he is, and is never more than his own limited ego before the One who dwells within him, whose form has no knowable boundaries, who encompasses him on all sides, fathomless as the abysms of the earth and vast as the sky."[235]

It is this background of the Apocalypse of John that provides the proper perspective on Salome's "You are Christ" and Jung's ancestress' "You are the redeemer." It also explains the motif of the woman reading from the Apocalypse in Jung's dream. In effect, we today have been set a task that should fill us with the utmost humility and modesty. Only the future will reveal if we have been able to cope with this task. But what we know for sure, and what our dreams clearly show, is that unifying symbols that point to the self, and thus to the union of opposites, are on the increase. This makes Jung's dream in Geneva extremely relevant. It is no coincidence that in both *The Red Book* and in this dream it is a woman who gives Jung this message. It is an age-old truth that the "fall of man," both then as now, and the renewal of consciousness begin with the feminine.

235 C.G. Jung, "Answer to Job," CW 11, § 758.

9. Jung's Great-Grandmother, the Ghost Woman, and Other Beings

Anima Haunting

As we saw above, only two days after his heart attack in Geneva, Jung wrote to Hedy Wyss that she had become an instrument of fate for him which had freed him from "the dark doom that had been weighing on [his] soul up to now." Without her, he "would probably never have been able to fathom this mystery."[236] This is astounding. One wonders why she, of all people, was able to awaken in Jung the memory of his alleged ancestral connection to Goethe to such an extent that it helped him to solve the curse of the House of Atreus. Resolving it, as he himself admits, nearly cost him his life. In view of his severe heart symptoms of that night, this could well have happened!

What, then, does this peculiar entanglement between Jung and his analysand portend? From the letters we learn that Hedy Wyss must have held a "special resemblance" to Jung's great-grandmother: "It is probably an aesthetic sensibility, or lack thereof, which appears so charmingly in you ..." [237] Her sensibility reminded Jung of the "lively artistic personalities" of the Ziegler sisters, that is, of his great-grandmother and her sister, as Jung mentions in a letter to his cousin Ernst Jung.[238] Her particular resemblance, Jung thinks, may well have prompted him to transfer this great-grandmother fantasy onto Hedy Wyss. Yet, soon after, the matter becomes more complicated. Only two weeks later, in a further letter, he comes back to this "anima haunting," and he sounds a note of caution:

236 Letter of March 31, 1943.
237 Letter of April 16, 1943.
238 Letter to Jung's cousin Ernst [not Ewald] Jung, *Letters*, vol. 2, 30 December 1959, pp. 527-529.

Bollingen, 1 May 1943

Dear Hedy Wyss!

Strange! I did not recognize your handwriting on your letter and, as a result, it has been left unanswered. Even stranger! When you were in Geneva, you were lost to me here. It was as if you were dead, as if your back were turned toward me, and the place where the swan was hatching was empty, and your handwriting was unrecognizable, or it was extremely unlikely that you would write. These phenomena are somewhat alarming. The anima-haunting is behind it. Caution and consideration seem indicated ...

At the beginning of my vacation, I was overcome with fatigue; the suffering of the world, small, large, near, far, sank like a lead-laden iron ship to the bottom of my sea, leaving the world empty, a stomping ground for ancestral souls and field spirits that hopped around like goats in ruins. It was eerie; and you were drowned, irretrievably it seemed, in the Calvinist, melancholic hole called Geneva ...

I am grateful if I do not disturb you too much. I hope you have recovered from Geneva.

In the meantime,
With my best regards,
Your faithful,
C.G. Jung

Jung laments the fatigue that has overcome him. The world's suffering weighs heavily on him, and he speaks of the 'ancestral souls and field spirits that hopped around like goats in ancient ruins.' And then he implicates Hedy Wyss, as if she, too, had played a part in this anima haunting. But why? Simply because she had stayed for a few days with her sister-in-law in Geneva and was therefore not available to him! "It was eerie; and you were drowned, irretrievably it seemed, in the Calvinist, melancholic hole called Geneva ..."[239]

Here is what the haunting was all about: Jung had received a letter from Hedy Wyss from Geneva, but as he did not recognize her handwriting, he had laid it aside and the letter went unanswered. Meanwhile, Hedy Wyss was staying with her brother's family in Geneva, where she was, indeed, very unhappy, lost in a melancholic stupor. For Jung, it was "as if she were

239 Letter of May 1, 1943.

dead, as if her back were turned toward him, and the place where the swan was hatching was empty, and her handwriting unrecognizable."[240] This haunting, orchestrated by the anima, alarmed Jung and made him extremely cautious.

Hedy Wyss, for her part, did not endorse this anima haunting. Rather, in *Lohengrin's Black Swan*, she reports that during her unhappy visit to her sister-in-law, she had become so self-repudiating and estranged from herself, she had, indeed, become inaccessible. Even her own mother would not have recognized her handwriting at that time.[241] As is so often the case, both versions are not without a certain truth, which suggests a *mutual* entanglement.

In the following two months, things go haywire. Hedy Wyss delves deeply into Goethe's relationships with women, perhaps quite intentionally. She wants to understand why Jung has projected his great-grandmother fantasy onto her, of all people. Her investigations clearly annoyed Jung. His criticism that, as an artist, she was not conscious enough of her work had plunged her into the aforementioned "solar eclipse." But after an SOS phone call, everything seems to be quite harmonious again. She paints a lot, uncanny subjects, such as 'a blonde woman in a newborn dreamscape giving water to a man with a gaping wound; a lion girl, a kind of childlike sphinx;' and an illustrated letter to Jung of a 'naked girl in front of three horses,' and so on.

Their relationship becomes increasingly complicated. Jung warns her not to believe too much in *his* feelings for her. Doubts arise in him, for this 'great-grandmother projection' still stands between them, even after the crisis in Geneva, when, according to Jung, he had freed himself from the curse of the House of Atreus. He again asks himself why this fantasy is connected with Hedy Wyss in particular. He suspects that it might also have to do with *her* ancestors. However, Hedy Wyss' research into her own ancestral history offers no explanation for this peculiar phenomenon of transference.

The tension between them was finally eased after Jung wrote another extraordinarily substantial letter to her. Jung composed it on the day before his vacation, presumably in a state of great exhaustion. Notwithstanding the incomparable beauty in Jung's remarks about "all mere human love," the letter does not bode well. Irrespective of the quality of its content, its recipient is shocked by it. She is particularly at a loss to understand why Jung suggests she 'has gone to war with him.' In fact, Jung's letter is testimony to his great and self-critical honesty in his dealings with himself. Because its

240 Ibid.
241 *Lohengrin's Black Swan*, p. 101.

description of the problem of the transference is so impressive and in some ways unique, the letter is repeated here with only a few omissions:

Küsnacht-Zürich 2 July 1943

Dear Hedy Wyss!

You are absolutely right: You have never "said all that there is to say". That's why I reminded you several times that starting a conversation would be desirable. You were surprised that I apologized for that great-grandmother fantasy (even inwardly asked for forgiveness for it); I knew why. Votre coup a porté. I have to take the blame. I am now turning 69, and there are still things to be destroyed in me that I cannot master. Arrow wounds heal. The modern cannon shot has a more lasting effect – and it is indescribably painful. Un coup de grâce [death blow] – this is how "transferences" are resolved, and never have they been resolved otherwise, except in the sackcloth and ashes of one's own accursedness. The monstrous pain of all living beings is the inexorability of their death. For God's sake, is there no gentle shroud that one could spread over the carrion of beauty biting the dust? I know that you suffer – suffer terribly – the recoil of the cannon! Both the slayer and the slain are one and the same. I ask you and I ask myself not to carry through with the slaying, but for your sake, for my sake, for the sake of the eternal divinity, let us rise again, because one must prove oneself to oneself despite oneself. We are untrustworthy, not credible and not worthy. Why on earth am I even talking? I am only able to devour myself.

Didn't you know that there is something else besides "transference"? Have we never heard of "love" that "bears all things and endures all things," that "does not insist on its own way"[242] but submits? I must believe in this love: without it all our beginnings are meaningless and invariably end in the catastrophe of the transference. And because I believe in it, I must, in spite of my own human weakness, in spite of the most hideous misunderstandings, try again and again to overcome the "transference," the sinister entanglement in the force of destiny [heimarmene], through that most difficult art: to love a human being. For me, this means first and foremost to allow someone the dignity of making their own decision. I cannot believe you are so very different that you would not be able to understand such things. I cannot believe I was so wrong about you.

242 See 1 Corinthians 13:5-7.

(Nevertheless – the great-grandmother. Forgive this voice from the sidelines; it is aimed at me!) In the same way that "the innermost nature of all grain is wheat, and of all metal, gold," all merely human love bespeaks a higher state, the attainment of which leads into suffering and through the Crucifixio ...
... I am unable to forget the time that we are living in, the immensity of suffering! Why do you wage war against me? I know you are under attack by the devil and that you feel abandoned ... but no one can protect us from our own hell. Only the ability to suffer can help, namely to defy all longing to suffer.
Yours,
C.G. Jung

The beginning of the letter is not at all pleasant. Hedy Wyss had complained to Jung that she could 'never say all that there is to say' in analysis, for there was always someone knocking on the door, wanting something from him. Jung replies somewhat dryly that she was quite right. She never does stop talking, and he would, indeed, welcome it if the conversation could finally begin. Jung wants to get down to the nitty-gritty of the relationship, but in doing so he seems to be overtaxing, and probably overestimating, Hedy Wyss. She obviously cannot always follow him and his lively spirit, which is not surprising given the breadth and depth of Jung's letters.

To be sure, the problem lies not only with her. Jung apologizes for the great-grandmother fantasy that keeps creeping into their relationship in an irritating way: at almost 69, there are still things that he has not been able to master and needs to rid himself of. Thus, he takes the blame for any misunderstandings upon himself. From these arrow wounds one can heal, he tells her. But then, an even bigger shot is fired – indeed, a veritable cannon shot, which has a longer-lasting effect – *un coup de grâce*, a mercy shot, which seems to be the only way to solve the problem of the transference – if such a thing is even possible!

At first it is unclear for whom this tremendously painful *coup de grâce*, which threatens all living things, is intended. Is it aimed at Jung, who wants to resolve the curse of the House of Atreus once and for all, or is it aimed at her projection onto him, as her analyst? As it turns out, the shot hits both of them equally grievously, albeit in different ways.

When Jung goes on to talk about the 'inexorability of death' and the 'carrion of beauty biting the dust,' he probably has the increasing frailty of old age in mind. But that is not the end of the story, and thus, as is often the case, there follows an enantiodromia, from the 'carrion of beauty biting the dust' to the beautiful saying of Meister Eckhart: "In the same way that 'the innermost nature of all grain is wheat, and of all metal, gold,' all merely human love bespeaks a higher state, the attainment of which leads into suffering and through the *Crucifixio*."[243]

It is worth taking a closer look at this quotation that Jung refers to often, and particularly, at its context. Meister Eckhart says:

> If any should ask me, wherefore do we pray, wherefore do we fast, wherefore do we do all manner of good works, wherefore are we baptized, wherefore did God become man, I would answer, So that God may be born in the soul and the soul again in God. Therefore were the Holy Scriptures written. Therefore did God create the whole world, that God might be born in the soul and the soul again in God. The innermost nature of all grain is wheat, and of all metal, gold, and of all birth, man![244]

Whenever Jung quotes from ancient or medieval sources, either consciously or unconsciously their context resonates, too. This is also the case here. In his letter to Hedy Wyss, Jung mentions en passant the transformation of grain into wheat and of metal into gold. But Meister Eckhart sees in it the birth of God in the empirical human being, which Jung certainly knew and alludes to in his letter. His real message to Hedy Wyss, then, is, 'All merely human love bespeaks a higher state, namely *the birth of God in humankind*.' And just as this birth led to the crucifixion at Calvary, so, too, can this greater love, that no longer covets and desires, only be attained through the painful doubt and suffering of the *meaning of love* itself.

In his commentary on this utterance of Meister Eckhart in his essay "The Philosophical Tree," Jung expounds upon the meaning of the birth of God

243 Letter of July 2, 1943.

244 C.G. Jung, *Psychological Types*, CW 6, § 425. See also, id., "The Philosophical Tree," CW 13, § 372, and id., *Visions, Notes of the Seminar Given in 1930-1934*, ed. by Claire Douglas in two volumes, Princeton: Princeton University Press, 1997, Seminar of May 6, 1931, p. 341. A slightly different version of this quote in: Meister Eckhart, *Works*, vol. 1, translated by C. de B. Evans, London: John M. Watkins, 1947 [1924], p. 80: "When anyone asks me, Why do we pray or why do we fast or do our work withal, I say, So that God may be born in our souls. What were the scriptures written for and why did God create the world and the angelic nature? Simply that God might be born in the soul. All cereal nature means wheat, all treasure nature means gold, all generation means man."

in humankind. To begin with, he elaborates on the identity of microcosms and macrocosms, then he goes on to say that, "... the little, single individual becomes the 'great man,' the homo maximus or Anthropos, i.e., the self. The moral equivalent of the physical transmutation into gold is *self-knowledge*, which is a remembering of the *homo totus*."[245]

One may wonder, however, to what extent Hedy Wyss was able to understand Jung's hidden messages. Jung, for his part, is certainly aware of her terrible suffering, rather less from what she herself says and more from the nature of her relationship to him. He is aware of 'the recoil of the cannon' caused by her projection, but he asks her 'not to carry through with the slaying for her sake, for his sake, for the sake of the eternal divinity.' There is something beyond transference, and that is this higher state of love. He poses his next question in a strange we-form, "... have we never heard of 'love' that 'bears all things and endures all things, that 'does not insist on its own way.'"[246] It is as if he is posing this question also to himself, but then he continues, "I must believe in this love: without it all our beginnings are meaningless and invariably end in the catastrophe of the transference." And that is why he "must try again and again to overcome the 'transference,' the sinister entanglement in the force of destiny [*heimarmene*], through that most difficult art: to love a human being."[247]

"The Ghost Woman Is in You"

What particularly shook Hedy Wyss was Jung's assumption that she was waging war against him, for she, for her part, could not recall anything that might explain his assertion. But then she dreamed of a mysterious figure (the ghost woman!), who, like a sleepwalker, creeps into her grandfather's house. It was a dazzlingly beautiful, black-haired woman. She was looking for a key that she wanted to steal from her paternal grandfather's house. The dreamer observes her, without making her presence known. Upon waking, Hedy

245 C.G. Jung, "The Philosophical Tree," CW 13, § 372.

246 See Paul's so-called Song of Love, "Love is patient and kind; love does not envy or boast; it is not arrogant or rude. It does not insist on its own way; it is not irritable or resentful ... love bears all things, believes all things, hopes all things, endures all things." 1 Corinthians 13:4-5 and 7.

247 Letter of July 2, 1943.

Wyss thought this figure must have been her paternal great-grandmother or grandmother.[248]

From his tower in Bollingen where he had begun his vacation only a few days earlier, Jung once again writes her a long letter.

Bollingen, 7.VII.1943

Dear Hedy Wyss!

I am very grateful for your kind letter. Why should you wage war against me? I do not want to deceive you, take advantage of you, exploit you, enslave you, rape you, bully you, or anything else against which war should be waged ... The ghost woman is in you. By virtue of her existence, my unconscious could project the great-grandmother. The ghost woman is the mother-anima of your father. This reveals the key parallel with my "guru" who called himself Philemon. He is equivalent to the father-animus of my mother, who had a pronounced father complex. Philemon is the sage who is in possession of the secret of the self. The key is to open the "introitum ad occlusum Regis palatium"[249] [entrance to the locked palace of the king], that "castrum sapientiae"[250] [house of wisdom] which is the seat of the self. The figure of your grandmother likewise fetches the keys from the "father" (who is indeed the representative of sapientia) in order to open the gate to the self. She is the father-anima form of your self, which wants to free itself from the form of the father-anima. Since I am the unenviable bearer of the father-image, your resistances are thus directed against me, as if I were your prison guard. This is a very natural and instinctive reaction ... Please, do not think that the above is nothing but prosaic science. In reality, it is a desperate attempt to hold on to Ariadne's thread of consciousness in overwhelming darkness. These things are demonic, fateful and of incalculable danger. Terms like "transference" and the like are hopelessly inadequate to express the mysterious nature of this event, or even to banish it into a formula. I know from my own innermost experience how terrible these forces can be, and therefore, whenever I see these "super-personal personalities" or whatever one wishes to call them – at work, I try to help. No knowledge, no art helps; only one's own humanity, which one lays on the scales,

248 *Lohengrin's Black Swan*, p. 115.

249 This is the title of a treatise of Philaletha: "*Introitus apertus ad occlusum Regis palatium.*" See C.G. Jung, *Mysterium Coniunctionis*, CW 14, § 27.

250 For the "*castrum sapientiae*" see C.G. Jung, ibid., CW 14, § 731.

fully conscious of the danger of doing so. One can only hope and pray that everything will turn out well. It's not a "love affair" that you could whisper about with your girlfriends, but a diabolical test of whether you can ultimately stand and bear yourself. Being alone with oneself, staring oneself in the face with no possibility of escape, that's what it's all about. Being alone has two meanings: it also means being al[l]-one.
... I believe that there is some meaning in my efforts on your behalf. I don't want to acquire or buy you, as it were; I simply want you to blossom like the woodruff, or to become what you are. I cannot stand by and watch plants that could bear beautiful flowers or fruit wither away. Mere weeds are of no interest. I think you will agree with me on that ...
In the meantime, best regards from your rest-seeking,
C.G. Jung

Image 12: Hedy Wyss: Minotaur and the Blonde Citizen Girl, 1943/50 (Plate IX). This picture seems to have made a particular impression on Jung. Hedy Wyss considered it to be one of her strongest paintings.

Why, indeed, should his analysand wage war against him? He does not want to deceive her, take advantage of her, exploit her, or anything else for which a war should be waged. But what he really wants, as he expressed in an earlier letter and to which he now refers, is to 'solve the Ariadne-like clew [Hedy Wyss] by which the Minotaur-slayer [C.G. Jung] is entangled.'[251] This, however, is not at all an easy task, but rather "a desperate attempt to hold on to *Ariadne's thread of consciousness* in overwhelming darkness."[252] The image of the Minotaur-slayer and the Ariadne thread, that leads out of the labyrinth of unconsciousness, clearly points to the main problem: their *mutual* entanglement in the unconscious. Jung wonders how, like Theseus und Ariadne, they might find a way out of this entanglement.

There is no way around the ghost woman mentioned in the letter, who, as Jung notes, is in Hedy Wyss. This is not about Jung's ancestress – his great-grandmother – but rather the figure from *her* dream, whom she believed to be her paternal great-grandmother or grandmother. Jung interprets the ghost woman as the "mother-anima" of her father – Hedy Wyss' grandmother, or *the image that her father had of his mother*. But why does Jung say that the ghost woman is in Hedy Wyss? This statement is ambiguous, as is so often the case with Jung. Primarily, of course, it refers to the woman in her dream who has crept into her grandfather's house, apparently looking for the key to the house of wisdom. Jung's allusion, however, extends far beyond this obvious meaning.

The key for which the ghost woman is searching has *magical* qualities: it can unlock the *introitum ad occlusum Regis palatium* [the entrance to the king's locked palace] and the *castrum sapientiae* [the castle of wisdom].[253] It gives the owner access to the 'higher' world, psychologically speaking, to the original primordial human being, that is, to the self. Fatally, however, the key in Hedy Wyss' dream is still in the possession of the father – of the old king and his mother-anima, which is why the house of wisdom remains locked to the dreamer! As a thief, she will never be able to open the *castrum sapientiae*, for there is too much calculation involved.[254] Psychologically speaking, this

251 Letter of January 15, 1942.

252 Letter of July 7, 1943 (emphasis AS).

253 This, too, is a term from alchemy. Like the *spiraculum vitae aeternae* it alludes to the higher world, the 'world of worlds,' i.e., the *mundus potentialis* of Gerhard Dorn. C.G. Jung, *Mysterium Coniunctionis*, CW 14, § 731.

254 To the thief who sneaks in the alchemical opus see Jung's comment in *Mysterium Coniunctionis*, CW 14, §§ 186-196. Here he states, "The thief, as we saw, personifies a kind of self-robbery. He is not easily shaken off as it comes from a habit of thinking

means that while the key remains entwined with the "mother-anima form" of her father, it will never be found. This is what the ghost woman means for the dreamer alone.

If we now take the analytic relationship into consideration, which Jung obviously did, things get much more complicated. Added to this is the fact that because of the existence of the ghost woman in Hedy Wyss, Jung, or, as he puts it, 'his unconscious,' projects his great-grandmother onto his analysand. What an unholy entanglement! Jung's attempt to unravel the tangle of threads and to hold on to the Ariadne thread of consciousness seems very sincere. His explanations sometimes remain puzzling nevertheless. This is, perhaps, not so surprising, for where the dead are concerned, things do tend to become both demonic and fateful, and in this instance, we are dealing with both Hedy Wyss' and Jung's ancestors.

For both Jung and Hedy Wyss, it is the paternal grandparents who are involved. Jung wants to get to the bottom of these "super-personal personalities." Neither Jung's broad knowledge nor Hedy Wyss' artistic skills can help: there is "only one's own humanity, which one lays on the scales, fully conscious of the danger of doing so. One can only hope and pray that everything will turn out well." This is no "love affair," for ultimately one is alone with it. But being alone has a double meaning for Jung. He sees it as being al[l]-one.[255] One is simultaneously both alone and at one with everything – united with the All, the universe. This, in turn, refers to the oneness of microcosm and macrocosm.

Jung's letter ends with a confession: he believes in the deep meaning of analytical work; he *must* believe in its meaning. His only wish is for Hedy Wyss to blossom like the woodruff, to become who she is meant to be, for he cannot bear to watch a plant that could bear beautiful blossoms or fruit wither away. This image of blossoming woodruffs references a dream that Hedy Wyss had, in which she saw a forest suffused with sunlight and full of woodruffs encircling the trees. Jokingly, she later wrote to Jung that she would like to encircle him like blossoming woodruff, to which Jung amiably replied, ["I simply want you] to become what you are." This was not about him, not about her encircling him, but rather about furthering the growth of her own self. No one, no matter how strong and beloved, can replace one's own center, one's own tree of life and its growth.

supported by tradition and milieu alike: anything that cannot be exploited in some way is uninteresting – hence the devaluation of the psyche." Ibid., CW 14, § 194.

255 Letter of July 7, 1943.

C.G. Jung's Grandfather Karl Gustav Jung

Their entanglement, however, was far from being resolved. Only a few weeks later, at the end of July 1943, Hedy Wyss dreamed of C.G. Jung's grandfather, *Karl Gustav Jung*. Like his father's own father, Franz Ignaz Jung, who had been a medical practitioner in Mannheim, Karl Gustav turned to medical studies, first in Heidelberg and later in Berlin. Karl Gustav, however, became embroiled in a political murder. In spring of 1819, the dramatist and writer August von Koetzebue was assassinated by a student of theology. This murder was the undoing of Karl Gustav Jung, for having been befriended with some members of the murderer's fraternity in Jena, he was suspected of being complicit in the act. He was subsequently imprisoned, along with several other young fellows. He was released only after thirteen months and in the wake of the event, he was expelled from Prussia and barred from teaching at German universities. Thus, through no fault of his own, his promising career was interrupted.

He eventually continued his studies in Paris, where he came to the attention of the famous Alexander von Humboldt. Humboldt recognized the young German's talents and offered him a lectureship in surgery, anatomy, and obstetrics at the University of Basel, which is how Jung's grandfather came to Switzerland. Various legends of a grandiose nature have grown up around this encounter between Karl Gustav Jung and Humboldt.[256] Although C.G. Jung was always somewhat embarrassed by the rumor of an alleged kinship with Goethe, his "illustrious ancestor," as he used to call him, he seems to have relished to some degree these rumors about his great-grandfather.

In her dream, Hedy Wyss[257] saw C.G. Jung's grandfather surrounded by various gentlemen who had gathered for a meeting. Speaking High German, he politely told her, 'It is better not to inquire about certain things, for they could be fatal.' The dream elicits an astonishing confession from Jung. In response to her letter, he wrote that he had always envied his grandfather: "If I had *his* extraversion, I would be better able to present myself."[258] His grandfather knew how to present himself in a dignified manner, which is

256 On Jung's grandfather Karl Gustav Jung see C.G. Jung, *Memories, Dreams, Reflections*, p. 35, fn. 1, and H. M. Koelbing, "Die Berufung Karl Gustav Jungs (1794–1864) nach Basel und ihre Vorgeschichte" [The Appointment of Karl Gustav Jung to the University of Basel and its Prehistory], pp. 318-330.

257 *Lohengrin's Black Swan*, p. 117.

258 Letter of July 22, 1943.

why he was well received and admired wherever he went. Whereas C.G. Jung, on the other hand, always felt "crushed by the enormity of the things" he could not master. Because he had seen too much and too many monstrous things, he constantly struggled with his overwhelming sense of ineptitude. Her dream, Jung continued, quite correctly says that there are thoughts that can kill. "There are murderous problems for the sake of which there is, even now [in the midst of the war], so much murder in the world. I do not feel up to this demonic situation, and that is why I cannot muster up any decent self-confidence."[259] When people asked Jung why he did not publish this or that thought, he knew it was because of his great-grandmother and his illustrious forebear (Goethe). Unlike the latter with his vast oeuvre, Jung chose not to publish certain things. He did not want to imitate Goethe: he was a scientist, not an artist.[260]

In 1943, C.G. Jung accepted a chair in medical psychology at the same university in Basel where his grandfather had once taught. 1943 must have been a year of enormous internal and external pressure for Jung. It began at the end of March with the dream in Geneva that deeply agitated him and brought on his first threatening heart symptoms. Although Jung had spoken on alchemy in 1935 and 1936 at the Eranos conference, it was in January of 1943 that he completed *Psychology and Alchemy,* his first major alchemical work.[261] No sooner was this work done than he turned to his *opus magnum, Mysterium Coniunctionis.*[262] The first chapters were written even before his heart attack, in February 1944. Hedy Wyss reports in *Lohengrin's Black Swan* that Marie-Louise von Franz worked on Jung's manuscript while he was in hospital. This is confirmed in Barbara Hannah's biography of Jung: "[Marie-Louise von Franz] collaborated with him on that book before and after his illness, and had continued her research without interruption during the time he was in the hospital."[263] In addition, there were several deaths of some friends who were close to him: in March 1943, as already mentioned,

259 Ibid.

260 Thus Hedy Wyss in *Lohengrin's Black Swan*, p. 106.

261 See Foreword to the Swiss edition by C.G. Jung, in: *Psychology and Alchemy*, CW 12, p. x. The first publication appeared one year later, in 1944. Jung's Eranos lectures on "Dream Symbols of the Process of Individuation" (1935), and "The Idea of Redemption in Alchemy" (1936), are included in revised and expanded form as Part II and III of *Psychology and Alchemy.* To this, Jung added an elaborate introduction on the archetype of the Christian and alchemical god-image, as well as the "Epilogue" dealing with the Faustian hubris of modern man.

262 See B. Hannah, *Jung. His Life and Work*, pp. 275 and 284.

263 *Lohengrin's Black Swan*, p. 140 and B. Hannah, *Jung. His Life and Work*, p. 284.

the Indologist Heinrich Zimmer died; then Rudolph Staehelin, who had been a fellow student, passed away; and in September Peter Baynes,[264] with whom he had been in Africa and who had translated C.G. Jung's first works into English, died. These losses took a heavy toll on Jung.

Image 13: C.G. Jung's Grandfather Karl Gustav Jung (1794-1864)
Drawing by Ernst Fries, Heidelberg

264 Peter Baynes died on September 6, 1943. Ibid., p. 276.

10. C.G. Jung, Hedy Wyss, and Bourgeois Morality

Hideous Paradoxes

"It is frightening, as it were, to see the ways and methods the dream uses to educate us to be honest." Thus begins Jung's letter from Bollingen of September 10, 1943, that references a dream Hedy Wyss had sent to him beforehand. Hedy Wyss was painting a lot at that time, perhaps out of her desire to express her strong feelings for Jung. Two paintings in particular were among this work: "Dionysos and Ariadne in the Underworld" and "Laozi and the Dancer." Dionysos and Ariadne as a metaphor that played a significant role in the analytic work of C.G. Jung and Hedy Wyss will be discussed below. According to legend, Laozi, the ancient Chinese master, is regarded as the author of the *Dao de jing*. He is said to have lived in the sixth century B.C., and, along with Zhuangzi, is considered the most important representative of Taoism. Tradition has it that he foresaw the decline of the empire, whereupon he freed himself from all official tasks and retired to the western mountains, accompanied by a young female dancer. It is quite possible that Hedy Wyss unconsciously identified with the role of the dancer at the side of the old sage. In any case, she once asked, 'Where is he now, my old Lao Tzu? In Niflheim[265] again, in the snowed-in tower, with ☉ and ☽ ?'[266]

What Jung describes as somewhat "frightening" in his letter of September 10, 1943, was a phallic dream motif that placed the dreamer in intimate proximity to her analyst.[267] Jung could have taken the easy way out and spoken only of the creative power of the unconscious, for this is how the symbol of the phallus is generally interpreted. But instead, as he probably often did, he began by considering the symbolic image as something very real. Accordingly, the phallus points to the human – the all-too-human –,

265 The icy world of Hel, the goddess of death, in Northern mythology.
266 Thus her entry in the *Little Book of Monologues* of January 3, 1944. For this, see below chapter 11, "The Little Book of Monologues." Her reference to Sol and Luna refers to Jung's work at the time on the first part of the *Mysterium Coniunctionis*.
267 See Hedy Wyss *Lohengrin's Black Swan*, p. 122.

concupiscentia, the impulsivity to which the ego can fall prey at any time. Thus, in his reply, Jung speaks firstly of the person who is caught up in herd mentality, who is neither a confirmed saint nor a Luciferian criminal, but rather a quite ordinary man with a shadow. Since this respectable man is usually "neither god nor pig," he could easily be tempted to cherish illusions about his decency.

Image 14: Hedy Wyss: Dionysos and Ariadne in the Underworld, 1943 (Plate X)

The moral problem, however, cannot be disposed of by blindly following collective norms and doing what everybody else does out of supposed respectability, nor by disregarding these norms altogether! Jung ponders on the sins God might punish more: those one has committed, or those, perhaps, that one has *not* committed? Be that as it may, the paradoxes of life – and of love – at times put collective morality seriously to the test. This may sometimes mean we have to endure the conflict between collective adaptation and inner truth until a solution emerges, as it were, from within our own nature. For how would we ever know whether the good we intend to do is really good, and the evil that we try to avoid is really evil? Thus, in his response to Hedy Wyss' intimate dream, Jung emphasizes that when the truth is *completely true*, it usually has a diabolical edge to it.[268]

In *Mysterium Coniunctionis,* Jung interprets a lengthy passage from the supposedly Jewish treatise of Abraham Eleazar *Uraltes Chymisches Werk* [Age-old Chymical Work].[269] The author elaborates at length on the black Shulamite whose blackness persists despite her enlightenment. This apparently imperfect state, however, equates with the state in which the alchemists sought to unite the opposites; the Shulamite's outer blackness compensates her inner illumination, her "inner beauty."[270] Grieving over her blackness, the Shulamite exclaims, "What shall I say? I am alone among the hidden; nevertheless, I rejoice in my heart, because I can live privily, and refresh myself in myself. But *under my blackness I have hidden the fairest green.*"[271] While blackness may indeed be a torment – for life generally also has a diabolical note, as Jung says to Hedy Wyss – there is also some secret happiness concealed within it. The alchemists called the latter, to which our text also refers, the *benedicta viriditas*, the blessed greenness. It signifies on the "one hand the 'leprosy of the metals,' but on the other, the secret immanence of the divine spirit of life in all things."[272]

If Jung speaks of bourgeois morality and urges Hedy Wyss to accept the necessity of a moral standpoint, he does so in the spirit of the alchemists who

268 Letter of September 10, 1943. On the relativity of good and evil see St. Paul, "For I do not do the good I want, but the evil I do not want is what I keep on doing." (Romans 7:19) Jung had an intensive discussion about the question of good and evil with Erich Neumann after Neumann's publication of *New Ethic.* See Erich Neumann, *Depth Psychology and a New Ethic*, English translation by Eugene Rolfe, New York: G.P. Putnam's Sons, 1969. On the dialogue between C.G. Jung and Erich Neumann see *Analytical Psychology in Exile. The Correspondence of C.G. Jung and Erich Neumann*, ed. by Martin Liebscher, translated by Heather McCartney, Princeton: Princeton University Press, 2015, especially Appendix II, C.G. Jung: "Corrections and amendments to Erich Neumann's *New Ethic*," pp. 361-369.

269 C.G. Jung, *Mysterium Coniunctionis*, CW 14, §§ 591 ff. and §§ 606 ff. Abraham Eleazar, *Uraltes Chymisches Werk*, 2nd Edition, Leipzig, 1760. The author pretends to be Jewish in order to hide his Christian background. This pseudonym gives him the liberty to make statements that would have not been possible for a Christian; too real was the danger of being accused of being a heretic.

270 See C.G. Jung, *Mysterium Coniunctionis*, CW 14, § 609.

271 Ibid., CW 14, § 622.

272 C.G. Jung, ibid., CW 14, §§ 622 f. (emphasis AS).

always sought to perceive and reconcile the opposites. This is particularly well expressed in Jung's commentary on the passage by Abraham Eleazar mentioned earlier:

> It is, unfortunately, far truer to say that a change for the better does not bring a total conversion of darkness into light and of evil into good, but, at most, is a compromise in which the better slightly exceeds the worse.[273]

Because a change for the better is, at most, a compromise, Jung always pointed out the "hideous paradoxes" to Hedy Wyss. It is not a euphemism to say that beneath the agony of life there lies "a secret happiness"; it is the knowledge of wholeness, which consciousness can only perceive as a paradoxical phenomenon. This is expressed in the paradox of the self, as the alchemists, the philosopher and theologian Cusanus, and many others always emphasized. In his work *Aion,* Jung presents a fascinating hypothesis regarding this:

> The self is a true "*complexio oppositorum*" [Cusanus], though this does not mean that it is anything like as contradictory in itself. It is quite possible that the seeming paradox is nothing but a reflection of the enantiodromian changes of the conscious attitude which can have a favorable or an unfavorable effect on the whole.[274]

It could well be, he continues, that the frightening figures that occur in our dreams every now and then may have their origin in the conscious mind's fear of the darkness of the unconscious. The brighter the conscious mind, the more it provokes the dark side of the unconscious. This is probably the reason why Jung repeatedly makes enantiodromia-like U-turns in his letters. He knows about the danger of any attitude that is too one-sided, be it too high or too low, too optimistic or too gloomy.

273 C.G. Jung, ibid., CW 14, § 611.
274 C.G. Jung, *Aion*, CW 9/2, § 355 (emphasis AS).

On the Need for a Moral Standpoint

Doubts about her analysis never left Hedy Wyss. Sometimes it was 'a bit too much of a preaching tone' that irritated her about Jung, while at other times, 'a playing with fire' that frightened her. One is struck by how dismissive she was of any criticism, no matter how cautiously it was offered by Jung. Her reaction to Jung's remarks on bourgeois morality is a good example. Hedy Wyss had given Jung her diary to read, since 'he had always told her that he never knew what she was thinking.'[275] Concerned about some of her entries, he sent the diary back to her, together with a four-page, handwritten letter.[276] In it, he warned her not to disregard the collective standpoint. This letter, which is once again of extraordinary density, 'knocked her for six, even if it did not knock her out.'[277]

It is not always easy to follow Jung's train of thought. He seems to accuse Hedy Wyss of having no morals, that is, of underestimating the need of having a moral standpoint. What she sees as bourgeois morality, which she tries to defy, is, according to Jung, "not 'morality,' but a psychological medium of a certain average – and therefore exceedingly collective – way of feeling and seeing things."[278] She is, therefore, overlooking the fact that the collective point of view is also a part of us, a part of every human being, for it cannot be totally eliminated. And then he continues:

> ... any violation of the collective standpoint is a serious matter: it causes a dissociation and a disturbance in the psychic equilibrium ... Any violation of the norm constitutes a debt; it is felt as such, and plays out as such. No "spiritual freedom" exempts one from this; only self-deception feigns the moral high ground. Nature itself makes it all so seemingly easy and then, with an almost diabolical reversal of viewpoint, later presents the bill. Faint (?) portents of this earthquake are already vibrating in your diary entries and especially in your points of view. Be glad that I feel and realize this moral conflict on your behalf, and please, do not deceive yourself about the fact that your apparently conflict-free feeling is simply a means of bringing about that very situation in which your inner collective man will demand his payment with even greater force. I will pay my debt by

275 *Lohengrin's Black Swan*, p. 121.
276 Letter undated, presumably September 15, 1943.
277 *Lohengrin's Black Swan*, p. 125.
278 Letter undated, presumably September 15, 1943.

standing by you for as long as you need me. But I will not pay your debt, my dear, for no one else can do that for you ...[279]

Individuation and Guilt

In response to his reading of Hedy Wyss' diary, Jung revisits a topic that had preoccupied him many years earlier, namely the question of human guilt necessarily bound up with individuation. Whether we like it or not, we have to accept the collective standpoint of bourgeois morality, and yet we also have to find the courage to follow our own individual path. While this may sometimes create a painful conflict, carelessly disregarding bourgeois morality does not free us from guilt. On the contrary, it will cause guilt to manifest all the more painfully in our life.

In 1964, two typescripts were discovered in the archives of the Psychology Club Zurich, bearing the title of "Adaptation, Individuation, Collectivity." Signed by Jung in his own handwriting and dated "Oct. 1916," they are his notes on two lectures that he gave at the Psychology Club in October 1916. These papers are now published in volume 18 of his *Collected Works*, though unfortunately only in the abridged form. It is a difficult but exceedingly substantial text about which Elisabeth Rüf, co-editor of the *Collective Works*, once commented, "This text hits the reader like a hammer."[280]

The first part discusses the psychological need for many forms of adaptation to outer and inner conditions. But as the path of individuation is aimed at an inner center of the personality, older than the ego, an initial distancing from both the inner (the unconscious) and outer (society) collectivity is necessary. This creates a threatening disturbance of psychic equilibrium. To a certain extent, this is unavoidable, for the individual must separate him or herself from collective morals, as well as from the prevailing image of God. Only in this way can one's singular destiny, that is, the uniqueness of one's life, be fulfilled. This burdens the individual with a tragic, yet inevitable, guilt.[281]

279 Ibid.

280 C.G. Jung, "Adaptation, Individuation, Collectivity," in: *The Symbolic Life*, CW 18, §§ 1084 ff. The information about Elisabeth Rüf I owe to Regine Schweizer-Vüllers.

281 Ibid., CW 18, §§ 1094 f. In June 1916, some months before C.G. Jung's lecture, Emma Jung gave a talk at the Psychology Club Zurich on the problem of guilt. This manuscript is in the archive of the Psychology Club.

How the individual deals with this conflict between individuation and collectivity, and how the associated guilt can be redeemed, is the topic of the second part of Jung's lectures.[282] This will not be discussed here.[283] Instead, we return to Jung's reaction to his reading of Hedy Wyss' diary in the aforementioned letter of September 15, 1943, in which he revisits this problem of guilt, specifically on "the moral debt to the norm." In this letter, Jung formulates more clearly than in his lecture notes of 1916 the conflict around the individuation process, of having to adapt to the outer collective on the one hand, while orientating oneself toward one's own inner center, the self, on the other.

Jung's point of departure is Hedy Wyss' *problematic position on bourgeois morality,* that is, the alleged freedom with which she (as an artist?) wants to flout bourgeois morality. To him, this is a self-deception that leads to a belief in one's own superiority. He, on the other hand, emphasizes that we must consider the collective point of view simply because it is inherent in us. Any violation of the collective standpoint causes a dissociation and disturbance of the psychic equilibrium, which usually manifests as ego inflation. We then project our own bourgeois or collective parts onto other people, who, it must be said, lead a dreadfully bourgeois and boring life compared to our own. This illusory feeling of superiority, however, does not free us from moral debt to the norm, because any violation of the norm constitutes a new debt. No "spiritual freedom," however enticing, exempts us from this debt. Jung warns Hedy Wyss that sooner or later, nature will present her with the bill "with an almost diabolical reversal of viewpoint." Her "inner collective man will demand his payment with even greater force."

Jung goes on to speak of the guilt that is *imposed* on us. By this he means the guilt inherited from our ancestors that we cannot shake off, which, he adds in parentheses, in the case of Hedy Wyss are the sins that her father did *not* commit! In the end, it does not matter whether we are exceedingly moral and virtuous, or whether, in our so-called youthful freedom, we have no regard for rules at all. In both cases, the balance is disturbed. Thus, Jung

282 Ibid., CW 18, chapter 2, "Individuation and Collectivity," §§ 1099-1106.

283 See also the discussion of this text by Marie-Louise von Franz in her book *Muhammad ibn Umail's Hall ar-Rumuz*, Egg: Fotorotar, 1999, pp. 39-41, and Theo Abt (ed.), *Book of the Explanation of the Symbols Kitāb Hall ar-Rumūz* by Muhammad Ibn Umail. Psychological Commentary by Marie-Louise von Franz, Zurich: Living Human Heritage Publication, 2006 (Corpus Alchemicum Arabicum, Volume I A), §§ 38-46.

feels compelled to ask, "Why was it ever made possible for us to forget the terribly true doctrine of the *peccatum originale*?"[284]

What he resolutely requires of his analysand, though no less of himself, is the greatest possible honesty toward one's own shadow aspects, and the consequent acceptance of one's own guilt. To make this less abstract, Jung gives concrete advice on how we can deal with our own shadow: "... if you feel that you are in error somewhere, please stick with it and confess to it, for then you will pay off at least a little of the debt imposed upon you."[285] Unsparing honesty toward one's shadow and owning one's guilt can have a tremendously purifying and healing effect. Of course, one may be ashamed – even terribly ashamed – of this or that, but ultimately, openness to shame can generate a self-confidence that is firmly rooted in the fertile soil of our human and animal nature, i.e., in the realm of our instincts. A tree whose roots reach down into the dark deep of the earth is more likely to withstand the storm than one with only superficial roots.

Only after repeated warnings, summarized here very briefly, not to underestimate bourgeois morality, does it become clear what Jung is really getting at. Ultimately, he is not concerned with morality, but with establishing the psychological equilibrium necessary for the process of individuation to progress and flourish. His analysand's self-deception jeopardizes this equilibrium and compromises the trust she could have in Jung and, in turn, herself. Jung wants to provide their relationship with a vessel that, out of mutual respect, would allow *them both* to remain true to themselves.

In *Lohengrin's Black Swan,* it is noticeable that Hedy Wyss is often very quick to judge other people in an unflattering way. As much and as often as she also doubts herself, she doubts her fellow human beings. This is equally true the other way around; the more she sees her fellow human beings in an unduly critical light, the more she seems to hate herself. This isolates her from the people around her. Even her relationship with Jung is never entirely free of doubt. Her comments about her analyst in her diary entries that are transcribed in *Lohengrin's Black Swan* are often contradictory in regard to her analyst. Her notes sometimes reveal a subliminal distrust of Jung, and, at other times, a degree of inflation on her part.

284 Letter undated, presumably September 15, 1943.
285 Ibid.

For his part, Jung begs her to perceive him without wishful fantasies and to take *his* reality into account.[286] Clearly, what he reads in her diary does not make him feel understood – so 'fictitious and futile!' "Where, for example," he asks, "do you get the idea from that you have beguiled my mind? A woman can beguile my heart, but a whole world cannot beguile my mind. My feeling is amenable, but my mind is a tougher nut to crack."[287] Putting these critical undertones aside, this letter on bourgeois morality ends, as his letters so often did, in cheerful, almost hymnal, strains:

> Hence, O Diotima, I have bowed most profoundly before your feeling, so that I do not devalue this great divine power. Where it is concerned, I shall be careful not to interfere. But when it comes to your understanding! That is the matter at hand now.
> I greet the swans and horses and whatever else hoots and scoots.
> I trust you will understand! "Don't fall!"
> Your ever-devoted,
> C.G. Jung[288]

286 In a short, very early letter to the 'Dear Miss Hedy Wyss,' which Jung wrote to her before her first visit to Bollingen, he asks her to perceive him as far as possible without wishful fantasies, "Not only didn't I smile, but I got the creeps from the involuntary God-likeness. Please, no adventure fantasies! I will be able to say 'good day' and 'hm, hm' to you [in the Bollingen tower], as one does, perhaps with a cup of tea and a sandwich." Letter undated, postmarked 17.VII.39. The visit actually took place on the 1st August 1939.

287 Letter undated, probably, September 15, 1943.

288 Ibid. The animals that "hoot sand scoot" refer to the subjects of her paintings.

11. The Little Book of Monologues

The *Little Book of Monologues,* as the story goes, came into being quite playfully. During a Club lecture given by Cornelia Brunner[289] in December 1943, Jung pulled out of his pocket a small, yellow vanilla notebook with a red spine and began to make some entries. It was a notebook that belonged to Hedy Wyss with diary and dream entries which she had left behind a year earlier and had forgotten about. According to Hedy Wyss' manuscript *Lohengrin's Black Swan,* Jung's entries during the lecture were comments partly on the lecture of Cornelia Brunner and partly on the dreams of his analysand. A short while later he sent the little book back to its owner by mail, enriched with an initial, longer contribution, the *Monologue in December 1943*. He wrote this monologue from his tower in Bollingen, from where he complains of his suffering the winter cold. This little notebook went back and forth between them until it was full. The third and last entry by Jung, the *Epilogue,* was again written in Bollingen. For Hedy Wyss, it was, in retrospect, 'a lovely, teasing intermezzo with the dubious little book.' It certainly has this aspect, but Jung's entries are again so profound and wide-ranging that one only discovers their true depth and breadth after reading them several times.

"Once again, she's writing a beautiful story in the blossom country of the south." With this reference to Richard Wilhelm's book on the Taoist Zhuangzi, Jung began his longer entry, entitled *Monologue in December 1943.*[290] In what follows, however, there is at first nothing of the serenity of the Chinese sage, nothing of the equanimity of the Taoist of old. On the contrary! Warming his hands by the hearth fire in his tower with only 12° C, Jung ponders plugging draughty cracks tormenting his rheumatic limbs, and wonders if his rickety old heart might endure a little longer.

289 Cornelia Brunner lectured at the Psychology Club on December 11, 1943 on an essay of Gertrud von Le Fort entitled "*Die ewige Frau* [*The Eternal Woman*]." She was president of the Club from 1952-1977.

290 R. Wilhelm, *Dschuang Dsï* [Zhuangzi], *Das wahre Buch vom südlichen Blütenland* [The True Book of the Blossom Country of the South].

Galatea's Throne

After this lament about the arduousness of life in the wintry tower of Bollingen, however, Jung draws on unlimited resources. His heart "has become frail, like the thinnest of glass" and within "sits a Homunculus that shall not shatter a second time at Galatea's throne."[291] This is an allusion to the Aegean Feast in Goethe's *Faust,* to the scene at the end of the classical Walpurgis Night, in which Homunculus, in his glow and desire, crashes and shatters against Galatea's shell-bedecked throne.[292] Hidden behind Galatea's throne is the goddess of love. Jung is concerned that this karma should not be repeated, that love should not be destroyed once again.

Here, Goethe draws on Ovid's story about the savage creature Polyphemus: "Even he understood what love means. Seized by violent passion, his heart on fire," he becomes inflamed with burning passion for the nymph Galatea. She, however, "a sweeter flower than any in the meadows, more tall and stately than the alder, more radiant than crystal," spurns his love. While *he* extols his beloved with beautiful verses and sings a wonderful hymn to love, *she* rests in the arms of her beloved, the handsome boy Acis, who holds all of her affections. What a betrayal! In blind passion Polyphemus takes revenge on his beloved by slaying the youthful shepherd with a rock.[293] Too violent is the giant in his passion, and, as a result, burning love is followed by murder and slaughter. This disaster, by which the youthful god is shattered or killed, is what Jung wants to avoid.[294] "This time, he [the youthful god]

291 *Monologue in December 1943.*

292 J.W. von Goethe, *Faust. A Tragedy.* Part II, Act II, verses 8450 and 8472.

293 Ovid, *Metamorphoses,* Book XIII, 738-897.

294 In Goethe's *Faust* Thales is the first to see the disaster coming:

Thales:

Homunculus is it, by Proteus ensnared ...
These symptoms betoken imperious craving,
The clamorous drone of an agonized raving;
He'll crash at her glittering throne and be shattered;
It's flaming, now flashes, already is scattered.

The scene ends with the Sirens' hymn to nature and Eros, who had devised the play of the elements:

Sirens:

What lights us the billows, what fiery wonder
Sets blazing their clashes and sparkling asunder?
It lightens and wavers and brightens the height:
The bodies they glow on the courses of night,
And ringed is the whole by the luminous wall;
May Eros then reign who engendered it all!

must come into being, while on his journey into the beyond,"[295] he writes to Hedy Wyss in the *Little Book of Monologues.*

In October, 1949, Jung gave a lecture at the Psychology Club Zurich on "Faust and Alchemy."[296] Here, in view of the Aegean Feast, he compares Galatea, within whom Aphrodite or Venus is concealed, to the *Lapis vivus*, the living stone. In this he sees a chance to heal the catastrophic death of Homunculus. By being too strongly drawn to the sensual, concrete aspect of love, Homunculus is shattered against the gleaming throne of the goddess. Their conjunction goes up in flames, destroyed in the fire of desire, and, burning together, they finally drown in the sea. Thus, for the time being, the union of the opposites remains an event that has taken place solely in the unconscious. Jung, however, sees in this encounter a prefiguration of the marriage of Faust and Helena,[297] that is, of the *coniunctio oppositorum*, the realization of which will be but a future possibility.

The end of the classical Walpurgis Night suggests "that something new has arisen in the unconscious and can become operative from there." The new, or as Jung called it, the "prelude to healing, [is] obviously Eros, because it is Eros who is to rule from now on, as that power of the unconscious which sets everything in motion."[298]

> May Eros then reign who engendered it all![299]

It is this quality of Eros with which Jung is concerned in his seemingly incidental reference to Galatea's throne, the throne against which Homunculus should not shatter. Hidden within the allusion to the ancient story is Jung's

Hail the sea, the ocean swelling!
Wreathed in sacred fiery torrents:
Hail the fire, the waters welling!
Hail the singular occurrence!
All in union:
Hail the gentle airs benignant!
Hail the deeps with secrets pregnant!
Solemnly here be ye sung,
All four elements as one!
(*Faust. A Tragedy*, Part II, Act II, 8469-8487)

295 *Monologue in December 1943* (emphasis AS).

296 C.G. Jung, „Faust und die Alchemie", Lecture at the Psychology Club Zurich, October 8, 1949, in: I. Gerber-Münch, *Goethes Faust*, pp. 13-37 (not yet translated).

297 C.G. Jung, „Faust und die Alchemie," p. 31 (translation mine).

298 I. Gerber-Münch, *Goethes Faust*, p. 349 (translation mine).

299 J.W. von Goethe, *Faust. A Tragedy,* Part II, Act II, verse 8479.

fervent admonition and heartfelt plea to Hedy Wyss that she set aside desire, wishing, striving; in short, that she set aside the *concupiscentia* and honor *Eros* instead as the *numen of human relationship* that can or could reveal itself, particularly in the analytic relationship.

The Fragility of the *Vitrum Sphaericum*

In the *Monologue in December 1943*, Jung writes that his heart has become frail, like the thinnest of glass. In addition to the very real threat that existed just a few months before his second heart attack, a further allusion is hidden here – to the alchemical vessel. In January, 1943, only a month after this entry, Jung completed his work *Psychology and Alchemy*. Here he wrote:

> The glass corresponds to the *unum vas* of alchemy and its contents to the living, semi-organic mixture from which the body of the lapis, endowed with spirit and life, will emerge – or possibly that strange Faustian figure who bursts into flame three times: the Boy Charioteer, the Homunculus who is dashed against the throne of Galatea, and Euphorion (all symbolizing a dissolution of the "center" into its unconscious elements). We know that the lapis is not just a "stone" since it is expressly stated to ... consist of body, soul, and spirit; moreover, it grows from flesh and blood.[300]

This time, it is the Homunculus in Jung's heart that should not dissolve into thin air, as it did in Goethe's *Faust*; the heart should not break "on his journey to the beyond."[301] Even now, Jung carefully safeguards this fragile *vitrum sphaericum*, and allows no one to touch it: *Noli me tangere*![302] Again this is an allusion to the hermetic vessel, this time, however, to its *cosmic*

300 C.G. Jung, *Psychology and Alchemy*, CW 12, § 243.

301 *Monologue in December 1943*. The becoming of the Homunculus on his journey to the beyond may also refer to C.G. Jung's *Mysterium Coniunctionis*, the work with which Jung struggled with all available energy for more than ten years.

302 The risen Christ appears to Mary Magdalene and says to her: "*Noli me tangere*" – "Do not cling to me, for I have not yet ascended to the father." (John 20:17) For a psychological interpretation of this passage see, Laurel Howe, "Redeeming Mary Magdalene – The Feminine Side of the Death and Resurrection Archetype," in: Andreas Schweizer and Regine Schweizer-Vüllers (eds.), *Wisdom has Built her House. Psychological Aspects of the Feminine*, Contributions to Jungian Psychology by The Psychology Club Zurich, vol. 2, Einsiedeln: Daimon, 2019, pp. 136 f.

meaning. "For the alchemists the vessel is something truly marvelous: a *vas mirabile.* Maria Prophetissa asserts that the whole secret lies in knowing about the Hermetic vessel. '*Unum est vas*' (the vessel is one) is emphasized again and again. It must be completely round, in imitation of the spherical cosmos, so that the influence of the stars may contribute to the success of the operation ..."[303]

Psychologically, the *rotundum,* or roundness, points to wholeness i.e., to the symbol of the primordial cosmic man, or Anthropos. This ranges from the animal man in us, the archaic world of drives and instincts, to the *homo altus,* the greater inner man whose liberation from the narrowness of blind desire and yearning is the goal of individuation. Ultimately, individuation is not so much concerned with reaching a goal, but rather with circumambulating a mysterious center wherein lies the uniqueness of every human being. This circumambulation, however, is not ego-driven; on the contrary, it is, as Marie-Louise von Franz once put it, "the precondition for genuine relatedness and a sustainable social attitude,"[304] especially for a sustainable love relationship that in no way patronizes the other. This is reminiscent of the often-quoted beautiful description of love Jung wrote in a letter to the American Mary Mellon:

> This love is not transference and it is no ordinary friendship or sympathy. It is more primitive, more primeval and more spiritual, than anything we can describe. That upper floor is no more you or I, it means many, including yourself and anybody whose heart you touch.[305]

Expressible only in highly paradoxical words, the *vitrum sphaericum,* like love, is exceedingly fragile, and yet it lifts man above everyday life. In this vein, from his wintry tower in Bollingen, Jung writes further in his monologue, "I am already dead to this age. To the moment, I am no longer bound, nor even a year, but to centuries only." This, once again, is an allusion to Faust, initially to his wager with the devil:

303 C.G. Jung, *Psychology and Alchemy,* CW 12, § 388 (emphasis AS). A footnote to this paragraph says, "*domus vitrea sphaeratilis sive circularis*" – the spherical or circular house of glass, ibid., fn. 13.

304 See Marie-Louise von Franz, "The Cosmic Man as Image of the Goal of the Individuation Process and Human Development," in: id., *Archetypal Dimensions of the Psyche,* Boston & London: Shambhala, 1999, p. 153.

305 C.G. Jung, *Letters,* vol. 1, Letter to Mary Conover Mellon, Bollingen, April 18, 1941 anno miseriae, p. 298.

If the swift moment I entreat:
Tarry a while! You are so fair!
Then forge the shackles to my feet,
Then I will gladly perish there![306]

It is as if love, so carefully guarded in the *vitrum sphaericum*, is able to overcome the young person's attachment to the moment – to their desires, yearnings, and their hopes, gradually at first, but increasingly as they grow older. *Faust* is Goethe's *opus magnum*. The time of Sturm und Drang has long since passed, and so have *The Sorrows of* [Goethe's] *Young Werther,* who was unable to withstand the pain of love. The fetters of fate became so unbearable for the latter that only violent death could provide a way out. The young, Jung continues, cannot imagine what it means to have bid "goodbye at every turn to that other who would like to, who could, who should, who hoped, who feared, and anticipated." "[The young person] does not understand the rising waters of timelessness and therefore does not understand the ecstasy of old age."

At the end of his life, however, Faust seems to have known about the water of timelessness. In his last words before his death, he again mentions the beauty of the moment, although he uses the subjunctive, "I might entreat the fleeting minute" – but he also knows that 'his path on earth' cannot be destroyed:

I might entreat the fleeting minute:
Oh tarry yet, thou art so fair!
My path on earth, the trace I leave within it
Eons untold cannot impair.
Foretasting such high happiness to come,
I savor now my striving's crown and sum.[307]

These are powerful words, indeed. But they suggest the insight that beyond the gods of the moment, there is another reality that can only be intuited. A hundred years later, C.G. Jung, considering this reality, spoke of the *objective psyche* or *objective cognition* that "lies hidden behind the attraction of the

306 J.W. von Goethe, *Faust. A Tragedy*, Part I, verses 1699 ff.
307 Ibid., Part II, 11581 ff.

emotional relationship."[308] This is a realization that no longer adheres to the moment, because it is associated with centuries or even eons.

Jung writes to the fabulously young Hedy Wyss while in the blossom country of the south – she spent some days in the southern part of Switzerland at that time – "the old have already left the blossoming times and summer lands, their longings and their attachments. All, all, has become remembrance and inklings."[309] Psychologically, this corresponds to a shift from the ego to the self, from the limitations of the relative narrowness of personal psychology to the larger personality or, as Jung called it, the Great Man within us.

The awakening to the Great Man in us can happen gradually, like a blossom slowly unfolding, but it can also be brought about by a sudden, often entirely unexpected, numinous event, an eruption from the hidden world of the unconscious that has, it must be said, a certain violence. Jung had experienced such an eruption twenty-seven years earlier, on January 16, 1916, when his house in Küsnacht appeared to be haunted. This was the beginning of Jung's encounter with the dead that was to have a lasting influence on him for the rest his life, and on the development of analytical psychology as a whole. Thus, before continuing our discussion of the *Little Book of Monologues,* we shall pause to discuss this event. Hedy Wyss read Jung's document of his encounter – the *Septem Sermones* with great enthusiasm.[310]

308 C.G. Jung, *Memories, Dreams, Reflections*, p. 297.
309 *Monologue in December 1943.*
310 See C.G. Jung's letter to Hedy Wyss of December 23, 1939.

12. Digression: The Haunting of Jung's House and the Septem Sermones ad Mortuos

The Haunting

We begin with Jung's report as recorded in his *Memoirs*:

> It began with a restlessness, but I did not know what it meant or what 'they' wanted. There was an ominous atmosphere all around me. I had the strange feeling that the air was filled with ghostly entities. Then it was as if my house began to be haunted. My eldest daughter saw a white figure passing through the room. My second daughter, independently of her elder sister, related that twice in the night her blanket had been snatched away; and the same night my nine-year-old son had an anxiety dream [...] Around five o'clock in the afternoon on Sunday [January 16, 1916] the front-door bell began ringing frantically. It was a bright Sunday[311]; the two maids were in the kitchen [...] Everyone immediately looked to see who was there, but there was no one in sight [...] The whole house was filled as if there were a crowd present, crammed full of spirits [...] Then they [the dead] cried out in chorus, "We have come back from Jerusalem where we found not what we sought."[312]

This last statement marks the beginning of the *Septem Sermones ad Mortuos* (Seven Sermons to the Dead). Jung recalled:

> Then it began to flow out of me, and in the course of three evenings the thing was written. As soon as I took up the pen, the whole ghostly

311 Here the text of *Memories, Dreams, Reflections* has been translated erroneously, "It was a bright *summer* day." According to the *Protocols* it should read, "It was a bright Sunday." The date of January 16, 1916 is confirmed by the sketch of the "*Systema mundi totius*," that Jung made the same evening as part of a long imagination. See C.G. Jung, *The Black Books*, vol. 5, p. 175. Jung's entries of that day in German begin, ibid., p. 169. For the English text see pp. 269 ff.

312 C.G. Jung, *Memories, Dreams, Reflections*, pp. 190 f.

> assemblage evaporated. The room quieted and the atmosphere was clear. The haunting was over.[313]

The original text of the *Sermones* flowed out of him, or rather out of 'the monstruous flood of the unconscious,' which explains the peculiarly antiquated language. The text unfolded, however, not over the course of three evenings, as described in Jung's *Memoirs*, but in six entries in volumes 5 and 6 of *The Black Books* between January 29 and February 8, 1916, that is, over the span of a full week. On the Sunday evening of the haunting, Jung drew the sketch of the *Systema mundi totius* and wrote the corresponding text. These first entries are an impressive testimony to his entire experience.

That same year, 1916, he transcribed this first version of the *Sermones* in calligraphic writing and, in a slightly modified, separate document, added the following introduction to the title:

> The Seven Sermons to the Dead written by Basilides in Alexandria, the City where the East toucheth the West. Translated from the Greek original into German.[314]

Jung lays no claim to being the author of the text, but states instead that it is Basilides, the second century Gnostic who lived in Alexandria. In that Egyptian city on the Mediterranean coast, Egyptian, Jewish, Hellenistic, and later Christian cultural traditions met in a fascinating and vibrant way.[315] Jung had this modified version of the *Sermones* privately published. In the *Protocols*,[316] he reported that he had had it printed on the occasion of the founding of the Psychology Club Zurich (February 26, 1916). It was to be a gift to Edith McCormick-Rockefeller, the generous benefactor who had made possible the acquisition of the magnificent clubhouse in the center of Zurich.

313 Ibid., p. 191.

314 See ibid., Appendix V, p. 378. Unfortunately, since the private prints of the *Septem Sermones* are not dated, neither in the family archive nor in the library of the Psychology Club Zurich, the exact date of their origin cannot be determined.

315 For a detailed discussion of the *Septem Sermones* see Stephan A. Hoeller, *The Gnostic Jung and the Seven Sermons to the Dead*, Wheaton, Illinois: Theosophical Pub. House, 1982. The author elaborates on the historical background of this text, mainly on its various allusions to Neoplatonic and Gnostic thought.

316 C.G. Jung, *Protocols*, p. 26.

"From Then On, My Life Belonged to the Generality"

It was through these parapsychological events, out of which the text of the *Septem Sermones ad Mortuos* had spontaneously emerged, that Jung realized the supremacy and autonomy of the inner images. This breakthrough was preceded by years in which Jung, after his separation from Freud, intensively worked on his dreams, visions, and imaginations. He first recorded his fantasies in *The Black Books*, out of which emerged *The Red Book*. Through his descent into the unconscious, the presence of the dead became more and more clear to him. Their voices addressed what had remained for his ancestors 'unanswered, unresolved and unredeemed.' These questions from the inner world were tied to his destiny, and he felt compelled to answer them as fully as possible. "It was then that I ceased to belong to myself alone, ceased to have the right to do so," he recalled near the end of his life. "From then on, my life belonged to the generality."[317] Jung's entry in Hedy Wyss' *Little Book of Monologues*, in the so-called *Monologue in December 1943,* refers back to this experience. Here he writes that "he is already dead to this age." After this encounter with the dead, time could no longer exist for him in the now – no "Tarry a while! you are so fair!"[318] – but only within the context of centuries.

After the spirits of the dead filled Jung's house on Seestrasse in Küsnacht in January 1916, and again in March 1943, when his ancestress appeared to him in a dream and, to his great annoyance, all kinds of stupid and impudent laughing people entered his home, Jung could no longer evade the spirits of the dead and his ancestors. He had to find an answer to their unanswered questions. For this reason, at least some of the central contents of the *Septem Sermones* will be discussed here. They shed light on the problematic nature of transference and perhaps might also illuminate why Hedy Wyss struggled with it so very much. It should be noted that in the later version of the *Septem Sermones* recorded in *The Red Book* (presumably 1917/1918), it is no longer Jung who instructs the dead, but the white-robed priest and sage Philemon. Here, Jung has incorporated the *Septem Sermones* into a much broader, more comprehensive, commentary in his attempt to better understand the

317 C.G. Jung, *Memories, Dreams, Reflections*, p. 192.
318 Faust's wager with the devil.

messages from the beyond. This text is a real help in understanding the *Sermones*.[319]

The World of Fullness and the *principium individuationis*

"We [the dead] have come back from Jerusalem, where we did not find what we sought."[320] These are the opening words of the First Sermon. In Jerusalem, once the prosperous center of the Judeo-Christian world, the dead clearly were given no answers to the questions that beset them about the image of God today. Disappointed, they return from the city once sacred to them. Perhaps Nietzsche was right after all with his prophecy "God is dead! God remains dead!"[321] Philemon proclaims this not to be so at the beginning of the Second Sermon, "God is not dead. He is as alive as ever. *God is creation* ..."[322] The God-image that Philemon reveals, however, does not meet with the expectations of the dead and the ancestors. As the dead had been Christians, a great commotion broke out after Philemon's Second Sermon. This was not at all the Christian God-image of old, according to which Christ redeemed humankind by submitting to being crucified and then ascending to the Father. If God is creation, it means that he suffers, like all human beings, from the painful inner turmoil of everything that exists. He is not above the opposites; he contains them, and this, in turn, would mean that the devil is thereby included.

God as creation is differentiated from the Pleroma. The Pleroma is a concept often mentioned in the first two Sermons, and it plays a large role in the Gnostic systems, including that of Basilides. It designates the world of primordial fullness, an original wholeness that existed *before* the creation of the world with its limitations through space and time, and continues to exist beyond everything that has been created. The Gnostics yearn for this world of the beginning; they want to immerse themselves in it. But this must not

319 Drawing from the *The Black Books*, Sonu Shamdasani incorporated this text and Jung's imaginations in his edition of *The Red Book* under the title "Scrutinies," as the third book of the *Liber Novus*.

320 C.G. Jung, *The Red Book*, p. 346b [*The Red Book. Reader's Edition*, pp. 507 f.].

321 Friedrich Nietzsche, *The Gay Science*, ed. by Bernard Williams, translated by Josefine Nauckhoff, Cambridge: Cambridge University Press, 2001, Book Three, Aphorism 125, "The madman," p. 120.

322 C.G. Jung, *The Red Book*, p. 348 b [*The Red Book. Reader's Edition*, p. 516] (emphasis AS).

be understood as a return or a regression. The deep longing of the Gnostics is rather the renewal and recreation of the human being.

From his deep study of Gnostic texts, Jung held fast to this Gnostic world of fullness and the oneness of all being. But it was only decades later, while studying the phenomena of synchronicity, that he devoted several years of scientific research to this world of oneness. Synchronistic phenomena point to an underlying unity of matter and psyche and thus to "a psychically conditioned relativity of space and time."[323] Symbolically, the Pleroma has been expressed for millennia through the archetype of the cosmic man or Anthropos, or by the *anima mundi,* which the alchemists equated with Mercurius.[324] In radical contrast to the Pleroma, God as creation encompasses all opposites and contradictions, good as well as evil, yes and no, day and night, etc. This, then, is why the created world requires the *principium individuationis,* that is, the discriminating consciousness through which the opposites can be recognized as such and integrated as far as possible.[325]

In the second of the *Septem Sermones,* the Godhead that contains good and evil, God and the Devil, is equated with the Gnostic Abraxas. He "is the God who is difficult to grasp."[326] Jung was now confronted with an entirely paradoxical God-image. More than thirty years passed before Jung returned

323 C.G. Jung, "Synchronicity: An Acausal Connecting Principle," in: *The Structure and Dynamics of the Psyche,* CW 8, § 840, and id., "On the Nature of the Psyche," CW 8, §§ 343 ff. See especially ibid., CW 8, § 418: "... it is not only possible, but fairly probable, even, that psyche and matter are two aspects of one and the same thing." Originally published as "Der Geist des Psychologie" [The Spirit of Psychology], *Eranos Jahrbuch 1946,* Rhein Verlag, Zurich 1947. For Barbara Hannah this was one of Jung's best lectures. B. Hannah, *Jung. His Life and* Work, p. 292.

324 C.G. Jung, "On the Nature of the Psyche," CW 8, § 393, "Mercurius was interpreted now as *anima mundi* and now as the Holy Ghost." Regarding the cosmic man see M.-L. von Franz, "The Cosmic Man," in: id., *The Archetypal Dimensions of the Psyche.*

325 To the best of my knowledge, it is here, in the First Sermon to the Dead that Jung speaks of the *principium individuationis* for the first time. C.G. Jung, *The Red Book,* p. 347b [*The Red Book. Reader's Edition,* p. 512].

326 Ibid., p. 350a [*The Red Book. Reader's Edition,* p. 520]. Jung knew Abraxas from Albrecht Dieterich's book *Abraxas, Studien zur Religionsgeschichte des späteren Altertums* [Studies to the History of Religions in Late Antiquity], B.G. Teubner, Leipzig 1905. On January 16, 1916, in the evening of the day on which his house was haunted by the dead, Jung made a sketch of the *Systema mundi totius,* which depicts Abraxas' world surrounded by the Pleroma. See C.G. Jung, *The Black Books* 5, p. 175. Not much later, the mandala *Systema mundi totius* emerged from this sketch (Plate IX). In the outer circle of the Pleroma and equally in the innermost center, the opposites dissolve, whereas the two white middle circles contain the world of Abraxas, i.e., all imaginable opposites.

to this image of God that had erupted like a volcano in his *Sermones*, to write about it in detail in his "Answer to Job" (1952):

> God has a terrible double aspect: a sea of grace is met by a seething lake of fire, and the light of love glows with a fierce dark heat of which it is said "ardet non lucet" – it burns but gives no light. That is the eternal, as distinct from the temporal, gospel: one can love God but must fear him.[327]

Image 15: C.G. Jung, Systema mundi totius (Plate XI)

327 C.G. Jung, "Answer to Job," CW 12, § 733. On the fear of God in the eternal gospel see Revelation 14:6-7, "Then I saw another angel ... with an eternal gospel to proclaim ... and he said with a loud voice, Fear God and give him glory ..."

A Lonely Star in the Zenith

The following chapters of the *Sermones* present lengthy explanations of the almost unsurpassable paradoxes of the new God-image and the image of man. In psychological terms, this corresponds to the self as a *complexio oppositorum* that contains all opposites within itself. Here, however, only the content of the seventh and last sermon shall be discussed, although it is actually no longer a teaching, but rather a moving *hymn to the image of the star* as a symbol of the self:

> At immeasurable distance a lonely star stands in the zenith.
> This is the one God of this one man, this is his world, his Pleroma, his divinity.
> In this world, man is Abraxas, the creator and destroyer of his own world.
> This star is the God and the goal of man.
> This is his one guiding God,
> in him man goes to his rest,
> toward him goes his long journey of the soul after death, in him everything that man withdraws from the greater world shines resplendently.
> To this one God man shall pray.
> Prayer increases the light of the star,
> it throws a bridge across death ...
> Man here, God there.
> Weakness and nothingness here, eternally creative power there.
> Here nothing but darkness and clammy cold
> there total sun.
> But when Philemon had finished, the dead remained silent. Heaviness fell from them, and they ascended like smoke above the shepherd's fire, who watches over his flock by night.[328]

This text is unique beyond the beauty and poetry of the language. "At immeasurable distance a lonely star stands in the zenith." This *One Star* is the God and the goal of *this One Man,* which constitutes the uniqueness of

328 C.G. Jung, *The Red Book*, p. 354a [*The Red Book. Reader's Edition*, pp. 534 f.]. See also *The Black Books,* vol 6, 8.II.16, p. 227, where this text is slightly different. Here the last part, "But when Philemon had finished ...," is missing.

his individual destiny.[329] From the image of the One Star emerges the divine child, born in the soul of man. This, however, does not suggest that the individual can escape his responsibility for the collective. On the contrary: the closer a person comes to their star – the more they live their own unique and individual destiny – the more their life no longer belongs to themselves, but to the collective!

A particularly impressive example of this can be seen in the life and prenatal vision of a star of the Swiss hermit Niklaus von Flüe, canonized in 1947. His biographer Heinrich Wölflin (ca. 1501) reports, "Still in his mother's womb, he saw a star in the sky shining above all others, and the whole world was illuminated by its rays ..." And from the time he lived in his hermitage in Ranft, he had always seen a star that resembled him, "so that he believed it was the same one, that he saw in his mother's womb."[330] In her book *The Visions of Niklaus von Flüe,* Marie-Louise von Franz suggests that this star is "a symbol of the *alchemical Mercurius* as the *principium individuationis.*"[331] Subsequently, she refers to a passage in Jung's essay *The Spirit Mercurius,* where he describes Mercurius "as the shining and shimmering planet, appearing like Venus close to the sun in the morning or evening sky ... like her [he is] a Lucifer, a light-bringer (φωσφόρος). He heralds, as the morning star does, only much more directly, the coming of the light."[332] In the same way, the vision of the star signifies an archetypal destiny to Niklaus von Flüe, peasant and later saint. His prenatal vision can, therefore, be seen as an anticipation of his later destiny and vocation.

Likewise, there are certain childhood dreams remembered in adulthood that can point to a future destiny, to the unique, singular meaning of this particular individual's life. Another question, however, is whether the task

329 Three weeks later, Jung explains in a letter to Joan Corrie how he understands this passage: "The primordial creator of the world, the blind creative libido, becomes transformed in man through individuation and out of this process, which is like pregnancy, arises a divine child, a reborn God ..." C.G. Jung, *The Red Book*, p. 354, fn. 123 [*The Red Book. Reader's Edition*, p. 535, fn. 123].

330 Robert Durrer (Ed.), *Bruder Klaus. Die ältesten Quellen über den seligen Niklaus von Flüe, sein Leben und sein Einfluss* [Brother Klaus. The Oldest Resources of the Blessed Niklaus von Flüe. His Life and Influence], Sarnen: 1917, reprint, 1981, Vol. 1, p. 531, (translation mine).

331 Marie-Louise von Franz, *Niklaus von Flüe and Saint Perpetua: A Psychological Interpretation of their Visions*. Translated from the original German manuscript by Alison Kappes and Barbara Davies, Volume 6 of the *Collected Works of Marie-Louise von Franz*, Ashville: Chiron Publications 2022, p. 16.

332 C.G. Jung, "The Spirit Mercurius," CW 13, § 273.

indicated by such a dream will be understood and thus realized in the life of the person concerned, for initially it is only a *potential* slumbering in the soul. Just how such a destiny can manifest in a person's life can be seen in the childhood dream of Marie-Louise von Franz, dreamed at the age of three and a half.

In this dream, reproduced here in abbreviated form, she is on a walk with her family when she suddenly sees two men appear in the distance and walk toward her. Her father calls out in horror, "Those are the gods! They're coming to test us!" Then he explains to the little child that each person possesses an enameled plaque with their name, date of birth and date of death; if the plaque is damaged, the person in question falls into the hands of the gods. They all run home. But the enamel of the little girl's plaque is damaged! She is horrified. At that moment, a round, brilliant light appears in the corner of the ceiling. She leaves her body and for a brief moment becomes one with the light. This gives her courage. She returns to her body and thinks, "Okay, fine, so I'll just go meet the gods." Then she wakes up with a scream.[333]

Marie-Louise von Franz discusses this dream in her essay "The Unknown Visitor," but without referring to it as her own. When sharing the dream with Jung, he reminded her of the Gnostic tradition according to which every soul receives a tablet from the celestial powers, a "letter of debt." The Christian Gnostics believed that Christ freed souls from the compulsion of the stars by pinning the letter of debt to the Cross. In the childhood dream of Marie-Louise von Franz, it was not Christ, but a light that she saw above her, which gave her the courage to meet the gods, to consciously take upon herself her individual destiny on the path of individuation, trusting in the round light in which, from the standpoint of psychology, we recognize the self. "All the same," she wrote, "it is terrifying to fall into the hands of the living God. That is why the child is frightened."[334]

333 M.-L. von Franz, "The Unknown Visitor," in: *Archetypal Dimensions of the Psyche*, p. 71.
334 Ibid., p. 72.

"It Is Difficult to Remain True to Love"

The image of the lonely star in its zenith refers to the singular guiding god of the individual, as mentioned in the seventh and last Sermon to the dead. Like the round light in Marie-Louise von Franz's dream, it heralds an archetypal transformative process of the Christian self-symbol, the extent of which cannot yet be estimated. Soon after the hymn to the One Star, following the *Septem Sermones*, the Dark One appears in Jung's imaginations, who is apparently a shadow aspect of Philemon. After a long address, he announces to Jung, "You will go to men as one veiled. Your light shines at night. Your solar nature departs from you and your stellar nature begins." Whereupon Jung answers, "You are cruel ... With these words the mysterious dark one vanished."[335]

Years later, while working on various contributions on the symbolism of the self in the Christian context, C.G. Jung delved into this transformation of the God-image. In this context, *Christ* is the symbol of the self. However, while the self represents a person's psychic totality, the figure of Christ "lacks the nocturnal side of the psyche's nature, the darkness of the spirit, and is also without sin."[336] Sooner or later, the symbol of Christ must be made complete by the inclusion of the dark side. This could be what was meant by the Dark One's announcement, which heralds a shift from solar nature to stellar nature.

It is only much later that Jung realizes what both the Dark One and Philemon want from him, namely that he remain faithful to love, because only through a love that desires nothing from the other can the fateful commingling with the world of Abraxas, with the world of eternal becoming and passing away, be overcome. Commingling always denotes bondage; it is not yet a voluntary devotion that expects nothing more.[337] Only through voluntary devotion do I "attain bonding with the great mother, that is, the stellar nature, liberation from bondage to men and things ... Only thus does

335 C.G. Jung, *The Red Book*, p. 355a [*The Red Book. Reader's Version*, p. 538].

336 C.G. Jung, "A Psychological Approach to the Trinity," CW 11, § 232. On the impeccancy of Christ see id., *Aion*, CW 9/2, § 70, where it says, "He [Christ] represents a totality of divine or heavenly kind, a glorified man, a son of God *sine macula peccati*, unspotted by sin."

337 C.G. Jung, *The Red Book*, p. 355b [*The Red Book. Reader's Version*, p. 540]: "I gathered from Philemon's words that I must remain true to love to cancel out the commingling that arises through unlived love. I understood that the commingling is a bondage that takes the place of voluntary devotion."

the light of the star grow, only thus do I arrive at my stellar nature, at my truest and innermost self, that simply and singly is."[338]

However, this love does not denote the Christian concept of loving one's neighbor. Rather, it is a love that, under certain circumstances, requires one to consciously commit a sin, for it is above collective morality.[339] Philemon now addresses his dark master and brother, which is obviously a shadow aspect of Christ which has little in common with the conventional conception of Christ. He kneels down, touches the earth, and says, "My master and my brother, praised be your name ..." And after a long oration, he asks the Dark One, "Have you not forgiven the adulteress? Did you not sit with whores and tax-collectors? Did you not break the command of the Sabbath? You lived your own life, but men fail to do so, instead they pray to you ..." They pray to Christ that He might redeem them. However, Christ's "work would be completed [only] if men managed to live their own lives without imitation."[340] "The time has come when each must do his own work of redemption. Mankind has grown older and a new month has begun."[341] Thus ends the speech of Philemon.

This "new month" points to a new Platonic month, meaning the end of the Aion of Pisces and the beginning of the new Aquarian Aion.[342] An important feature of the new Aion, however, is proclaimed in Philemon's address, as well as in, almost thirty years later, the declaration of Jung's ancestress in his dream. The new Aion signifies that today, we must work towards our own redemption or, to put it more accurately, we must hold ourselves responsible for this work. This is what the statement "You are the redeemer" made by Jung's ancestress in his dream in Geneva means. The time has come for everyone to do their own work of redemption. We can no longer delegate this work to Christ. After two thousand years of traditional Christian belief that Christ redeemed us on the cross and that we can participate in this redemption through Him, the message of Philemon and the

338 Ibid., *The Red Book*, 356a [*The Red Book, Reader's Version*, p. 541].

339 Reflecting on Philemon's speech Jung states, "It is difficult to remain true to love since love stands above all sins." Ibid.

340 Ibid., 356 [*The Red Book, Reader's Version*, p. 542].

341 Ibid., 356 b [*The Red Book, Reader's Version*, p. 543].

342 Regarding the incoming Aquarian Aion, see Liz Greene, *The Astrological World of Jung's* Liber Novus. *Daimons, Gods, and the Planetary Journey*." London, New York: Routledge, 2018, p. 87, where the author discusses Phanes "as the God of the new Aquarian Aion," and continues, saying that "Phanes thus appears to be a reborn and transformed Saturn as a ruler of Aquarius ..." See also ibid., pp. 82 f. and 168-171.

ancestress is so new that it threatens to burst Jung's heart, his fragile *vitrum sphaericum*.

As we hear at the end of the *Septem Sermones*, prayer is a part of this work: "Prayer increases the light of the star, it throws a bridge across death."[343] More is revealed in the introduction to the two volumes of Jung's *Visions Seminar*, with his interpretation of Christiana Morgan's visions. Jung advised his analysand Christiana Morgan to record all of her material from the unconscious as beautifully and carefully as she could – in a beautifully bound book – as he had done in *The Red Book*. She could always then go back to the book and leaf through the pages; this would be her church, her cathedral, the silent places of her spirit where she could find renewal. If she were to believe anyone who told her that this was morbid or neurotic, she would suffer a loss of soul for she had poured her soul into this book.[344]

By giving careful consideration and elaboration to the daily images we receive from the unconscious, be they threatening or fascinating, we are engaging in a form of prayer. This aligns with the etymological roots of the word 'religion' which goes back to the Latin *religere* – to consider something conscientiously –, or, according to the classical lexicon of *Georges*, 'to consider something devotedly.' In this sense, any true love would be a prayer.

This brings us back to Jung's first entry into the *Little Book of Monologues*.

343 C.G. Jung, *The Red Book*, p. 354b [*The Red Book, Reader's Version*, p. 534].
344 See C.G. Jung, *Visions*, vol. 1, Introduction, p. xiii.

13. The Little Book of Monologues (Continuation)

"A Stone of Gold for Your Mosaic"

After his encounter with the dead, Jung remained connected with the world of the ancestors and thus with the timelessness of all life. This relativity of space and time pervades Jung's letters and messages to Hedy Wyss. We find a noteworthy example of this in the *Monologue in December 1943*, Jung's first longer entry in the so-called *Little Book of Monologues*. Here it says:

> Everything, including what is most recent and immediate, is remembrance from times inconceivably distant, and the inkling of innumerable summers and winters, births and deaths of coming eons. No here, no now, no upswing, no collapse, no hot desiring and no rigid no, no you and no me.[345]

Jung then presents a new image for the process of becoming whole:

> I have to think my life, and life in general, through to the end. I must assemble the mosaic out of a thousand little stones, while she sits on a branch in this land of blossoms where it is so hot and so sad, trilling and lamenting, so hot and so sad, and seems to know nothing of the transalpine Niflheim,[346] of the old people who warm their hands by a fire in the dusky hearth, while thinking of cracks to plug against cold rheumatic drafts; of apprehensive rest that one must grant to one's rickety old heart so that it might endure a little longer and not disturb too much while one works on the mosaic, work that is oh!-so indispensable.[347]

345 *Monologue in December 1943.*
346 In Christian times, the icy world of Hel, the goddess of death in Northern mythology, was equated with hell.
347 *Monologue in December 1943.*

To my knowledge, despite the fact that this image of working on a mosaic being a very apt expression of the individuation process, Jung never used it elsewhere in his scientific work to describe the process of becoming whole. While it is true that we can never grasp the full picture, except perhaps in visionary experiences and near death, nevertheless, if we dare to do the work of redemption and devote ourselves over many decades to fully living our lives – taking it as far as we possibly can –, and if we turn to our dreams and inner images for guidance, we begin to see the outline of something like a painting emerging, a landscape of the soul whose colors and diversity reflect our own unique life in the best possible way. Perhaps – and indeed, we might wish – that death occurs when the last piece of the mosaic tile is laid.

Jung returns to the image of the mosaic toward the end of the monologue when he writes to Hedy Wyss:

> But what can this mortal do? He writes in this diary to remind you. May he be a ray of sunshine that broke through the clouds, a stone of gold for your mosaic. But down here is this curse-laden, fog-afflicted earth upon which God's work is done.[348]

Even if we are committed to life and the unconscious images of the soul, we are not alone in laying the tiles of our mosaic. Others with whom we are connected, be it through love or hostility, also fill in the spaces of our mosaic. The stones need not always be brightly hued, like the sun. To complete the entire picture, dark and painful tiles are also needed on the journey toward wholeness. Jung, however, wants his *Monologue in December 1943* to be a ray of sunshine, a golden stone for the mosaic of his analysand.

The golden stone is an allusion to the philosopher's stone, about which the alchemists assert, "*aurum nostrum non est aurum vulgi*, our gold is not, as the stupid suppose, the ordinary gold, it is the philosophical gold or even the marvelous stone, the *lapis invisibilitatis* (the stone of invisibility) ..."[349] Jung, the "saturnine, wobbly old man,"[350] has long known that this gold does not deliver him from the curse-laden, fog-afflicted earth. He knows, it is a supreme treasure, or as the alchemist Petrus Bonus stated, "a gift of God."[351] So, once again, we encounter the paradox of the fragility of human life on

348 Ibid.
349 C.G. Jung, *Psychology and Alchemy*, CW 12, § 343.
350 *Monologue of December 1943.*
351 C.G. Jung, *Psychology and Alchemy*, CW 12, § 462.

the one hand, and its supreme, eternal value on the other. In Jung's first entry in the *Little Book of Monologues* to the young woman in the blossom country of the south, he seems to be saying that it is precisely here on this accursed earth that God's work wants to be accomplished.

Sol and Luna

Meanwhile, the *Little Book of Monologues* went back and forth between C.G. Jung and Hedy Wyss. In his second entry, dated January 1, 1944, Jung writes, "She, H.W., has dived in a little deep, to the point where ☉ and ☽ [Sol and Luna] are one and the same thing. That's going a bit too far." The circumstances that led to this remark are as follows.

Throughout the years of his correspondence with Hedy Wyss, Jung was deeply engaged in his studies on alchemy. In January 1943, he began intensive work on the first volume of the German edition of *Mysterium Coniunctionis.*[352] As the subtitle of his *opus magnum* suggests, he was struggling with the difficult problem of "... the Separation and Synthesis of Psychic Opposites in Alchemy." In these studies, he was particularly preoccupied with the symbolism of Sol and Luna. In a letter to Hedy Wyss of September 24, 1943, he writes that he had had to neglect everything because of this work which was difficult and emotionally draining. Jung casually adds that the subject of his examination is "the nature of the relationship men and women have to each other when one or the other says, 'I simply love you!'" He follows up with some blasphemies and the statement, "how bitter the water of wisdom [and death] tastes,"[353] a conclusion with which Hedy Wyss herself might well be familiar.

Hedy Wyss struggled with her love for C.G., her preferred form of address in her diary. It sometimes seems she was a little too identified with him and his work. For example, simply because *he* was working on the difficult problem of Sol and Luna, she believed this particular problem was also constellated for her. In her mind, this explained why the sun and moon were often the subject of her paintings. She once said to 'dear, dear C.G. Jung' in an apologetic manner that this was simply how things were: he

352 The German version of *Mysterium Coniunctionis* is edited in two volumes. The first volume contains chapters I to III.

353 Letter of September 24, 1943. See also Jung's chapter on Sal (III,5) and its bitterness, in: *Mysterium Coniunctionis*, CW 14, §§ 234 ff.

should see her thoughts on the moon as a reflection of his own light dazzling her.[354] It was only when she continued to speculate upon Sol and Luna that Jung responded with the above-mentioned entry of January 1, 1944 in the monologue booklet, saying that she had dived into the matter a little too deeply which, in view of her youthful age, was definitely too far.

The Epilogue

Jung's third and last entry in the *Little Book of Monologues*, the *Epilogue*, begins as follows, "In misty rain and slush. Amen. He sits in the tower, pondering death and life, partaking in Dionysos-Ariadne." Since Jung uses the mythological metaphor of Ariadne, Dionysos, and the Minotaur quite often in his letters, a chapter will be dedicated to it here.

Dionysos and Ariadne or the Apotheosis of an Earthly Woman

As Hedy Wyss reports in her manuscript, the whole story began when Jung once whispered in her ear in jest, "I am your labyrinth, Ariadne." This is a quote from a poem by Nietzsche, with the title "Ariadne's Lamentation," in which Dionysos responds to the bitter lament of the deeply shaken Ariadne: "Be clever, Ariadne ... Must one not first hate oneself, in order to love oneself? ... *I am your labyrinth.*"[355]

Jung mentions Dionysos and Ariadne for the first time in mid-January 1942. Prior to this letter, Hedy Wyss had written a long letter of complaint about her family, particularly her father (Ariadne's complaint!). Jung replied that they should see each other again face to face, and not merely ...

354 *Lohengrins Black Swan*, p. 131.

355 Jung quoted this poem several times in his work, for instance, in the Zarathustra Seminar of October 24, 1934. C.G. Jung, *Nietzsche's Zarathustra, Notes of the Seminar Given in 1934-1939*, ed. by James L. Jarrett, London: Routledge, 1989, vol. 1, p. 189. Here the quotation is in relation to Nietzsche's lamentation over the lost god. In his essay on "Wotan" (1936), Jung also mentioned Ariadne's lament, stating that like Ariadne, Nietzsche had fallen victim to the "God-hunter" (Wotan), "... Hunted by thee, O thought, / Unutterable! Veiled! horrible one! / Thou huntsman behind the clouds. / Struck down by thy lightning bolt ..." C.G. Jung, "Wotan," CW 10, § 381.

in the rather dark mirror of your letter. Dionysos could have said to the lamenting Ariadne, whom the Minotaur-conquering Theseus had deserted, "I am your band-aid" (instead of "labyrinth"), and it would have been true, for I am hellishly ill-suited to be an orphan's father. Since writing letters only creates labyrinthine squiggles of the soul that hopelessly entangle the Minotaur-slayer in an Ariadne-like clew, I will hereby bring my good intentions to an end.

Wishing you a happy and eventful New Year,
I remain,
Your ever-devoted,
C.G. Jung

Ariadne means the "utterly pure,"[356] which, according to Karl Kerényi, was originally an epithet of the Great Goddess. But in the legend of the Minotaur, the former Goddess descended into the world of humans. As the daughter of the Cretan king Minos, she became mortal. She fell in love with Theseus and by means of her famous thread, she helped him to escape from the labyrinthian netherworld of the Minotaur. Various tales tell of Ariadne's further destiny. It is said that Theseus took her with him after killing the Minotaur – his act of liberation, but that he later abandoned her on the island of Dia (Naxos) while she was sleeping. Dionysos found her on the shore and awakened her from deep sleep. Inflamed with love, he chose her, a mortal, as his bride. Other sources suggest Dionysos abducted her.

Accounts of Ariadne's death also vary. According to *Homer,* she was killed by Artemis when Theseus attempted to bring her to Athens, for Ariadne, as a mortal, would have violated the virgin goddess' divine sphere of power. *Hesiod* contradicts this in his *Theogony.* He, "correcting Homer, tells us of the mercy of Zeus, who granted Ariadne immortality and eternal youth." From him "she received the wreath that gleams in the heavens as the 'wreath of Ariadne,' the *corona borealis* [the Northern Crown]."[357] But all these tales around her death share one common idea: "For," as Kerényi puts it, "the entire ancient world, which had forgotten the original Cretan myth,

356 Karl Kerényi, *Dionysos. Archetypal Image of Indestructible Life*, tr. from the German by Ralph Manheim, Princeton: Princeton University Press, 1976, p. 99, about Ariadne see particularly pp. 89-125.

357 Ibid., p. 109. See Hesiod, *Theogony*, transl. with an introduction and notes by Martin L. West, Oxford: Oxford Press, 2008, 947-949, and Homer, *Odyssey*, Book 11, 321-325.

the marriage of Dionysos and Ariadne was the fulfillment and *apotheosis of an earthly woman*."[358]

A somewhat contrasting aspect of the Dionysos-Ariadne myth has its origin in the world of the Hellenistic mystery cults. This is important because the initiation rituals of these cults significantly influenced Jung's understanding of the analytic relationship and the individuation process. This seems to be confirmed by Karl Kerényi in his work on Dionysos, published posthumously. Here it says, "Just as Dionysos is the archetypal reality of *zoë*, so Ariadne is the archetypal reality of the bestowal of soul, of what makes a living creature an individual [individuation]."[359] In the mystery cult of Dionysos, Ariadne used her thread to lead the dancers through the labyrinth, while the dancers honored the "mistress of the labyrinth" with their cultic ritual dances that led them more deeply into the labyrinth, that is, into the realm of death, into the underworld or, in psychological terms, into the unconscious, and out of it again through an inner conversion of the initiate (metanoia). This reflects the death and renewal of the initiates into the mysteries of the underworld.

By seeing himself in the role of Dionysos and his analysand in the role of Ariadne, Jung reveals much about his understanding of psychic development within the analytic process: it is a religious initiation comparable to the ancient mysteries. This process leads one through the death of one's old, former person to the realization of what constitutes 'indestructible life,' that is, in psychological terms, to the realization of one's greater, eternal person – the self. The realization of the self brings about a considerable increase in consciousness. As Marie-Louise von Franz once put it in her book *On Dreams & Death*, this process involves

> [the transformation of the everyday ego] into an interiorized, spiritual consciousness. This is the "fruit" which is being preserved after the destruction of the body in death, the "one grain and corn."
> Accordingly, therefore, this "body" which survives death would, in psychological terms, be made up of everything from the collective unconscious which the individual had, in life, brought into consciousness. That which our everyday ego thinks, does, feels, etc. throughout the day escapes into the outer world and finally gets lost there. But when something meaningful, which can be recognized by means of a strong

358 K. Kerényi, *Dionysos*, p. 109 (emphasis AS).
359 Ibid., p. 124.

> emotion, breaks into our life, then there is a chance for us to make its archetypal (that is, spiritual) meaning conscious. In this way a piece of something eternal and infinite is realized in our earthly existence, and that means, in a literal sense, that it has become real.[360]

It is this aspect of indestructible life that Jung is inferring with his various references to Dionysos. In contrast, Ariadne's love embodies a feminine psychic energy that enables the individual – whether man or woman – to *realize* the eternal and indestructible (Dionysos) *in concrete life*. Such love, however, requires the arduous work of a lifetime.

"Moved by Ariadne's lament, even a god looked back," Jung writes in the *Little Book of Monologues*, and he wonders, "How should a mortal fare any better?"[361] How can he, a mortal, avoid becoming hopelessly entangled in the Ariadne-like threads of a loving woman? The archetypal background of the Dionysos and Ariadne metaphor is the sacred marriage. For Jung, this requires an attitude of the utmost humility. How could he possibly respond to her, a woman, without presuming some likeness to God? For this reason, he humbly asks Ariadne [Hedy Wyss]: "God grant that you may also understand the mere-human about me."[362] He himself is almost torn apart by the *complexio oppositorum,* between the archetypal background and that which is merely human. It is this problem of uniting the opposites that Jung wrestled with in the *Mysterium Coniunctionis* with all of his strength for so many years.

And Dionysos? The revival of the god of wine was crucial to Jung. In *Psychology and Alchemy*, he writes that the unconscious attempts "to restore the lost Dionysos who is somehow lacking in modern man (pace Nietzsche!) to the world of religion."[363] Jung, too, was concerned with the Dionysian elements of emotionality, ecstasy and rapture, all of which played a major role in the mystery cult of the god of wine. They continued to play a role in the medieval church carnival festivals before they were ultimately banned by ecclesiastical authorities.

Jung hoped to awaken a Dionysian zest for life in Hedy Wyss as well, which, he thought, might be more beneficial to her than complaining

360 Marie-Louise von Franz, *On Dreams & Death. A Jungian Interpretation*. Translated by Emmanuel Kennedy-Xipolitas and Vernon Brooks, Chicago and La Salle, Illinois: Open Court, 1998, pp. 118 f.

361 Monologue of December 1943.

362 Letter of March 26, 1943.

363 C.G. Jung, *Psychology and Alchemy*, CW 12, § 181.

about her family and her father. This is what he was getting at when he remarked, "Dionysos could have said to the lamenting Ariadne, whom the Minotaur-conquering Theseus had deserted, 'I am your band-aid' (instead of labyrinth), and it would have been true, for I am hellishly ill-suited to be an orphan's father."[364] He can give her comfort, but what he cannot and does not want to do is to replace her father, for he is "hellishly ill-suited to be an orphan's father." He also prefers direct encounters with Hedy Wyss, "since writing letters only creates labyrinthine squiggles of the soul"; all too easily the Minotaur Slayer becomes entangled in the Ariadne-like clew while reading the letters![365]

But the Dionysian element was not always short-changed. In *Lohengrin's Black Swan*, Hedy Wyss reports the following from the Eranos conference in 1941, to which Karl Kerényi also contributed:

> Jung's theme was the symbol of transformation in the Mass, whereby he also included the transformation in the ancient mystery cults. In the evening of the next day, Hedy Wyss observed Jung sitting in a circle of participants, radiant, with his glass full of red wine raised high, he who the day before had spoken in such a deep and moving way about the sacrifice of the Mass, about the elevation of the chalice – and now this Dionysian feast ... To be filled once with God, whoever this God may be, Christ, Dionysos ...
>
> Jung, as she remembers, called her 'Queen of the Night' back then. But she sadly adds: 'But ever and ever again, I feel as if I had lost my crown and had to wander around the country barefoot as a beggar girl.'[366]

This is Ariadne. This touching account and self-reflection on the part of Hedy Wyss show something of the spirit of Dionysus and Ariadne, of Jung's enthusiasm and joy, but also of her own sensitivity and sorrow. In one of his letters, Jung comments on this aspect of Hedy Wyss: "You are quite correct inside – much more correct than I find easy and like." And then, turning as it were to Ariadne, he adds, "But this inner correctness, though justified in God's eyes, stands in opposition to this diabolical world to which we are bound by our very existence as human beings. One needs to be both correct

364 Letter of January, 15, 1942.
365 Ibid.
366 *Lohengrin's Black Swan*, p. 44.

and not correct, which is why I am both correct and not correct with you. But let's not make things too difficult for each other."[367]

A Festival of Life and Death (Epilogue)

It is as if Jung had anticipated his own proximity to death in his last entry in the *Little Book of Monologues*, the Epilogue of January 12, 1944.

> In misty rain and slush. Amen. He sits in the tower, pondering death and life, participating in Dionysos-Ariadne. "But Hades and Dionysos are the same, to whom they rave in bacchic frenzy," Heraclitus.[368]

Jung sits in his tower, v/o [vulgo, i.e., commonly called] private nuthouse, probably freezing as always in the midst of a cold winter. He seems to vacillate between thoughts of death and of life. Exactly one month later, on February 11, 1944, he broke his foot on one of his daily walks. He was taken to hospital where, some ten days later, he suffered a very bad thrombosis of the heart, probably from lying in bed for such a long period. "Jung was at death's door and remained so for several weeks."[369] As Jung indicates in his Epilogue, he now experienced in all its brutality how Hades and Dionysos – death and indestructible life – are two sides of the same coin. But in these near-death experiences, he had unfathomably impressive visions of the mystical wedding – the *hierosgamos* – to which, because of the beauty of Jung's own description in his *Memoirs,* nothing can be added.[370]

While still recovering from his heart attack in Zurich Hirslanden Clinic, he writes to Hedy Wyss to thank her for her concern. Then, as if remembering Ariadne's lament, he adds that he must meditate daily on the words of St. Ambrose: *In patientia vestra habetis animas vestras* – through your patience,

367 Letter of September 19, 1943.

368 "For if it were not to Dionysos that they made a procession and sang the shameful phallic hymn, they would be acting most shamelessly. But Hades is the same as Dionysos in whose honor they go mad and rave." *The Fragments of the Work of Heraclitus of Ephesus on Nature*, translated by John Burnet, 1920, Fragment 15, wikisource.org > Fragments of Heraclitus.

369 B. Hannah, *Jung. His Life and Work*, p. 277.

370 C.G. Jung, *Memories, Dreams, Reflections*, Chapter X, "Visions," pp. 289 ff.

your souls prove themselves.[371] It has always been the goal of the mystery cults, including the Dionysian mysteries, to remember the soul that has sunk into oblivion.

The symbolism of the mythological image of Dionysos and Ariadne and the dynamics contained therein aptly reflect important aspects of the analytic relationship. Only two years later, in his discussion of the alchemical series of images in the *Rosarium philosophorum* in "The Psychology of the Transference," Jung once more focusses on the mystery behind this relationship. He published this paper in 1946 and dedicated it to his wife, Emma Maria Jung-Rauschenbach. He is aware of the ultimately insurmountable difficulties of this undertaking, which is why he expressly underlines in the preface that his investigation is provisional.

Coniunctio Solis et Lunae

Towards the end of the second chapter of Jung's commentary on the *Rosarium*, entitled "King and Queen," we hear of two aspects of individuation which are different in principal and yet necessarily related to each other. Firstly, individuation "is an internal and subjective process of integration, and secondly, it is an equally indispensable process of *objective* relationship," for the soul "can live only in and from human relationships." By the latter, Jung understands "the conscious acknowledgment and acceptance of our fellowship with those around us [without whom] there can be no synthesis of personality."[372] The subjective aspect, on the other hand, requires an unceasing effort on the part of the individual to understand the world of the unconscious, i.e., the archetypal factors that largely shape one's life, as much as possible. Jung repeatedly urged Hedy Wyss to focus on both aspects, on the conscious relationship to the other person as well as on the struggle to understand the images rising from the unconscious.

Only conscious understanding is able to create the inner consolidation of the individual, that provides protection from the devastating psychic consequences of mass-mindedness.[373] But the more the unconscious reveals its

371 Letter of May 12, 1944. The same quote is also in two other letters, of September 24, 1943, and July 19, 1944. The quote refers back to Luke 21:19, which the Vulgate translates: "In patientia vestra possidebitis animas vestras" – "by your endurance you will gain your life."

372 C.G. Jung, "The Psychology of the Transference," CW 16, §§ 448 and 444.

373 Ibid.

treasures, and the greater the increase in psychic knowledge, the more real is the danger of a false spirituality and serenity growing. This in turn can lead to the neglect of secular and daily obligations.

The other danger – and this also holds true for "the bond established by the transference" – is to drag the objective relationship down to a primitive level. This includes all those voices that say, 'it's nothing but,' 'it's just a professional relationship,' 'it's only an illusion,' and the like. This destroys the numinous aspect of any objective relationship. "Between this Scylla and that Charybdis there is a narrow passage, and both medieval Christian mysticism and alchemy have contributed much to its discovery."[374] Then follows Jung's profound concluding comment on the *coniunctio Solis et Lunae*. Perhaps when he referred to the psychotherapist's struggle "with difficult transference problems," Jung may also have had in mind his experiences with Hedy Wyss.

> Looked at in this light, the bond established by the transference – however hard to bear and however incomprehensible it may seem – is vitally important not only for the individual but also for society, and indeed for the moral and spiritual progress of mankind. So, when the psychotherapist has to struggle with difficult transference problems, he can at least take comfort in these reflections. He is not just working for this particular patient, but for himself as well and his own soul, and in so doing he is perhaps laying an infinitesimal grain on the scales of humanity's soul. Small and invisible as this contribution may be, it is yet an *opus magnum*, for it is accomplished in a sphere *but lately visited by the numen*, where the whole weight of mankind's problem has settled. The ultimate questions of psychotherapy are not a private matter – they represent a supreme responsibility.[375]

For the alchemists, that sphere "lately visited by the numen" was, for centuries, the deep mystery that they described as *coniunctio Solis et Lunae*, the union of sun and moon, of man and woman, of one human being to another. It is impossible to say how much they projected their experience into matter, or, like Gerhard Dorn, anticipated, or even recognized, it as an inner-psychic process. But one thing seems to be clear, namely that the mystery of the

374 Ibid., CW 16, § 448.
375 Ibid., CW 16, § 449 (emphasis AS).

union of the opposites is exceedingly constellated in the unconscious of women and men today, and, accordingly, it wants to be heeded.

Image 16: The Bollingen Stone (Plate XII)

14. Reborn to the World – The Time After 1944

After his heart attack at the beginning of 1944, Jung spent weeks in a state of perpetual bliss, but only at night; during the day he was mostly depressed. Looking back at the end of his life, he shied away from using the word "eternal" to describe this experience, and yet it was, as he recounts in his *Memoirs*, "the ecstasy of a non-temporal state." "This is eternal bliss," he thought. "This cannot be described; it is far too wonderful!" A magical atmosphere, accompanied by inexpressibly beautiful visions of the *hierosgamos* and other images, surrounded his sickbed and the room was filled with the purest bliss.[376]

Jung's realization of these visionary images having an 'absolute objectivity' brought a caesura into his life. It took him almost a year to recover from the heart attack. The visions of the sacred or mystical marriage that he experienced at the time of his illness remained with him for the rest of his life. It was probably the inner vigor of these images from the unconscious that enabled him to commit himself to his creative daemon in a new and open way. Thus, he reports in *Memories, Dreams, Reflections*:

> After the illness a fruitful period of work began for me. A good many of my principal works were written only then. The insight I had had, or the vision of the end of all things, gave me the courage to undertake new formulations. I no longer attempted to put across my own opinion, but surrendered myself to the current of my thoughts. Thus one problem after the other revealed itself to me and took shape.[377]

Looking back upon the days and weeks after his heart attack when he was still deeply submerged in the depths of the unconscious, Jung "told Marie-Louise von Franz that he first reexperienced his body as *that of a big fish.* This was such a realistic experience that for some time, whenever he was fed with spoonfuls of soup, he felt anxious about whether it would not flow out again at his gills!"[378] The image of the fish is reminiscent of the Indian myth of

376 C.G. Jung, *Memories, Dreams, Reflections*, pp. 293-296.
377 Ibid., p. 297.
378 B. Hannah, *Jung. His Life and Work*, p. 284.

Vishnu who, in the form of a fish, brought up the ancient scriptures of the Vedas from the depths of the sea, where a demon had carried them during an enormous flood. Jung mentions this myth earlier, in *Symbols of Transformation*, as if he had anticipated by decades the vision he later experienced during his heart attack. "If the libido manages to tear itself loose and force its way up again," he writes, "something like a miracle happens: the journey to the underworld was a plunge into the fountain of youth, and the libido, apparently dead, wakes to renewed fruitfulness."[379] This "fertilization" by the creative spirit of the unconscious engendered in Jung a newfound trust in his stream of thoughts and fantasies. Like a fish in water, he allows himself to drift, and brings up to the light of consciousness the insights and wisdom gleaned from the dark, watery depths.

Initially, Jung blamed himself for his broken foot and subsequent heart attack. He thought 'that there was something wrong with his attitude and that he was to some extent responsible for the mishap.'[380] But gradually, he began to realize that he was *not* responsible. He later added the insight, not always easy to realize, that one must accept life as it is, without personal objections.

> ... when one follows the path of individuation, when one lives one's own life, one must take mistakes into the bargain; life would be incomplete without them. There is no guarantee – not for a single moment – that we will not fall into error or stumble into deadly peril. We may think there is a sure road. But that would be the road of death ... Anyone who takes the sure road is as good as dead.[381]

It took Jung almost a whole year to recover from his heart attack of February 1944. The letters of this year to Hedy Wyss are correspondingly short. As Barbara Hannah recounts in her biography of Jung, he did not resume his work on alchemy until the spring of 1945. "He worked on *Mysterium Coniunctionis* with great enthusiasm, but was not strong enough to do more than two hours a day at the most."[382] Mentally, however, he was completely immersed in his work. In January, 1945 he wrote to Hedy Wyss, "Very

379 C.G. Jung, *Symbols of Transformation*, CW 5, § 449 (first published in 1912; extensively revised in 1952).
380 C.G. Jung, *Memories, Dreams, Reflections*, p. 297.
381 Ibid.
382 B. Hannah, *Jung. His Life and Work*, p. 284.

slowly, I am feeling a little better ... I am caught in the snares of Rex, which I am trying to untangle, going from one entanglement to another ... *o beata confusio – o confusa beatitudo* [o happy confusion – o confusing happiness]! That's pretty much how I feel."[383]

While he was determined to bring *Mysterium Coniunctionis* to its conclusion, an almost endless series of new problems and unsolved questions arose from his studies of these ancient, fascinating alchemical texts. As a result – even before the publication of the second volume of the German edition (Chapters IV to VI) – a whole wealth of further works came about, some of which he originally planned to integrate into his *opus magnum*. Only the most important ones will be mentioned here: 1944 "Psychology and Alchemy"; 1946 "The Psychology of the Transference"; 1946/1947 "On the Nature of the Psyche"; 1951 *Aion. Researches into the Phenomenology of the Self*; 1952 "Synchronicity: An Acausal Connecting Principle," and 1952 "Answer to Job." Only after writing all of these preliminary (!) works could he conclude *Mysterium Coniunctionis* with chapter VI, "The Conjunction." Jung's letters to the young artist are permeated with his wrestlings with the secret of the union of opposites and thus with the numen of human relationship in general, or, to put it in alchemical terms, his strivings toward the *hierosgamos*. Forming the background to all of this was Jung's deep concern that *this* work – the work of achieving a love that 'does not insist on its own way' may – succeed.

But back to those first years of convalescence. Like a bolt out of the blue and in the midst of his studies on alchemy, Jung had a further heart attack in November 1946. Once again, he hovered over death's abyss, and it took him several months to find his way back to his creativity. He told Barbara Hannah, "that he had an illness because he was faced with the mysterious problem of the *hierosgamos* (the *mysterium coniunctionis*).[384] Some insights can lead one if not actually into death, then up to its very door.

All this had a lasting impact on his relationship with Hedy Wyss. Jung's letters became shorter and less frequent. Their tone was no longer as familiar or intimate. For instance, a certain feeling of estrangement is reflected in the formal salutation of the September 1, 1944 letter which, as Hedy Wyss notes indignantly, he had not used for seven years: "My Dear *Miss* Wyss!" In this letter he confirms to her that he had, indeed, been silent, because all talk was

383 Letter of January 2, 1945. The "snares of Rex" refer to chapter IV, "Rex and Regina," of *Mysterium Coniunctionis*, CW 14, on which he was working at the time.
384 B. Hannah, *Jung. His Life and Work*, p. 294.

now burdensome to him and he felt he had talked too much in the first place. Then he continues, "I do not like the image of myself that you mirror back at me (unintentionally!), which I do not impute to you at all, but to myself."[385] Jung is referring to a dream Hedy Wyss had had in which he meets her 'tenderly – all too tenderly.'[386] That he takes the blame upon himself fails to reassure Hedy Wyss. Indeed, it has the opposite effect: she feels greatly distressed and suffers from his withdrawal: 'Silence, silence, silence ...'

Finally, as she makes a note of in *Lohengrin's Black Swan,* she finds consolation in some of his 'great-grandfather's' verses, namely, in a love poem Goethe wrote for Frau von Stein.[387] Nevertheless, she remains tormented by her boundless longing, aggrieved that he is no longer available to her as he used to be. After his illness, Jung had to reduce his analytical work to a minimum, and, as with his other analysands, he could see Hedy Wyss only on rare occasions. She, on the other hand, writes him a letter, among many others, the length of which frightens him and feels to Jung like "a too heavy a task." With some agitation, he suggests she write 'a proper letter (two kilometres long, if she likes) to the art commission, or whatever that animal with the many heads and the brains of a lizard is called. That is where her desire to write ought to run riot.'[388] The actual background of this remark is the rejection Hedy Wyss suffered when she submitted her art for an exhibition in Lausanne only to have it sent back to her without comment.

Jung appreciated her work as a painter. In response to Hedy Wyss' remarks concerning an exhibition of contemporary art in Basel, he said: "Instead of painting from eternity, these devils paint from our time; and instead of painting from the soul, they paint from the world ... Your pictures – namely those of Hedy Wyss – seem to me to be on the right track, so that I am personally irritated by the bungling of the art commission."[389] While Jung's anger may well have been aimed at the assessment her works had received, it may also have been aimed at certain trends in twentieth-century art as a whole.

385 Letter of September 1, 1944.

386 *Lohengrin's Black Swan*, p. 152a.

387 Charlotte von Stein. Ibid., p. 153. J.W. v. Goethe, „Aus den Briefen an Frau v. Stein," [From the Letters to Frau von Stein], *Werke*, München: C.H. Beck, [15]1994, vol. 1, p. 127. No English translation available.

388 Letter undated, probably October 13, 1944. The art commission that rejected her paintings.

389 Letter of October 31, 1944.

A Rose Nailed to the Cross

This was a difficult time for both Jung and Hedy Wyss, though for different reasons. Jung's heart condition required the greatest care. Being completely preoccupied with 'his ancient, fascinating texts,' he remained silent. Although Jung was now forced to take life at a slower pace, he was still urged from within to press on with his research, despite his frail body. "The world seems clouded, and it is only in the world of thought that the sun shines. My heart attack has really knocked the stuffing out of me, and it seems to me that the strength I still have must be used to express everything that comes into consciousness."[390]

Hedy Wyss, for her part, continued to wrestle with love. She is tossed to and fro by loneliness and ever renewed longing. In one of her rare encounters with Jung at that time, the symbol of the cross was mentioned on several occasions. Consequently, she painted a yellow rose nailed to the cross. Behind it was a red sea, for which, as she points out, she needed to use a lot of red paint in order to reinforce the impression of the cross with its rose. Her love is nailed to the cross. Or, to put it more cautiously, a shining aspect of love (the yellow rose) has been crucified. Because every love also has its darker aspects, perhaps she needed to sacrifice her sometimes too sunny feelings. But as the crucifixion and the blood-red sea suggest, such a sacrifice involves deep suffering. Beyond this suffering, however, lay the eternal and otherworldly aspect of the *mysterium coniunctionis,* the mystery that had preoccupied Jung for years. The extent to which Hedy Wyss succeeded in realizing this eternal and otherworldly aspect we do not know. She lived to be over 103 years old, outliving Jung by almost fifty years. We learn nothing about this in *Lohengrin's Black Swan* since the account breaks off in 1950, at the time she met her future husband.

But returning for the moment to the difficult time after Jung's illness, Hedy Wyss still experienced her old feelings of love for Jung in some of her encounters with him. Lyrically, she wrote: 'It is as if I were listening to a Haydn symphony which I have known for a long time, but which still grips me anew, as if I had never heard it before.' More than ever before, however, she now saw Jung as an old man, marked by age and death, as he himself had once said to her. His frailty pained her. Her previous confidence waned, and

390 Letter undated, probably October 13, 1944.

now she began to wonder whether love really was stronger than death (Song of Solomon 8:6).[391]

Despite their mutual best intentions, their increasingly irreconcilable differences could no longer be overlooked. This became especially clear in what Jung called the "fig-leaf problem." Returning to the theme of bourgeois morality, an ultimately insurmountable gulf opened up between them. It was Jung's critical remark, as recorded in Hedy Wyss' manuscript, about the 'flagrant openness and boldness of certain representations' in her painting that triggered their discussion on this topic.[392]

Adopting a Religious Attitude Toward Nature and the "Fig-Leaf Problem"

Jung's letter to Hedy Wyss from Küsnacht on February 1, 1945 is short, so short, in fact, that one could almost overlook its profundity. As it shows perhaps more than any other text Jung's profound awe of nature, it is reproduced here in its entirety.

> Küsnacht-Zürich 1 Febr. 1945
>
> Dear Hedy Wyss!
>
> Your letter comes as a reminder for me to apologize for laying the fig-leaf problem on the table yet again. I know that you know, and that your ethos compels you to give voice to nature. But what if nature is by nature taboo? Must not nature then also be kept secret? You know that it is not out of sheer prudishness that I do not believe in taboos where there are none. Giving full expression to nature is a constant violation of nature. Nature is an ἄρρητον [not to be spoken of]. Speaking about it unleashes its demonic aspect, and this harms the one who is giving voice to it. Nature wants to be, but not to be spoken of, named, designated, pointed to. This has the same effect on her as the evil eye: it annihilates her, and she will take its revenge. Don't look at her so directly; don't talk about her so straightforwardly, for otherwise it will seem as if you were not afraid of nature at all, and could easily conquer her by word or by gesture! In doing this, you are harming yourself by attracting daemons. I want to teach you a wholesome δεισιδαιμονία (fear of God), not some fig-leaf hypocrisy.

391 *Lohengrin's Black Swan*, p. 157 f.
392 Ibid., p. 159.

The reckless manner in which you speak about nature is forcing her to distance herself from you.
With best greetings,
From your incorrigible,
C.G. Jung

Jung had not been back to Bollingen since his illness. He still felt too weak to leave his house. However, fourteen months after his accident, at Easter, 1945, he returned to the tower, although only for a short time. When Barbara Hannah asked him after he had returned how it was, he said quite surprisingly, "It was pure hell."[393] Debilitated by his illness, Jung was forced to accept that he no longer had the strength to carry out the work that Bollingen required. This was a bitter realization for him. Perhaps it was this experience of his own frailty which prompted him to make the tremendously far-reaching statements in his letter on the need for adopting a deeply religious attitude toward nature.

Jung began by underscoring the demonic and gloomy aspects of nature which stand in dire contrast to the often astonishingly light-hearted approach of his analysand toward the inscrutable nature of the unconscious. But that is only one, and perhaps not the most important, aspect. Perhaps we need to understand Jung's remarks on the demonic aspect of nature in the light of the painful ambivalence and conflict he felt when he was confronted with his physical weakness and frailty on the one hand, and his experience of the immeasurably beautiful and delightful visions of the *hierosgamos* on the other. Both are a part of nature contained within what appear to be the diametrically opposed opposites of life and death.

Preceded by an apology for "laying the fig-leaf problem on the table yet again," Jung is prompted to ask in his letter what the 'right' or appropriate attitude towards nature might be. He knows that Hedy Wyss feels compelled from within to give voice to nature in her painting, but in view of the aforementioned boldness of certain representations, he continues, "But what if nature is *by nature* taboo? Must not nature then also be kept secret?" Jung's reference to the "fig-leaf problem" perhaps suggests that he was primarily concerned with her erotic depictions. But it is also possible that her rather liberal use of mythological motifs could have played a role in his critical

393 B. Hannah, *Jung. His Life and Work*, p. 285.

objection. In any case, he assures her that his objections are not based upon prudishness.

Image 17: Mutus Liber, The Mute Book, p. 8

And now follow the two sentences that are not only a warning to Hedy Wyss, but also reflect Jung's deep concern about the extraverted zeitgeist in general: "Giving full expression to nature is a constant violation of nature. Nature is an ἄρρητον [not to be spoken of]." Saying this out loud, he continues, unleashes its demonic aspect and harms the one who is giving voice to it. The Greek word Jung employs, ἄρρητον or ἀπόρρητον, has been used in the world of mystery religions since Herodotus (5th century B.C.) and refers to an ineffable divine mystery that the initiate encounters during the incubation ritual. Through this encounter with the deity, the initiate is transformed and becomes a 'new' person.[394] The secret of this renewal must be neither revealed nor spoken of.

Image 18: Mutus Liber, The Mute Book, p. 14.

Similarly, nature's secret must be preserved. If we do not pay her the necessary respect, if we interfere too much with her secrets, she will take her revenge. To an increasingly threatening extent, this is also true of the almost entirely extraverted approach of today's sciences to 'nature,' in which, with few exceptions, the religious or numinous – ultimately psychic – aspect of nature barely plays a role any longer. The use of single quotation marks around 'nature' is meant to indicate that our modern concept of nature as a quantitatively measurable factor reflects only a tiny fraction of what was once called creation, cosmos, universe, and the like. Today's prevailing statistical thinking is doing progressive damage to the soul and spirit of

394 I owe this reference to Laura Gemelli Marciano.

nature, which once hovered over the waters of the unconscious, yearning for creation.[395]

The way the alchemists dealt with nature was quite different. Their art was always a *secret lore*, not only because by doing their research they may have exposed themselves to the accusation of heresy, but also, and above all, because they were not permitted to expose the true content of their work. Two illustrations from the *Mutus Liber* (*Mute Book*) from the 17th century depict their art as a mystery.[396] In image 17, we see the alchemist and his *soror mystica*. Both figures are focused on the process of transformation in the alchemical furnace. While the man kneels in front of the *vas hermeticum*, as if absorbed in prayer, the woman points with her right hand to the transcendent mystery of the union of Sol and Luna in the philosophical vessel. The boy in the winged cap who imparts this secret is Mercurius in the form of the *puer aeternus*. The divine child embodies the new God-image.

In the lower left-hand corner of image 18, the figure is making a gesture for silence. Both the alchemist and the *soror mystica* are pictured with the fingers of their *left* hand placed on their lips while their *right* hand points upward to the transcendent mystery of the alchemical transformation. Clearly, this process of transformation also has a sinister (left hand) aspect that must be kept silent. Nature becomes unleashed when spoken of in a too naïve a manner, as Jung explained. In order to protect themselves from danger, the inscription between the alchemists recommends: *Ora lege lege relege labora et invenies* – pray, read, read, and reread, work, and you will find. We can realize the veracity of this legend by reading Jung's letters to Hedy Wyss and his works on alchemy. The more we read and reread these texts, the more we will understand. Similarly, the more we persist, the more we will be rewarded with the discovery of a gem which cannot be sought with intent or purpose, but rather is revealed unwittingly. It is common for us to say that *we* have realized something when, in truth, any insight comes to us from the inexhaustible sources of the collective unconscious; it happens *to* us, like receiving a precious gift.

From a psychological point of view, the ultimately ineffable, alchemical mystery of nature corresponds to the *objective-psychic* – to the archetypal

395 "The earth was without form and void, and darkness was over the face of the deep. And the Spirit of God was hovering over the face of the waters." Genesis 1:2.

396 *Mutus Liber – Alchemy and its Mute Book*. Reproduction of the first edition by La Rochelle 1677. Introduction and commentary by Eugène Canseliet, ed. by Moreh Derekh, translated by T. Bruemmer, Utrecht: Inner Garden Press, 2015.

– images of the unconscious, which operate outside of one's state of consciousness. When Jung speaks of this psychic realm, he does so with great respect and awe, for it is beyond any subjective arbitrariness. Every step toward consciousness, no matter how small, exacts its price. It is an *opus contra naturam*, as Jung stated in his introduction to *Psychology and Alchemy*:

> The essence of the conscious mind is discrimination; it must, if it is to be aware of things, separate the opposites, and it does this contra naturam. In nature, the opposites seek one another – les extrêmes se touchent – and so it is in the unconscious, and particularly in the archetype of unity, the self. Here, as in the deity, the opposites cancel out. But as soon as the unconscious begins to manifest itself, they split asunder, as at the Creation; for every act of dawning consciousness is a creative act ..."[397]

By calling it the "fig-leaf problem," Jung alludes to the expulsion of Adam and Eve from the Garden of Eden, and thus, to an *act of creation*. "Then the eyes of both were opened, and they knew that they were naked. And they sewed fig leaves together and made themselves loincloths." The serpent's prophesy was accurate: "For God knows that when you eat of it your eyes will be opened, and you will be like God, knowing good and evil." The knowledge they gained, however, exacted a high price, for now they *feared* God. (Genesis 3, 5-7.10)

Only now do they recognize this dark and demonic force as being the *other side* of the deity. By becoming separate and by being able to discriminate, they are now confronted with their nakedness, with the abysmal vulnerability of human *and* divine nature. Nature should not be approached carelessly, or, as Jung puts it in his letter to Hedy Wyss "[one must not] look at it so directly; [one must not] talk about her so straightforwardly, for otherwise it will seem as if you were not afraid of nature at all, and could easily conquer her by word or by gesture!" By being too nonchalant, one pushes nature (and thus also the objective-psychic) away from oneself. Jung wanted to instill in his analysand a wholesome fear of God, which he asks her not to misunderstand as fig-leaf hypocrisy.[398]

397 C.G. Jung, *Psychology and Alchemy*, CW 12, § 30.

398 Letter of February 1, 1945. Jung uses the Greek work δεισιδαιμονία which can mean both fear of daemons or fear of the gods.

Alienation

The manner in which Hedy Wyss reacted to Jung's commentary on the "fig-leaf problem" strongly reinforced their presumably inescapable alienation from each other. At a loss to understand Jung's letter, Hedy Wyss could 'only sway her head back and forth.' In *Lohengrin's Black Swan*, she declared that Jung had not got the point at all! In her view, she could no more be afraid of nature than she could be afraid of God. The malicious nature of people may frighten her, but not nature! She held the view that her love was right, in the same way that nature was right![399] Here we see the collision of two irreconcilable views on the nature of the divine, of love, of nature itself, and of the unconscious.

Hedy Wyss' reaction to Jung's objections opened up an ultimately unbridgeable gap. Their standpoints were simply too different. Perhaps this is the downside of any deeper relationship. Jung expressed it somewhat more dramatically two years earlier when speaking of "that ink into which life always leads."[400] Jung's letter about the "fig-leaf problem" and how to deal with nature coincided with the arrival of a man in Hedy Wyss' life who claimed all her attention and love. Her relationship with this man threw her 'into an overjoyed vortex of emotions, full of love and tenderness, a love, that was *allowed to be lived*'; into an 'amorous adventure and love's bliss that evoked a wonderful spring.' He was a married man and it was clear from the outset that he would return to his homeland after the war. Even though it was only a brief episode in her life, it was, as she said, 'one of the happiest.'[401]

When Jung addressed the problem of needing to fear God or demons in his letter, he was in the dark about his analysand's new love, which makes it all the more remarkable that he focused on the "fig-leaf problem" at that very moment Hedy Wyss was embarking upon this new relationship. As no one outside of a relationship has any legitimate basis to pass judgment on it, our focus is not upon whether her relationship to this man was right or wrong,

399 *Lohengrin's Black Swan*, p. 160.

400 Letter of April 16, 1943. On the "ink into which life always leads," see the following passage in C.G. Jung, *Mysterium Coniunctionis*, CW 14, § 609: "By the sin of Eve, she [the black Shulamite] is plunged, as it were, in ink, in the 'tincture,' and blackened ..." Referring to the treatise of Abraham Eleazar, Jung elucidates why the blackness of the Shulamite "seems to be rather more than a veneer, for it will not come off; it is merely compensated by her inner illumination and by the beauty of the bridegroom." Both sides belong to wholeness, and that is what Jung is aiming at with his warning.

401 *Lohengrin's Black Swan*, pp. 159 f.

moral or immoral. Without knowing the dreams of the lovers, how could one possibly know? Rather than being based on any moral judgment, Jung's intervention had its roots in his concern for her. Indeed, only a few months later, according to Hedy Wyss' account in *Lohengrin's Black Swan*, Jung guided her through her anguished farewell 'intelligently and helpfully,' to use her own words.

Far more than any of her relationships, Jung cared about how careless and unconscious his analysand was toward nature and God. His own approach to the unconscious and his own way of honoring nature comes from the archaic layers of the psyche. The archaic soul instinctively "knows" about the spirits and demons that lurk everywhere. Without this "knowledge," we would be blindly at their mercy. From the standpoint of psychology, the menace does not come merely from the spirits and demons that lurk externally in nature, but also and especially from those that threaten us *from within* –from our own demonic aspect. The more we neglect this aspect, i.e., the more we play down the demonic dark side of the psyche, the more we are at the mercy of the unconscious and our external environment. That is why it is so important to be aware of our own shadow and darkness.

In a lecture on the *Goose Girl* given at the Zurich Psychology Club in 1970, Marie-Louise von Franz stated, "[If] one knows one's own evil and darkness ... [then] the devil within, so to speak, warns you of the devil in other people. For of course, the devil smells the devil."[402] In other words, the more we know about the demonic both within and outside of ourselves, the more we perceive it, the better we can protect ourselves from it. Those who know the devil within can smell him when he sneaks up on them. One is warned before the devil attacks! It is also equally true, however, that we have to walk into his trap again and again, because he is also "part of that force which would do ever evil, and does ever good."[403]

From the moment they met, Jung encouraged Hedy Wyss to risk the experiment, the experiment of life. This requires, as we have seen, the ability to accept error and even one's own devils. A life without mistakes and errors would be inhuman. Honest love would certainly find no place in such a life. For it is the human, the all too human, aspects of life which bring us closer to one another – our smaller and larger shortcomings, our embarrassments and mistakes. There is no deep love without the fear of demons. We must

402 M.-L. von Franz, "The Goose Girl," in: A. Schweizer and R. Schweizer-Vüllers (eds.), *Stone by Stone*, p. 75.

403 J.W. von Goethe, *Faust. A Tragedy*, verses 1335 f.

therefore accept the demonic aspects of love and endure them, without giving up on love. To my mind, the deep secret behind our fear of daemons (δεισιδαιμονία) is that we hold on to love even in the knowledge of their presence.

The Objectivity of Love Beyond Emotional Ties

Jung's intense involvement with the unconscious, his wrestling with his dreams and active imaginations, in the years he spent working on *The Red Book* not only made his scientific work possible, but also significantly changed him, shaping his relationships with his fellow human beings and putting them in a different, a new, light. Those who have experienced the objectivity of the soul and the unconscious in such a profound way, who have accepted as far as they could the contents flowing from the unconscious, and who have experienced the reality of the other side, know this secret of an objective cognition, manner of relationship, and love.

At this point, it would be pertinent to mention once more Jung's letter of March 26, 1943, in which he so movingly speaks about love. "This has been the pain and sorrow of an entire life," he writes, "after realizing early on how women are able to love me, and then, how the Goddess herself descends into them and conjures up an ineffable springtime." And why? "Because I am not a brutal, but a shy and fleeting animal myself, in the grips of the God who cherishes all living things ... The deity is too big, and I am too small" to respond adequately to love. He can see the splendor of the eternal Deity in women – including Hedy Wyss –, and he knows that it is a God who spreads splendor around him. Marked now by this God, he is no more than a "friendly beast in the forest of this world ... Both God and animal come together in humankind, evoking suffering and beauty, and never the one without the other."[404] This *mysterium coniunctionis*, this great mystery, which Jung was gripped by for so many years and which took him to the very limits of his strength, is, indeed, very difficult to fathom.

In the chapter about the visions he had when he came close to dying after his heart attack in 1944, Jung writes about the objectivity of love, describing it as a mystery, a secret that can never be fully disclosed, and perhaps can only be approached upon the threshold of death. In this vein, he recounts a dream

404 Letter of March 26, 1943.

that he had after the death of his wife in which he saw her "in her prime ... Her expression was neither joyful nor sad, but, rather, objectively wise and understanding, without the slightest emotional reaction ..." This image, he states, contained all the years of marriage, including the end of her life. It is the image of a completed wholeness. And then he continues,

> The objectivity which I experienced in this dream and in the visions is part of a completed individuation. It signifies detachment from valuations and from what we call emotional ties. In general, emotional ties are very important to human beings. But they still contain projections, and it is essential to withdraw these projections in order to attain oneself and objectivity. Emotional relationships are relationships of desire, tainted by coercion and constraint; something is expected from the other person, and that makes him and ourselves unfree. Objective cognition lies hidden behind the attraction of the emotional relationship; it seems to be the eternal secret. Only through objective cognition is the real coniunctio possible.[405]

Objective cognition does not exclude feeling, as if it were unimportant. On the contrary, Jung explains in the *Protocols*,[406] feeling is eminently important because it involves us in relationships, and at the end of every relationship there is a projection that must be withdrawn. Only in this way, only in an honest relationship with a fellow human being, is it possible to know oneself. Only through this relationship do we gain the freedom of objective recognition.

It seems that this objectivity, be it in relationship to oneself, or to others, shines through again and again in the thousands and thousands of letters that Jung wrote over his lifetime. A meaningful example of this is seen in the aforementioned letter about love to Hedy Wyss. It is the earnestness with which Jung addresses people that is so striking. The two volumes of the previously published *Letters*, as well as his letters to Hedy Wyss, published here for the first time, are a treasure trove of his psychological contributions. That Jung always addresses the *individual* person, not from the distance, as if he were holding a lecture, but in a more personal way that includes himself, and often in an astonishingly self-critical manner, makes these letters so precious. What distinguishes him from the preacher or scholar is that he

405 C.G. Jung, *Memories, Dreams, Reflections*, pp. 296 f.
406 *Protocols*, pp. 180 f.

is aware of his own shadow and does not conceal or cover it up with polite words. This manner of his sometimes puts more sensitive natures, including Hedy Wyss' own nature, to the test. On rare occasions, he would raise his thunderous voice, but only when he felt criticized in an unjust, stupid, or too unconscious a manner.

15. Surrounded by Death – Jung's Last Letters to Hedy Wyss

The later letters, in the years following Jung's heart attack in late 1946, no longer seem to have the same quality of relatedness toward the addressee. Jung now needed all his strength to complete his major work, *Mysterium Coniunctionis*. In a letter dated September 12, 1954, in response to Hedy Wyss' complaints about her husband, Jung replied that he could not and would not respond to such laments any longer. For more than fifty years he had patiently listened to the wailing of the world. But now, if he were to have time to "contemplate [his] own shadow and its blackness," he needed to leave many people to their misfortune. He needed to protect himself, for it had been irrevocably confirmed that he had not been born the Redeemer, which would have been detrimental to his health. Furthermore, he added, while she was enjoying sunshine in Mallorca, "we have rain clouds and cold winds, pregnant with rheumatism." In short, "everyone has enough to do with their own devils and does not want to be annoyed by those of others to boot."[407] Jung does not beat around the bush.

Two Memorial Stones

Jung's last two letters to Hedy Wyss were written in 1956. In them, he adopted a more conciliatory tone. In many respects, they are farewell letters in which Jung talks about death and the dead. Between 1953 and 1956, Jung had suffered two heavy losses, and he himself had been brought to the brink of death. Toni Wolff died in March, 1953, and his wife Emma Maria Jung-Rauschenbach passed away in November, 1955.[408] Jung told Hedy Wyss that it had been particularly difficult for him to recover from his wife's death. The German version of his final book, *Mysterium Coniunctionis*, vol. 2 [chapters IV to VI], had just been published, or, as he put it, "is presently being wrapped in its first diapers."[409] Any concentrated mental effort now

407 Letter of September 12, 1954.

408 Letters of February 13, 1956 and October 31, 1956. Toni Wolff died on March 21, 1953 at the age of 64; Emma Jung-Rauschenbach on November 27, 1955 at the age of 73.

409 Letter of February 13, 1956.

tired him beyond measure, and his only endeavor was to rest and to find time for resting.[410] He now turned his attention to the deceased, to making memorial stones in their honor: a tombstone in the style of an ancient Greek temple for his wife; a stone slab with a ginkgo branch and a Chinese inscription for Toni Wolff; and a lengthy Latin inscription in stone at his tower for his ancestors. In a dream, Jung learned that these were "the paving stones on the way to the dark gate."[411]

Image 19: C.G. Jung, Memorial for Toni Wolff, 1956, front (Plate XIII)

410 Letter of October 1, 1956.
411 Ibid.

Image 20: C.G. Jung, Memorial for Toni Wolff, reverse (Plate XIV)

Toni Wolff

The five Chinese characters that Jung chiselled into the stone in remembrance of Toni Wolff are said to have the following meaning: To – ni – wolf – nun – mystery, which is usually translated as "Toni Wolff, *soror mystica*."[412] Next to it, however, is a branch of a ginkgo tree, a leaf falling to the ground, and a small old man who contemplates the falling leaf "in modest harmony with nature," as Jung writes to Hedy Wyss.[413] Jung placed the memorial stone under a ginkgo tree in his garden in Küsnacht, from where it was removed after his death. If we consider the composition of the picture as a whole, the translation might be a little different: In Toni Wolff, the

412 C.G. Jung, *The Art of C.C. Jung*, p. 172. On the translation of the Chinese characters see also Kevin B. Turner & Chia-Wei Yang, "Decoding Toni's Stone. C.G. Jung's Memorial for Toni Wolff," in: Jung Journal (Vol. 15, 2021, Issue 3). https://doi.org/10.1080/19342039.2021.1942758

413 Letter of February 13, 1956.

passion of love (ginkgo) and the religious devotedness of the nun were one; this is a great, inexpressible mystery. It is as if the old man leaning on his staff were meditating on the eternal *mysterium coniunctionis*, the moment of the falling leaf suspended between life and death.

On its reverse side, as Jung tells Hedy Wyss, is inscribed:

> D(iis) M(anibus) sacro arboris huius numini fec. et pos. C.G. Jung A[NN] O MCMLVI

> Dedicated to the spirits of the ancestors [and] to the sacred divine being of this tree. C.G. J[ung] created and placed [this stone] in the year 1956.[414]

The ginkgo tree references a poem that Goethe dedicated to Marianne von Willemer-Jung, who was very much his junior, when he was 66 years old. Earlier mention was made of her in connection with the legend of Jung's ancestry and Goethe. Since Goethe's day, because its shape is both divided into two while remaining one, the ginkgo leaf has been considered a symbol of friendship and love. And thus, in the middle verse of his poem "Gingo Biloba," Goethe sings the praises of the gingko leaf:

> Is it but one being single
> Which as same itself divides?
> Are there two which chose to mingle
> So that each as one now hides.[415]

The falling leaf that the old man is contemplating 'in modest harmony with nature,' is an image of immortality, often used in the Far East, from where the ginkgo tree came to Europe in the 18th century. It refers to the transience of life. The old man seems to know that precisely at the moment of greatest decay, the individual leaf returns to the eternal cycle of nature, to the origin of all life where everything becomes one again. Whoever looks at this and "knows" as the old man knows, is said to be enlightened: in the midst of the transient he recognizes the immortal and eternal.

414 C.G. Jung, *The Art of C.G. Jung*, p. 172.
415 J.W. von Goethe, *Poems of the West and East*, "Book of Suleika," p. 261.

Emma Maria Jung-Rauschenbach

There is a very touching story about Jung that illustrates this deep recognition of the eternal existing in close proximity to death. In November 1955, an Australian woman came to see Jung at his house on Seestrasse.[416] She had to wait quite a while because the doctor was in the house to check on Emma Jung. Finally, C.G. Jung appeared and, after a lengthy preliminary exchange, he asked her if there was anything she would like to know from him. Although she had prepared several dreams that she wanted to discuss with him, once she was in the presence of this great man she forgot all about them and asked him instead the seemingly nonsensical question of what the difference might be between herself and the table that stood in front of her. Jung was not at all irritated, quite the opposite: he leaned forward, tapped the table and said, "We are of the same substance as that table. Our discrimination, the 'I' awareness is the difference. The difference is the consciousness God has spent millions of years to bring about." He then spoke at length on God's experiment that has been going on for millennia; on archaic man; on the onset of culture with the invention of writing, and much more. He also expressed his deep concern about the alarming unconsciousness of people, which could once again destroy everything. The real problem, he told her, is the *collective shadow*. "The atom bomb is in the hands of unconscious people. It is like giving a baby a kilo of gelignite: it eventually blows itself up."[417]

Jung talked for a long time, until somebody knocked at the door. He then left the room and when he returned, he informed his visitor that the doctor had just told him that his wife would not survive her illness. The Australian woman was shocked and offered to leave. But Jung asked her to stay and began to talk about death. Among other things, he said, "Death is a drawing together of two worlds, not an end. We are the bridge."[418] For those who are able to perceive it, this is precisely what the falling ginkgo leaf means: the oneness of the ephemeral and the eternal, of life and death. Five days later, on November 27, 1955, Emma Maria Jung-Rauschenbach died.

416 M. Irene Rix Weaver (1902-1990) was the first Zurich-trained Jungian analyst from Australia.

417 *C.G. Jung, Emma Jung, Toni Wolff. A Collection of Remembrances*, ed. by Ferne Jensen, San Francisco: The Analytical Club of San Francisco, 1982. "An Interview with C.G. Jung" by M.I. Rix Weaver, pp. 90-95. Ibid. p. 92.

418 Ibid., p. 95.

Image 21: C.G. Jung, Memorial for Emma Jung-Rauschenbach (Plate XV)

To her, too, Jung dedicated a memorial stone. Today it stands in the courtyard of the Bollingen tower, next to the loggia. The inscription reads:

> In the capital: O VAS INSIGNE DEVOTIONIS ET OBOEDIENTIAE
> In the temple: DIIS MANIBUS ET GENIO CARISSIMAE ET FIDISSIMAE UXORIS MEAE EMMA MARIA VITAM PEREGIT PASSA MORTA LAMENTATA EST AETERNITATIS TRANSIVIT IN MYSTERIUM.

ANNO MCMLV
AET.S. LXXIII
On the pedestal: fec. et pos. MARITUS C.G. JUNG 1956

O incomparable vessel of dedication and obedience!
To the spirit of the ancestors and the soul of my so very much beloved and faithful wife Emma Maria. She completed her life. After her suffering and death, she was consoled. She passed over into the secret of eternity in the year of 1955. Her age [was] seventy-three.
Her husband C.G. Jung made and placed [this stone] here in 1956.[419]

Above the temple are the sun and moon. They indicate the *coniunctio Solis et Lunae*, the union of supreme opposites, in which the alchemists saw the crowning of the opus and the goal of the alchemical *peregrinatio*, the mystical journey. The wholeness suggested in the *coniunctio* is repeated in the sphere that is divided into four sections above the tripartite vessel. The latter could be an allusion to the mystery of the Grail vessel, the subject that had occupied Emma Jung to the end of her life.[420] The conjunction of sun and moon depicted on the stele, as well as the sphere with the four lines emanating from the center and building four quadrants, are reminiscent of Jung's description of Michael Maier's *peregrinatio* at the beginning of the chapter with the title "The Fourth of the Three," in *Mysterium Coniunctionis*. Here Jung describes the course of the alchemist's peregrination,[421] in which he journeyed to the four cardinal points: to Europe (north), America (west), Asia (east), and finally reached the fourth continent in the south, Africa. This is the darkest moment of his journey, a step towards the fourth dimension, which resembles death. Here, however, at the transition from the third to the fourth, Maier had a vision of paradise as a primordial image of wholeness. Thus, one could see in the symbolism depicted by Jung on the stone he chiseled for Emma Jung an image of individuation completed in death.

Addressing his last letter to "Dear Hedy formerly Wyss," he explains that this "formerly" is a reminder of the transience of all things. And later he adds, "One is a starting point whose beginning one doesn't quite know,

419 See C.G. Jung, *The Art of C.G. Jung*, pp. 172-173.
420 Emma Jung, Marie-Louise von Franz, *The Grail Legend*, translated by Andrea Dykes, Princeton: Princeton University Press, 1998.
421 C.G. Jung, *Mysterium Coniunctionis*, § 276.

and an end, and beyond it, one does not know. What happens within the spaceless and the timeless? Before and after?" It is as if, he says, his head has bumped up against a ceiling, while beneath him is an unfathomable deep into which, perhaps, one sinks.[422]

Suspecting that this might well be his last letter to Hedy Wyss, he adds a post scriptum:

> P.S. The arduous thing about old age – which I just now recall – is that if you do anything at all, you do it, or must do it, as if it were for the last time. Hence, this long letter!!!

422 Letter of October 31, 1956.

Appendix: Two Letters of Hedy Wyss to C.G. Jung

Just as the German and English manuscript for the final editions of C.G. Jung's letters to Hedy Wyss reached completion, two original letters of Hedy Wyss came to light from within the Jung archive of ETH Zürich. I am indebted to Carl Jung, the current Executive Secretary of the Works of C.G. Jung Zürich, for bringing them to my attention. It seems that these two letters alone have survived. They testify to the original, honest and self-critical manner with which Hedy Wyss met her analyst. The letters are reproduced here without further comment.

Zollikon, July 2023
Andreas Schweizer

*

[letter undated; before July 11, 1936]

Esteemed Professor,

I am writing to ask if you would grant me an audience. I have heard a lot about you recently through my friends, Marie-Louise v. Franz and Dr. Hans Wyss, which has given me the courage to ask.
My life, in a nutshell, is as follows: daughter of a doctor, academic milieu with the appropriate part-time university degree (Italian – art history); aside from this, the desire to paint; difficulties at home because of the latter – passive resistance and slow acceptance over the last ten years; now 30 years old, single, with my own studio, no desire to work, complexes about age, longing for love, etc. Going hand in hand with this is a long-standing friendship with an Italian writer, who is bound to a woman he does not love through a forced marriage. For my part, ever new attempts to break free of all these ties and insecurities by getting married, attempts that fail, of course.
You understand better than I that such a state of affairs is unbearable in the long term. That is why I am reaching out to you. Although I have always railed against psychoanalysis in the past, I occasionally came to your lectures

and found myself annoyed at the slightly ironic way you spoke about your cases.
My friends have instructed me otherwise. I am now a little more favorably disposed; I even have confidence in you.
When may I come?
I await your kind reply and send you, with respect, my greetings.
Yours,
Hedy Wyss

Atelier Wettingerwies 4 Zürich VII[423]

423 Just around the corner from the Psychology Club Zurich.

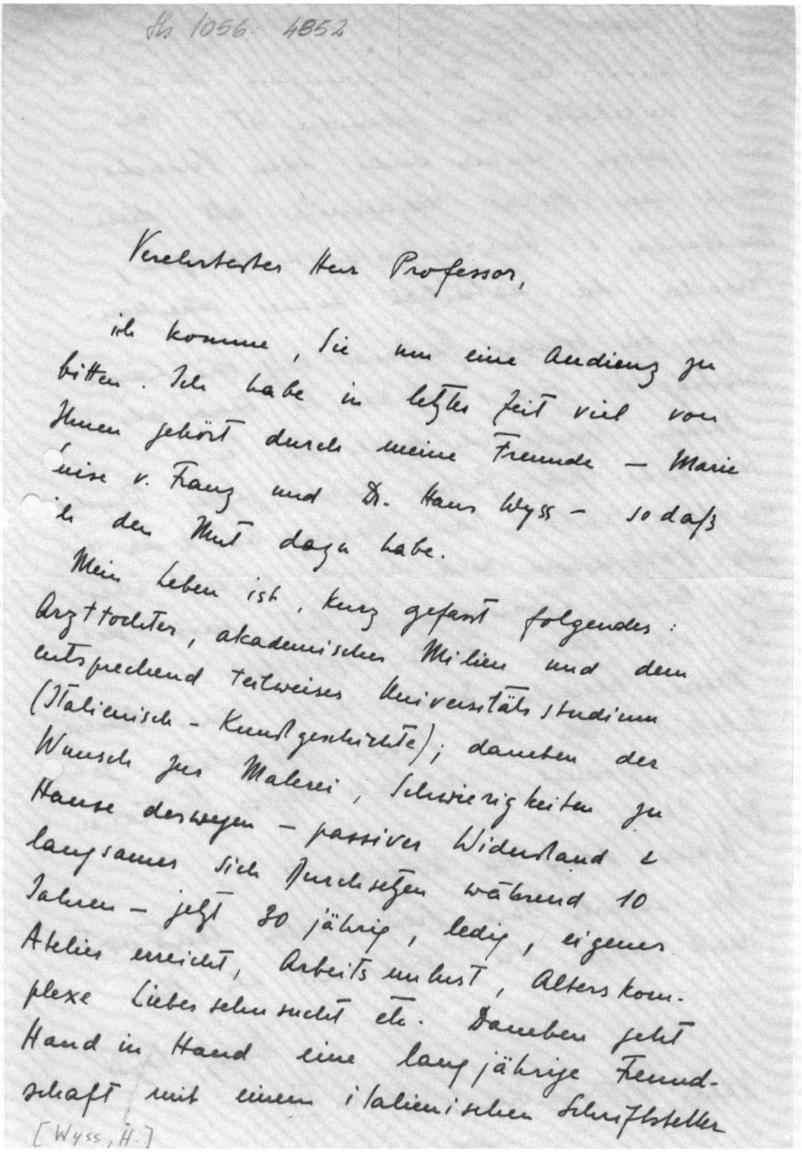

Verehrtester Herr Professor,

ich komme, Sie um eine Audienz zu bitten. Ich habe in letzter Zeit viel von Ihnen gehört durch meine Freunde – Marie Luise v. Franz und Dr. Hans Wyss – so daß ich den Mut dazu habe.

Mein Leben ist, kurz gefaßt folgendes: Arzttochter, akademisches Milieu und dem entsprechend teilweises Universitätsstudium (Italienisch – Kunstgeschichte); daneben der Wunsch zur Malerei, Schwierigkeiten zu Hause deswegen – passiver Widerstand & langsames Sich Durchsetzen während 10 Jahren – jetzt 30 jährig, ledig, eigenes Atelier erreicht, Arbeitsunlust, Alterskomplexe Liebessehnsucht etc. Daneben geht Hand in Hand eine langjährige Freundschaft mit einem italienischen Schriftsteller

Image 22a: Letter of Hedy Wyss to C.G. Jung, undated, front

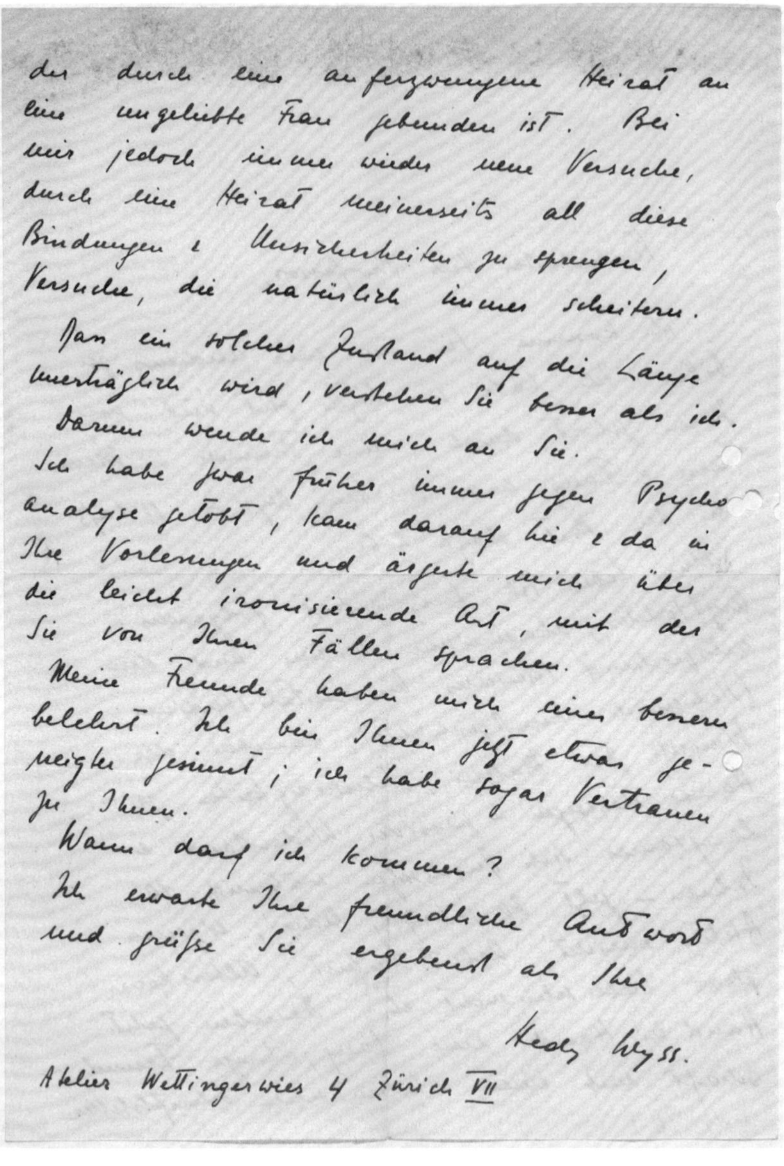

der durch eine aufgezwungene Heirat an eine ungeliebte Frau gebunden ist. Bei mir jedoch immer wieder neue Versuche, durch eine Heirat meinerseits all diese Bindungen & Unsicherheiten zu sprengen, Versuche, die natürlich immer scheitern.

Dass ein solcher Zustand auf die Länge unerträglich wird, verstehen Sie besser als ich.

Darum wende ich mich an Sie.

Ich habe zwar früher immer gegen Psychoanalyse getobt, kam darauf hie & da in Ihre Vorlesungen und ärgerte mich über die leicht ironisierende Art, mit der Sie von Ihren Fällen sprachen.

Meine Freunde haben mich eines bessern belehrt. Ich bin Ihnen jetzt etwas geneigter gesinnt; ich habe sogar Vertrauen zu Ihnen.

Wann darf ich kommen?

Ich erwarte Ihre freundliche Antwort und grüsse Sie ergebenst als Ihre

Hedy Wyss.

Atelier Wettingerwies 4 Zürich VII

Image 22b: Letter of Hedy Wyss to C.G. Jung, reverse

Atelier Wettingerwies 4
11th July, 1936

Esteemed Professor,

The "writer of this letter" is hereby resuming her harassment of you.
The day after my unfortunate encounter with you in Meilen, which, even though I would rather not admit it to myself, I suppose I do regret, I stumbled upon your essay on "Woman in Europe."[424] I read it immediately, in one sitting. And I was more than simply impressed – I was deeply stirred by it: it stirred my heart, not in a sentimental way, but rather crudely – physically, as it were.
Nevertheless, I thank you for it, and that is what I wanted to tell you. I shall have to talk to you about it in the fall. Now I am even more convinced that it is good. Because, you see, it is not a question of someone telling us: this is where you stand; rather, we want to know what we have to do. The question is: what must we do to be at peace with ourselves, or rather, so that we do not perish spiritually?
You see, I am not that keen on being a "woman of today"; I would much rather have lived a life from the past. But you yourself say that we don't have the choice. And the honesty towards oneself that art demands infects one's whole being: one can't fool oneself – or, unfortunately, anyone else – about anything.
I'm glad I'm still able to make my own decisions and need to talk to you.
I hope that by then you will have pardoned my rude unreliability; I know myself how much I am to blame for the so-called coincidence. Manque de Courage. Perhaps we are only in such a bad way because we lack courage.
There's a sentence in your essay, though, that I now mutter to myself like a prayer [mantra], "there are [always] renaissances,"[425] because, frankly, I find it offensive when someone claims that one belongs, personally or in general, to a declining era.
And so now, like a muttering mendicant monk, I will bide my time until your return [from America] in a few months' time.
And "no harm meant."

424 C.G. Jung, "Woman in Europe," CW 10, §§ 236 ff.
425 Ibid., § 237.

I wish you all the very best for America.[426] But do not forget old Europe, which needs you; those people who need you, including those who want to apologize for being women.
With my most humble greetings,
Yours,
Hedy Wyss

426 C.G. Jung and his wife traveled to the United States in August 1936, for Jung to receive an honorary doctorate from Harvard University, Massachusetts, and to deliver a lecture there. They did not return to Zurich until the end of October, after a stay in London. See D. Bair, *C.G. Jung*, pp. 417 ff.

Illustrations

Letters of C.G. Jung to Hedy Wyss © Foundation of the Works of C.G. Jung, Zurich.

Color Plates

Bibliography

Works of C.G. Jung

The Collected Works (CW) *of C.G. Jung and the Philemon Foundation Series* (20 Volumes) are quoted according to the edition of the Princeton University Press, Princeton.

C.G. Jung, *Symbols of Transformation*, CW 5.

C.G. Jung, *Two Essays on Analytical Psychology*, CW 7.

C.G. Jung, *The Structure and Dynamics of the Psyche*, CW 8.

C.G. Jung, *The Archetypes and the Collective Unconscious*, CW 9/1.

C.G. Jung, *Aion. Researches into the Phenomenology of the Self*, CW 9/2.

C.G. Jung, *Civilization in Transition*, CW 10.

C.G. Jung, *Psychology and Religion: West and East*, CW 11.

C.G. Jung, *Psychology and Alchemy*, CW 12.

C.G. Jung, *Alchemical Studies*, CW 13.

C.G. Jung, *Mysterium Coniunctionis. An Inquiry into the Separation and Synthesis of Psychic Opposites in Alchemy*, CW 14.

C.G. Jung, *The Practice of Psychotherapy*, CW 16.

C.G. Jung, *The Symbolic Life*, CW 18.

Letters, Lectures, and Seminars of C.G. Jung

C.G. Jung, *Letters*, selected and edited by Gerhard Adler, in collaboration with Aniela Jaffé, translations from the German by R. F. C. Hull, in two volumes, Princeton: Princeton University Press, 1973.

C.G. Jung, *Nietzsche's Zarathustra,* Notes of the Seminar Given in 1934-1939, ed. by James L. Jarrett in two parts, London: Routledge, 1989.

C.G. Jung, *Visions, Notes of the Seminar Given in 1930*-1934, ed. by Claire Douglas in two volumes, Princeton: Princeton University Press, 1997.

C.G. Jung, *On Psychological and Visionary Art,* Notes from C.G. Jung's Lecture on Gérard de Nerval's *Aurélia,* ed. by Craig E. Stephenson, Philemon Series, Princeton: Princeton University Press, 2015.

C.G. Jung, "Der Geist der Psychologie" [The Spirit of Psychology], in: *Eranos Jahrbuch 1946*, Zurich: Rhein Verlag, 1947.

C.G. Jung, "Faust und die Alchemie," Lecture at the Psychology Club Zurich, October 8, 1949, in: Irene Gerber-Münch, *Goethes Faust*. No English translation available yet.

The Red Books and The Black Books

C.G. Jung, *The Red Book, Liber Novus*, ed. and with an introduction by Sonu Shamdasani, New York /London: W.W. Norton & Company, 2009.

C.G. Jung, *The Red Book, Liber Novus, A Reader's Edition*, ed. and with an introduction by Sonu Shamdasani, New York /London: W.W. Norton & Company, 2009.

C.G. Jung, *The Black Books, 1913-1932. Notebooks of Transformation.* Edited by Sonu Shamdasani. Translated by Martin Liebscher, John Peck, and Sonu Shamdasani, Philemon Series. In collaboration with the Foundation of the Works of C.G. Jung, 7 volumes, New York/London: W.W. Norton & Company, 2020.

Memoirs

C.G. Jung, *Memories, Dreams, Reflections by C.G. Jung* recorded and edited by Aniela Jaffé. Translated from the German by Richard and Clara Winston. Revised edition. New York: Vintage Books, 1989.

Reflections on the Life and Dreams of C.G. Jung by Aniela Jaffé from Conversations with Jung, Einsiedeln: Daimon, 2023.

C.G. Jung, *The Original Protocols for Memories, Dreams, Reflections.* Edited by Sonu Shamdasani, with Thomas Fischer and Robert Hinshaw as consulting editors [will be published soon, status July 2023; see www.cgjung-werke.org].

Works about C.G. Jung

C.G. Jung Speaking. Interviews and Encounters, ed. by William McGuire and R.F.C. Hull, Princeton: Princeton University Press, 1977.

C.G. Jung, Emma Jung, Toni Wolff. A Collection of Remembrances, ed. by Ferne Jensen, San Francisco: The Analytical Club of San Francisco, 1982.

C.G. Jung, *The Art of C. G. Jung*, ed. by Foundation of the Works of C. G. Jung. Ulrich Hoerni, Thomas Fischer, Bettina Kaufmann. New York, London: W.W. Norton & Company, 2019.

Jung, C.G./ Neumann, Erich, *Analytical Psychology in Exile. The Correspondence of C.G. Jung and Erich Neumann*, ed. by Martin Liebscher, translated by Heather McCartney, Princeton: Princeton University Press, Princeton 2015.

Other works:

Abt, Theo (ed.), *Book of the Explanation of the Symbols Kitāb Hall ar-Rumūz* by Muhammad Ibn Umail. Psychological Commentary by Marie-Louise von Franz, Zurich: Living Human Heritage Publication, 2006 (Corpus Alchemicum Arabicum, Volume I A).

Bair, Deirdre, *Jung. A Biography*, Boston/New York/London: Little, Brown and Company, 2003.

Bishop, Paul, *Carl Jung*, London: Reaction Books, 2014.

Cocks, Geoffrey, *Psychotherapy in the Third Reich. The Göring Institute*, New Brunswick (USA)/London: Transaction Publishers, 1997.

Dieterich, Albrecht, *Abraxas, Studien zur Religionsgeschichte des späteren Altertums* [Studies to the History of Religions in Late Antiquity], B.G. Teubner, Leipzig 1905.

Durrer, Robert (ed.), *Bruder Klaus. Die ältesten Quellen über den seligen Niklaus von Flüe, sein Leben und sein Einfluss* [Brother Klaus. The Oldest Resources of the Blessed Niklaus von Flüe, His Life and Influence], Sarnen: 1917, reprint, 1981.

Eleazar, Abraham, *Uraltes Chymisches Werk [age-old Chymical Work]*, 2nd Edition, Leipzig, 1760.

Franz, Marie-Louise von, *C.G. Jung. His Myth in Our Time*, trans. from the German by William H. Kennedy, Toronto: Inner City Books, 1998.

Id., *On Dreams & Death. A Jungian Interpretation.* Translated by Emmanuel Kennedy-Xipolitas and Vernon Brooks, Chicago/La Salle, Illinois: Open Court, 1998.

Id., "Nike and the Waters of the Styx," in: id., *Archetypal Dimensions of the Psyche*, Boston & London: Shambhala, 1999.

Id., "The Unknown Visitor," in: id., *Archetypal Dimensions of the Psyche.*

Id., "The Cosmic Man as Image of the Goal of the Individuation Process and Human Development," in: id., *Archetypal Dimensions of the Psyche.*

Id., *Muhammad ibn Umail's Hall ar-Rumuz*, Egg: Fotorotar, 1999.

Franz, *Marie-Louise von,* "The Goose Girl," in: A. Schweizer and R. Schweizer-Vüllers (eds.), *Stone by Stone*, pp. 61–92.

Id., *Aurora Consurgens. A document Attributed to Thomas Aquinas on the Problem of Opposites in Alchemy*, ed. with a commentary by M.-L. von Franz, transl. by R.F.C. Hull and A.S.B. Glover, Toronto: Inner City Books, 2000.

Id., *Niklaus von Flüe and Saint Perpetua: A Psychological Interpretation of their Visions.* Translated from the original German manuscript by Alison Kappes and Barbara Davies, volume 6 of *The Collected Works of Marie-Louise von Franz*, Ashville: Chiron Publications, 2022.

Gerber-Münch, Irene, *Goethes Faust, Eine tiefenpsychologische Studie über den Mythos des modernen Menschen*, Egg ZH: Verlag Stiftung für Jung'sche Psychologie, 1997.

Goethe, Johann Wolfgang von, *Faust. A Tragedy*, Translated by Walter Arndt, 2nd ed., New York: W.W. Norton, 2001.

Id,, *The Works of J.W. von Goethe*, ed. by Nathan Haskell Dole, translated by Sir Walter Scott and others, London and Boston: Oxford Press, Vol. 9, *Poems of Goethe.*

Id,, *Poems of the West and East, West-Eastern Divan*. Bi-Lingual Edition of the Complete Poems. Verse Translation by John Whaley, Bern: Peter Lang, 1998.

Id., „Aus den Briefen an Frau v. Stein," [From the Letters to Frau von Stein]," *Werke*, München: C.H. Beck, 15 1994, vol. 1.

Greene, Liz, *The Astrological World of Jung's Liber Novus. Daimons, Gods, and the Planetary Journey*, London: Routledge, 2018.

Hannah, Barbara, *Jung. His Life and Work. A Biographical Memoir*, Wilmette, Illinois: Chiron Publications, 1997.

Heraclitus, *The Fragments of the Work of Heraclitus of Ephesus on Nature*, translated by John Burnet, 1920.

Hesiod, *Theogony*, transl. with an introduction and notes by Marin L. West, Oxford: Oxford University Press, 2008.

Hoeller, Stephan A., *The Gnostic Jung and the Seven Sermons to the Dead*, Wheaton, Illinois: Theosophical Pub. House, 1982.

Howe, Laurel, "Redeeming Mary Magdalene – The Feminine Side of the Death and Resurrection Archetype," in: A. Schweizer and R. Schweizer-Vüllers (eds.), *Wisdom has Built her House. Psychological Aspects of the Feminine*, pp.89–142.

Jung, Emma / Franz, Marie-Louise von, *The Grail Legend*, translated by Andrea Dykes, Princeton: Princeton University Press, 1998.

Kerényi, Karl, *Dionysos. Archetypal Image of Indestructible Life*, tr. from the German by Ralph Manheim, Princeton: Princeton University Press, 1976.

Kipling, Rudyard, *Just So Stories for Little Children*, Greenwood, Wisconsin: Suzeteo Enterprises, 2019.

Koelbing, Huldrych M., "Die Berufung Karl Gustav Jung (1794–1864) nach Basel und ihre Vorgeschichte" [The call of Karl Gustav Jung (1794-1864) to Basel and its Antecedents], in: *Gesnerus*: Swiss Journal of the history of medicine and sciences, vol. 34 (1977).

Meister Eckhart, Works, vol. 1, translated by C. de B. Evans, London: John M. Watkins, 1924.

Mutus Liber – Alchemy and its Mute Book. Reproduction of the first edition by La Rochelle 1677. Introduction and comments by Eugène Canseliet, ed. by Moreh Derekh, translated by T. Bruemmer, Utrecht: Inner Garden Press, 2015.

Neumann, Erich, *Depth Psychology and a New Ethic*, English translation by Eugene Rolfe, New York: G.P. Putnam's Sons, 1969.

Nietzsche, Friedrich, *The Gay Science*, ed. by Bernard Williams, translated by Josefine Nauckhoff, Cambridge: Cambridge University Press, 2001.

Ovid, *Metamorphoses.* Translated and with an Introduction by Mary M. Innes, Penguin Books, London, New York etc. 1955.

Plato, *The Dialogues of Plato*, volume II, "The Symposium." Translated with comment by R.E. Allen, New Haven and London: Yale University Press, 1991.

Priestley, J.B. and Hawkes, Jacquetta, *Journey Down the Rainbow*, New York: Harper and Bros, 1955.

Ruland, Martin, *Lexicon Alchemiae*, Hildesheim, Zürich, New York: Georg Olms, 1987 (Reprint of the original edition, Frankfurt 1612).

Safranski, Rüdiger, *Goethe & Schiller. Geschichte einer Freundschaft* [History of a Friendship], München: Carl Hanser Verlag, 2009 (no English translation available yet).

Id., *Goethe. Life as a Work of Art*, New York/London, W.W. Norton & Company, 2017.

Schweizer, Andreas, *The Fierce Dance of the Goddess – Dissolution, Chaos, and Renewal*, in: The Guild of Pastoral Psychology, No. 320, King's Lynn: Minuteman Press, 2015.

Schweizer, Andreas, and Schweizer-Vüllers, Regine (Eds.), *Stone by Stone. Reflections on the Psychology of C.G. Jung*, Contributions to Jungian Psychology by The Psychology Club Zurich, vol. 1, Einsiedeln: Daimon, 1917.

Schweizer, Andreas, and Schweizer-Vüllers, Regine (Eds.), *Wisdom has Built her House. Psychological Aspects of the Feminine*, Contributions to Jungian Psychology by The Psychology Club Zurich, vol. 2, Einsiedeln: Daimon, 2019.

Stein, Murray, "Jungian Psychology and the Spirit of Protestantism," in: A. Schweizer and R. Schweizer-Vüllers (Eds.), *Stone by Stone. Reflections on the Psychology of C.G. Jung.*

Turner, Kevin B. & Chia-Wei Yang, "Decoding Toni's Stone. C.G. Jung's Memorial for Toni Wolff," in: *Jung Journal* (Vol. 15, 2021, Issue 3).

Wilhelm, Richard, *Dschuang Dsï* [Zhuangzi], *Das wahre Buch vom südlichen Blütenland* [The True Book of the Blossom Country of the South], Zurich: Ex Libris 1972.

Wyss, Alma Hedwig, *Lohengrins schwarzer Schwan* [Lohengrin's Black Swan], unpublished manuscript.

Zhuangzi, Translation and Introduction by Hyun Höchsmann and Yang Guorong, New York: Longman, 2007.

Volume 1 of this series:

Stone by Stone
Reflections on the Psychology of C.G. Jung
Edited by Andreas Schweizer
and Regine Schweizer-Vüllers
352 pages, hardbound, illustrated in color
ISBN 978-3-85630-765-3

This volume comprises original contributions by Carl Gustav Jung and Marie-Louise von Franz, along with additional works addressing analytical psychology.

The accompanying frontispiece of this publication shows two masons engaged in placing the capstone on a building. Above this stone is the word "lapis" indicating the alchemical stone. To the alchemists, the lapis was infinitely precious. It healed illnesses, brought about miracles, endowed long life, but it was so mysterious and puzzling that they ascribed to it an endless number of names, and could only describe it through paradoxes. In psychological terms, it is an image of the Self, for the completeness or wholeness within us; in other words, for that never-to-be quite-realized mysterious inner value that embraces all parts of one's personality, even the minor, unsightly and despised aspects. Therefore, to the lapis and the alchemical process always belongs the encounter with the dark sides of one's own personality.

Volume 2:

Wisdom has Built her House
Psychological Aspects of the Feminine
Edited by Andreas Schweizer
and Regine Schweizer-Vüllers
260 pages, hardbound, illustrated in color
ISBN 978-3-85630-776-9

For the house of wisdom that already exists in the beyond – in the unconscious – to truly manifest within an individual human being, the whole of a person is required, along with all their four psychic functions of consciousness. This encounter with wholeness – with the divine – is a shocking event that leaves both parties – the human and the divine – renewed.

The essays in this volume by Marie-Louise von Franz, Rivkah Schärf Kluger, Gotthilf Isler, and Laurel Howe revolve around this encounter. They detail the possible union of the opposites – the divine with the human, the feminine with the masculine, the demonic with the redemptive. Ultimately, they are all about a new god-image in which the feminine – Wisdom in its feminine form – is united with the masculine. This development has been in the making within the collective unconscious for centuries and it wants to become a reality in our time.

Volume 3:

Encounters with C.G. Jung
The Journal of Sabi Tauber (1951–1961)
Editing and commentary
by Irene und Andreas Gerber
248 pages, illustrated in color, ISBN 978-3-85630-784-4

This volume presents the journal notes of Sabi Tauber, a young Swiss woman who recorded the experience of her encounters with C.G. Jung. She conscientiously noted Jung's responses to her questions and his comments on her dreams, mostly related to love, the creative principle, and the shadow.

In the years 1951–1961, Sabi Tauber often visited Jung in Küsnacht and in his secluded tower in Bollingen. Jung also went to her home in Winterthur a few times, where he spontaneously explained his views in the circle of the Tauber family and their friends.

A reader today will immediately be touched by C.G. Jung's living spirit, just as Sabi Tauber was then. While addressing her personal situation, Jung also repeatedly points to the archetype that he recognizes behind each problem. In this way, the scientific precision of Jung's thoughts is imbued with a unique feeling quality.

New from Daimon:

Aniela Jaffé
Reflections
on the Life and Dreams of C.G. Jung
Historical Commentary by Elena Fischli
400 pages, ISBN 978-3-85630-792-9

Aniela Jaffé presents thoughts and ruminations that Jung shared with her as they prepared *Memories, Dreams, Reflections by C.G. Jung*. These never-before-published revelations present a kaleidoscope of episodic, philosophical, humorous and enigmatic material, uniquely complementing and expanding on the widely acclaimed *MDR*.

The historical commentary by Elena Fischli illuminates the biographical work with C.G. Jung on the basis of source material. How did the conversations and the notes of Aniela Jaffé come about? What was the nature of the relationship and collaboration between her and Jung? How did others deal with their work? And finally, who was this woman who was so candidly given such a glimpse into Jung's inner life?

English Titles from Daimon

Ruth Ammann	- *The Enchantment of Gardens*
Susan R. Bach	- *Life Paints its Own Span*
Diana Baynes Jansen	- *Jung's Apprentice: A Biography of Helton Godwin Baynes*
John Beebe (Ed.)	- *Terror, Violence and the Impulse to Destroy*
E.A. Bennet	- *Meetings with Jung*
W.H. Bleek / L.C. Lloyd (Ed.)	- *Specimens of Bushman Folklore*
Tess Castleman	- *Threads, Knots, Tapestries*
	- *Sacred Dream Circles*
Renate Daniel	- *Taking the Fear out of the Night*
	- *The Self: Quest for Meaning in a Changing World*
	- *Psyche and Soma*
Eranos Yearbook 69	- *Eranos Reborn*
Eranos Yearbook 70	- *Love on a Fragile Thread*
Eranos Yearbook 71	- *Beyond Masters*
Eranos Yearbook 72	- *Soul between Enchantment and Disenchantment*
Eranos Yearbook 73	- *The World and its Shadow*
Eranos Yearbook 74	- *The Age of Immediacy at the Test of Meaning*
Eranos Yearbook 75	- *Life, Individual, Community, and the Thought of the Absolute ...*
Michael Escamilla	- *Bleuler, Jung, and the Schizophrenias*
Heinrich Karl Fierz	- *Jungian Psychiatry*
John Fraim	- *Battle of Symbols*
Liliane Frey-Rohn	- *Friedrich Nietzsche, A Psychological Approach*
Marion Gallbach	- *Learning from Dreams*
Ralph Goldstein (Ed.)	- *Images, Meanings & Connections: Essays in Memory of Susan Bach*
Yael Haft	- *Hands: Archetypal Chirology*
Fred Gustafson	- *The Black Madonna of Einsiedeln*
Daniel Hell	- *Soul-Hunger: The Feeling Human Being and the Life-Sciences*
Siegmund Hurwitz	- *Lilith, the first Eve*
Aniela Jaffé	- *Reflections on the Life and Dreams of C.G. Jung* *With a Historical Commentary by Elena Fischli*
	- *The Myth of Meaning*
	- *Was C.G. Jung a Mystic?*
	- *From the Life and Work of C.G. Jung*
	- *Death Dreams and Ghosts*
C.G. Jung	- *The Solar Myths and Opicinus de Canistris*
Verena Kast	- *A Time to Mourn*
	- *Sisyphus*
Hayao Kawai	- *Dreams, Myths and Fairy Tales in Japan*
James Kirsch	- *The Reluctant Prophet*
Eva Langley-Dános	- *Prison on Wheels: Ravensbrück to Burgau*
Rivkah Schärf Kluger	- *The Gilgamesh Epic*
Yehezkel Kluger & *Nomi Kluger-Nash*	- *RUTH in the Light of Mythology, Legend* *and Kabbalah*
Paul Kugler (Ed.)	- *Jungian Perspectives on Clinical Supervision*
Paul Kugler	- *The Alchemy of Discourse*
Rafael López-Pedraza	- *Cultural Anxiety*
	- *Hermes and his Children*
Alan McGlashan	- *The Savage and Beautiful Country*
	- *Gravity & Levity*
Gregory McNamee (Ed.)	- *The Girl Who Made Stars: Bushman Folklore*
	- *The North Wind and the Sun & Other Fables of Aesop*
Gitta Mallasz / Hanna Dallos	- *Talking with Angels*
C.A. Meier	- *Healing Dream and Ritual*
	- *A Testament to the Wilderness*
	- *Personality: The Individuation Process*

English Titles from Daimon

Haruki Murakami - *Haruki Murakami Goes to Meet Hayao Kawai*
Eva Pattis Zoja (Ed.) - *Sandplay Therapy*
Laurens van der Post - *The Rock Rabbit and the Rainbow*
Psychology Club Zurich - *Stone by Stone: Reflections on Jung*
- *Wisdom has Built her House*
- *Encounters with C.G. Jung. The Journal of Sabi Tauber*
Jane Reid - *Jung, My Mother and I: The Analytic Diaries of Catharine Rush Cabot*
Ingrid Riedel & Christa Henzler - *Painting Therapy on the Basis of C.G. Jung's Analytical Psychology*
R.M. Rilke - *Duino Elegies*
Miguel Serrano - *C.G. Jung and Hermann Hesse*
Helene Shulman - *Living at the Edge of Chaos*
D. Slattery / G. Slater (Eds.) - *Varieties of Mythic Experience*
David Tacey - *Edge of the Sacred: Jung, Psyche, Earth*
Susan Tiberghien - *Looking for Gold*
Ann Ulanov - *Spiritual Aspects of Clinical Work*
- *The Female Ancestors of Christ*
- *Healing Imagination*
- *Picturing God*
- *Receiving Woman*
- *Spirit in Jung*
- *The Wisdom of the Psyche*
- *The Wizards' Gate, Picturing Consciousness*
- *The Psychoid, Soul and Psyche*
- *Knots and their Untying*
- *Back to Basics*
Ann & Barry Ulanov - *Cinderella and her Sisters*
Eva Wertenschlag-Birkhäuser - *Windows on Eternity: The Paintings of Peter Birkhäuser*
Harry Wilmer - *How Dreams Help*
- *Quest for Silence*
Luigi Zoja - *Drugs, Addiction and Initiation*
Luigi Zoja & Donald Williams - *Jungian Reflections on September 11*
Jungian Congress Papers - *Jerusalem 1983: Symbolic & Clinical Approaches*
- *Berlin 1986: Archetype of Shadow in a Split World*
- *Paris 1989: Dynamics in Relationship*
- *Chicago 1992: The Transcendent Function*
- *Zürich 1995: Open Questions*
- *Florence 1998: Destruction and Creation*
- *Cambridge 2001*
- *Barcelona 2004: Edges of Experience*
- *Cape Town 2007: Journeys, Encounters*
- *Montreal 2010: Facing Multiplicity*
- *Copenhagen 2013: 100 Years on*
- *Kyoto 2016: Anima Mundi in Transition*
- *Vienna 2019: Encountering the Other*
- *Buenos Aires 2022: Analytical Psychology Opening to the Changing World*

Our books are available from your bookstore or from our distributors:

Baker & Taylor
30 Amberwood Parkway
Ashland OH 44805, USA
Phone: 419-281-5100
www.btpubservices.com

Gazelle Book Services Ltd.
White Cross Mills, High Town
Lancaster LA1 4XS, UK
Email: sales@gazellebookservices.co.uk
www.gazellebookservices.co.uk

Daimon Verlag - Hauptstrasse 85 - CH-8840 Einsiedeln - Switzerland
Phone: (41)(55) 412 2266 Email: info@daimon.ch
For detailed book descriptions visit our website: **www.daimon.ch**